# Nimble with Numbers

## Engaging Math Experiences to Enhance Number Sense and Promote Practice

**Grades 3 and 4**

*Leigh Childs, Laura Choate, and Karen Jenkins*

Originally published in 1999 by Addison, Wesley Longman, Inc.


First printing by Didax in 2011


Printed in the United States of America.

Order Number 912723
ISBN 978-1-58324-343-5

B C D E F 16 15 14 13 12

395 Main Street
Rowley, MA 01969
www.didax.com

# Table of Contents

## Subtraction



## Multiplication Facts



## Mixed Facts



## Blackline Masters

# Introduction to *Nimble with Numbers*

## Why This Book?

National recommendations for a meaning-centered, problem-solving mathematics curriculum place new demands on teachers, students, and parents. Students need a facility with numbers and operations to achieve success in today's mathematics programs. Basics for students today require a broadening of the curriculum to include all areas of mathematics. Students are being asked to demonstrate proficiency not just in skills, but in problem solving, critical thinking, conceptual understanding, and performance tasks. Consequently, the reduced time teachers devote to number must be thoughtful, selective, and efficient.

This book fulfills the need for high-quality, engaging math experiences that provide meaningful practice and further the development of number sense and operation sense. **These activities are designed to help students practice number concepts previously taught for understanding in a variety of contexts.** Besides meeting the need for effective practice, *Nimble with Numbers:*

- provides a variety of adaptable formats for essential practice;
- supplements and enhances homework assignments;
- encourages parent involvement in improving their child's proficiency with basic facts and computation; and
- provides motivating and meaningful lessons for a substitute teacher.

## Criteria for Preferred Activities

For efficient use of time devoted to the number strand, the book focuses on activities that are:

- Inviting (encourages participation)
- Engaging (maintains interest)
- Simple to learn
- Repeatable (able to reuse often and sustain interest)
- Open-ended, allowing multiple solutions
- Easy to prepare
- Easy to adapt for various levels
- Easy to vary for extended use

In addition, these activities:

- Require a problem-solving approach
- Improve basic skills
- Enhance number sense and operation sense
- Encourage strategic thinking
- Promote mathematical communication
- Promote positive attitudes toward mathematics as mathematical abilities improve

# Planning Made Simple

## Organization of Book

The activities of this book are divided into eight sections that cover high-priority number topics for third graders and fourth graders. The first two sections review the addition and subtraction facts. Procedures to minimize the number of addition and multiplication facts to learn are outlined at the end of the introductory section, on pages 10–11. Share these strategies with parents to help them use their available time efficiently.

The third section reinforces money concepts that give students an opportunity to practice real-life skills. The money section addresses a high-interest topic for parents and provides a relevant lead-in to the place value section. By devoting more time to the first four sections, students should experience more success with the addition and subtraction computation sections. Activities in the multiplication facts section allow practice of either the easier facts (through sixes) or all the facts. The multiplication facts are further reinforced in the concluding mixed facts section that involves more than one of the four basic operations. Throughout all sections, we make an obvious attempt to promote mental computation.

Each section begins with an overview and suggestions to highlight the activities and provide some time-saving advice. The interactive activities identify the specific topic practiced (Topic), the objective (Object), the preferred grouping of participants (Groups), and the materials required (Materials). At the end of many activities, "Making Connections" questions promote reflection and help students make mathematical connections. Tips are often included to provide helpful implementation suggestions and variations. Needed blackline masters are included with the activity or in the Blackline Masters section at the end of the book.

The introductory section concludes with a Matrix of Activities. The repeatable Sponges and Games are listed alphabetically with corresponding information to facilitate their use.

## Types of Activities

The book contains activities for whole group, small groups, pairs, and individuals. Each section provides:

- Sponges (S)
- Skill Checks (C)
- Games (G)
- Independent Activities (I)

## Sponges

Sponges are enriching activities for soaking up spare moments. Use Sponges with the whole class or with small groups as warm-up activities, or during spare time to provide additional math practice. Sponges usually require little or no preparation and are short in duration (3–15 minutes). These appealing Sponges are repeatable and, once they become familiar, can be student-led. Students are motivated to finish a task quickly when they know a favorite Sponge will follow.

## Skill Checks

The Skill Checks in each section provide a way to show students' improvement to the parents as well as to the students. With the exception of the *Making Cents* sheets, each page is designed to be duplicated and cut in half, providing six comparative records for each student. Before answering the ten problems in each Skill Check, students should respond to the starter task following the STOP sign. These starter tasks are intended to promote mental computation and build number sense. Some teachers believe their students perform better on the Skill Checks if the responses to the STOP task are shared and discussed before students solve the remaining ten problems. Most students will complete a Skill Check in 10 to 15 minutes. The concluding extension problem, labeled "GO ON," accommodates those students who finish early. We recommend that early finishers be encouraged to create similar problems for others to solve. By having students share and discuss their approaches and responses to the STOP task and to some of the problems, teachers help students discover more efficient mental computation strategies.

## Games

Initially a new Game might be modeled with the entire class, even though Games are intended to be played by pair players or small groups after the rules are understood. ("Pair players" refers to players who collaborate to play against another pair. This recommended arrangement promotes mathematical thinking and communication as students collaborate to develop and share successful strategies.) An excellent option is to share the Game with a few students who then teach the Game to others. To facilitate getting started, teachers may recommend some procedure for identifying the first pair or player. Most Games require approximately 20 to 45 minutes of playing time. Games are ideal for home use since they provide students with additional practice and reassure parents that the number strand continues to be valued. When sending gameboards home, be sure to include the directions.

## Games and Sponges

Games and Sponges provide students with a powerful vehicle for assessing their own mathematical abilities. During the Games, students receive immediate feedback that allows them to revise and to correct inefficient and inadequate practices. Because of their appealing and repeatable nature, these Sponges and Games are valuable as center activities. Sponges and Games differ from the Independent Activities since they usually need to be introduced by a teacher or leader.

## Independent Activities

Independent Activity sheets provide facts and computation practice for students. These sheets are designed to encourage practice of many more facts than would seem apparent at first glance. Some Independent Activity sheets allow multiple solutions. Most students will complete an Independent Activity sheet in 15 to 30 minutes. Independent Activity sheets can be completed in class or sent home as homework. Many Independent Activities provide two versions to accomodate different levels of difficulty and can be easily modified to provide additional practice.

# Suggestions for Using *Nimble with Numbers*

## Materials Tips

An effort has been made to minimize the materials needed. When appropriate, blackline masters are provided. The last section of the book contains more generic types of blackline masters, including patterns for various number cubes. The six-sectioned **spinners** (p. 150) can substitute for a number cube or die. The blank spinner can be used for the specially marked number cubes (4–9 or 3–5). A simple spinner, like the one shown, can be assembled using one of the blackline master spinner bases, a paper clip, and a pencil. To reduce the noise and confine the area where cubes are rolled, use a box with felt glued to its bottom or lid.

Some activities use the Digit Squares (p. 147). The familiar sets of 0–9 number tiles substitute well for Digit Squares. If not available, take time now to duplicate a Digit Square set on card stock for each student.

A few activities require Digit Cards (p. 146). Digit Card sets should also be duplicated on card stock. Digit Cards are also needed for some class Sponges. Teachers should cut two sets of Digit Cards apart, place them in an appropriate container (paper sack, coffee can, or margarine tub), and store in a handy place. Students will have more success with the money activities if they have access to play or real coins (p. 145).

Various materials work as markers on gameboards—different types of beans, multicolored cubes, buttons, counters, or transparent bingo chips (our preference due to the see-through feature). It is assumed that students have access to scratch paper and pencils. It is assumed that an overhead projector is available, but a chalkboard may be substituted.

## Recommended Uses

The repeatable nature of these activities makes them ideal for continued use at home. Encouraging children to use these activities at home serves a dual purpose: parents are able to assist their children in gaining competence with the facts and with mental computation, and parents are reassured as they see the familiar basics practiced. To support your work in this area, we have included a parent letter and a list of helpful open-ended questions.

Besides being a source for more familiar homework, these activities offer a wide variety of classroom uses. The activities can be effectively used by substitute teachers as rainy-day options or for a change of pace. Many activities are short-term and require little or no preparation, making them ideal for soaking up spare moments at the end or beginning of a class period. They also work well as choices for center or menu activities. When students are absent from school, include these activities in independent work packets. You may package these activities in manila envelopes or self-closing transparent bags to facilitate frequent and easy checkout. To modify the activities and to accommodate the needs of your students, you may easily change the numbers, operations, and directions.

## Getting the Most from These Activities

It is important to focus on increasing students' awareness of the mathematics being learned. To do this, pose open-ended questions that promote reflection, communication, and mathematical connections. For example, after using *Factors Pathway,* one colleague asked her students, "What mathematics are you doing?" Her third graders identified multiplication facts, repeated addition, finding factors, division, and algebra ("finding an unknown"). After using *Possible Equations,* a colleague asked her students to estimate the total number of facts they had practiced. The range of responses was great.

Having students work together as pair players is of great value in increasing student confidence. While working this way, students have more opportunities to communicate strategies and to verbalize thinking. When asked to identify and to share their successful Game strategies verbally and in writing, students grow mathematically. Also, it is worthwhile to ask students to improve these activities or to create new high-interest games.

Good questions help children make sense of mathematics, build their confidence, and encourage mathematical thinking and communication. A list of helpful, sample questions appears on page 9. Since the teacher's or parent's response impacts learning, we have included suggestions for responding. Share this list with parents for their use as they assist students with these activities and other unfamiliar homework tasks. This list was created by Leigh Childs for parent workshops and for inclusion in the California Mathematics Council's *They're Counting on Us, A Parent's Guide to Mathematics Education.* We have adapted the list for use with this book.

### Parent Involvement

Since most parents place a high priority on attention to the number strand, they will appreciate the inviting and repeatable activities in this book. Because most parents willingly share the responsibility for repeated, short periods of practice, the following items are designed to promote parent involvement: *Family Letter* (p. 8), *Questions Sampler* (p. 9), *Addition Facts Made Easy* (p. 10), and *Multiplication Facts Made Easy* (p. 11). The first home packet might include the *Family Letter*, the *Questions Sampler*, and *Place Value Paths* (pp. 69–71). To facilitate use, students should take home two sets of Digit Cards (p. 146) or Digit Squares (p. 147). More games require Digit Squares, so that might be the preferred choice for home use. Since many students will benefit by practicing the addition and subtraction facts, the next home packet might include *Addition Facts Made Easy* (p. 10) and *Uncover* (pp. 21–22) or *Sum and Subtract* (pp. 38–39). This packet should include materials for making two (three for *Sum and Subtract*) number cubes, each one labeled with digits 1–6 (p. 148). Advise students and their families to keep the number cubes and digit squares in a safe place for frequent use throughout the school year.

Students enjoy and benefit from repeated use of *Seeking Sums* (pp. 14–15) and *Possible Equations* (pp. 141–142) . These Sponge and Independent Activity sheets certainly lend themselves to home packets as well. The advantage of Independent Activity sheets and Sponges, unlike Games, is that many can be experienced while a monitoring family member prepares dinner, packs lunches, or attends to other household tasks.

### Concluding Thought

We hope that by using these materials, your students will develop more positive feelings toward mathematics as they improve their confidence and number competence.

# Family Letter

Dear Family,

To be prepared to work in the 21st century, all students need to be confident and competent in mathematics. Today the working world requires understanding of all areas of mathematics including statistics, logic, geometry, and probability. To be successful in these areas, students must know their basic facts and be able to compute. It is important that we be more efficient and effective in the time we devote to arithmetic. You can help your child in this area.

Throughout the school year, our mathematics program will focus on enhancing your child's understanding of number concepts. However, students must devote time at school and at home to practice and to improve these skills. Periodically, I will send home activities and related worksheets that will build number sense and provide much-needed practice. These games and activities have been carefully selected to engage your child in practicing more math facts than usually answered on a typical page of drill or during a flash-card session.

By using the enclosed *Questions Sampler* during homework sessions, you will be able to assist your child without revealing the answers. The questions are categorized to help you select the most appropriate questions for your situation. If your child is having difficulty getting started with a homework assignment, try one of the questions in the first section. If your child gets stuck while completing a task, ask one of the questions from the second section. Try asking one of the questions from the third section to have your child clarify his or her mathematical thinking.

Good questions will help your child make sense of the mathematics, build confidence, and improve mathematical thinking and communication. I recommend posting the *Questions Sampler* in a convenient place, so that you can refer to it often while helping your child with homework.

Your participation in this crucial area is most welcome.

Sincerely,

# Questions Sampler

### Getting Started

*How might you begin?*

*What do you know now?*

*What do you need to find out?*

### While Working

*How can you organize your information?*

*How can you make a drawing (model) to explain your thinking?*

*What approach (strategy) are you developing to solve this?*

*What other possibilities are there?*

*What would happen if . . . ?*

*What do you need to do next?*

*What assumptions are you making?*

*What patterns do you see? . . . What relationships?*

*What prediction can you make?*

*Why did you . . . ?*

### Checking Your Solutions

*How did you arrive at your answer?*

*Why do you think your solution is reasonable?*

*What did you try that didn't work?*

*How can you convince me your solution makes sense?*

### Expanding the Response

(To help clarify your child's thinking, avoid stopping when you hear the "right" answer and avoid correcting the "wrong" answer. Instead, respond with one of the following.)

*Why do you think that?*

*Tell me more.*

*In what other way might you do that? What other possibilities are there?*

*How can you convince me?*

# Addition Facts Made Easy

Since the tables go from 1 to 10, it appears there are 100 "facts" to memorize. However...

If you eliminate the easy 1s and 10s, you **eliminate 36 facts.**

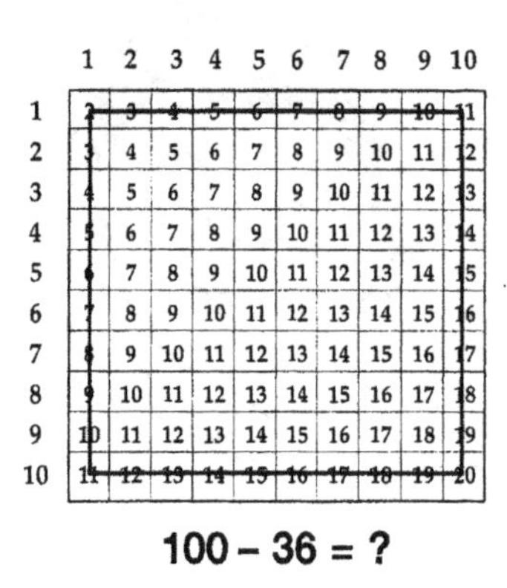

100 – 36 = ?

If you eliminate the 2s, which also seem easy, you **eliminate another 15 facts.**

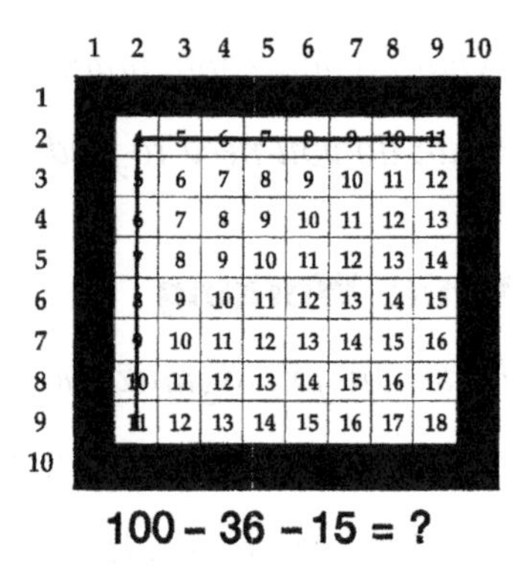

100 – 36 – 15 = ?

The **doubles,** like 4 + 4 and 6 + 6, seem easy to remember, so you can **eliminate another 7.**

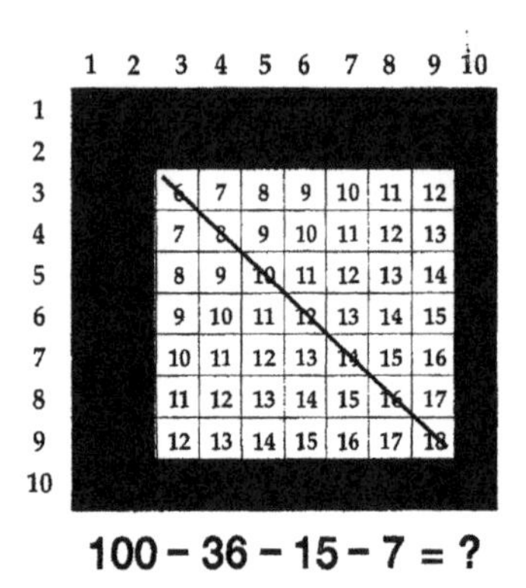

100 – 36 – 15 – 7 = ?

When you know the **doubles plus one** facts, you can **eliminate another 12.**

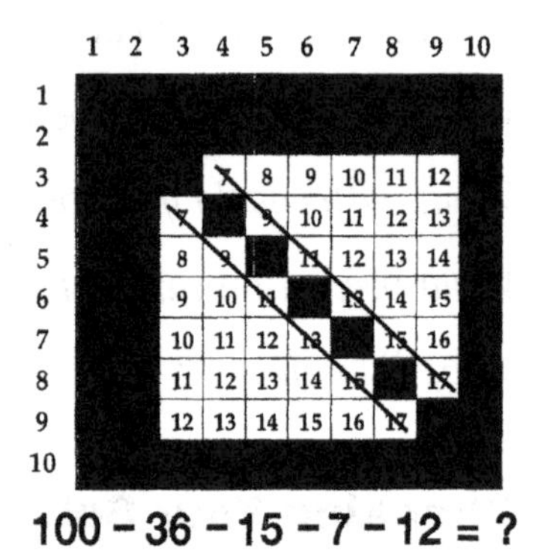

100 – 36 – 15 – 7 – 12 = ?

After you have learned the 9s, you can *reduce* the number of facts **by another 10.**

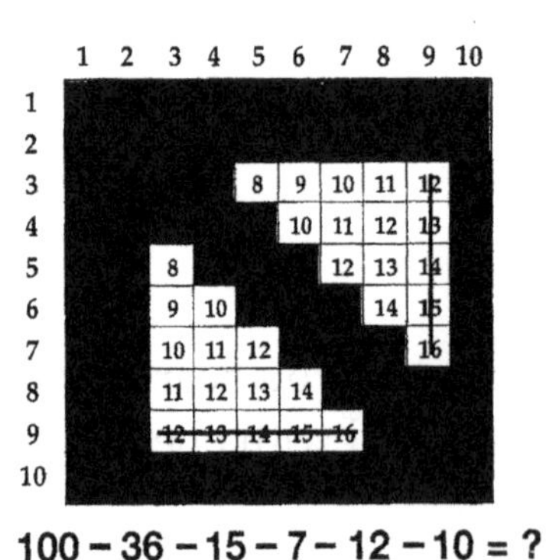

100 – 36 – 15 – 7 – 12 – 10 = ?

We still have duplicates like "3 + 5" and "5 + 3." So, we can cut the remaining 20 facts in half, **eliminating 10 more.**

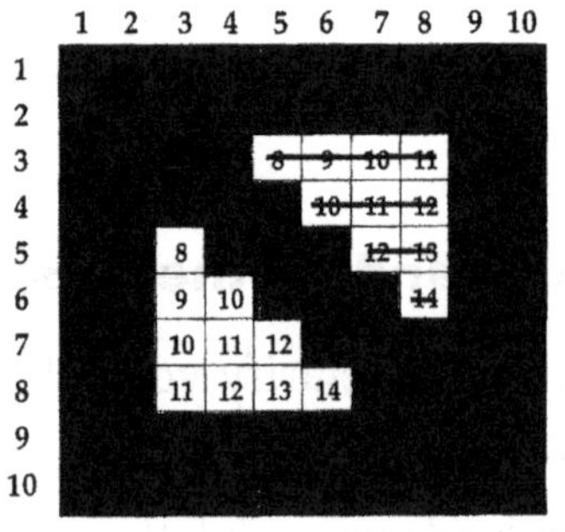

100 – 36 – 15 – 7 – 12 – 10 – 10 = ?

These remaining **"difficult" facts** are left to memorize.

| | | | | |
|---|---|---|---|---|
| 5 + 3 | 6 + 3 | 7 + 3 | 8 + 3 | 6 + 4 |
| 7 + 4 | 8 + 4 | 7 + 5 | 8 + 5 | 8 + 6 |

*It is **highly recommended** that students practice the **related subtraction facts** for quick recall. (For example, 8 – 3 and 8 – 5 are the related subtraction facts for 5 + 3.) For the ten facts listed above, there are 20 related subtraction facts.*

# Multiplication Facts Made Easy

Since the tables go from 1 to 10, it appears there are 100 "facts" to memorize. However...

If you eliminate the easy 1s and 10s, that's **36 fewer facts.**

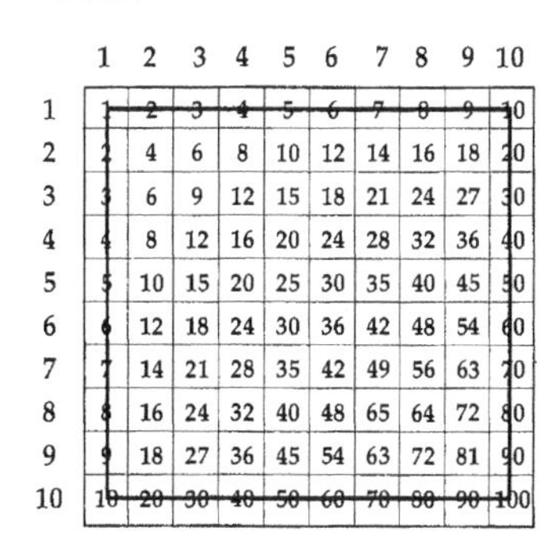

| | 1 | 2 | 3 | 4 | 5 | 6 | 7 | 8 | 9 | 10 |
|---|---|---|---|---|---|---|---|---|---|---|
| 1 | 1 | 2 | 3 | 4 | 5 | 6 | 7 | 8 | 9 | 10 |
| 2 | 2 | 4 | 6 | 8 | 10 | 12 | 14 | 16 | 18 | 20 |
| 3 | 3 | 6 | 9 | 12 | 15 | 18 | 21 | 24 | 27 | 30 |
| 4 | 4 | 8 | 12 | 16 | 20 | 24 | 28 | 32 | 36 | 40 |
| 5 | 5 | 10 | 15 | 20 | 25 | 30 | 35 | 40 | 45 | 50 |
| 6 | 6 | 12 | 18 | 24 | 30 | 36 | 42 | 48 | 54 | 60 |
| 7 | 7 | 14 | 21 | 28 | 35 | 42 | 49 | 56 | 63 | 70 |
| 8 | 8 | 16 | 24 | 32 | 40 | 48 | 65 | 64 | 72 | 80 |
| 9 | 9 | 18 | 27 | 36 | 45 | 54 | 63 | 72 | 81 | 90 |
| 10 | 10 | 20 | 30 | 40 | 50 | 60 | 70 | 80 | 90 | 100 |

If you eliminate the 5s and 2s, which also seem easy, you will have **28 less.**

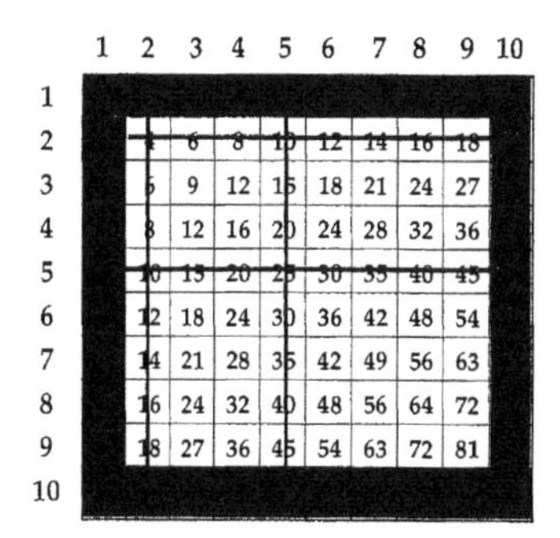

| | 1 | 2 | 3 | 4 | 5 | 6 | 7 | 8 | 9 | 10 |
|---|---|---|---|---|---|---|---|---|---|---|
| 1 | | | | | | | | | | |
| 2 | | 4 | 6 | 8 | 10 | 12 | 14 | 16 | 18 | |
| 3 | | 6 | 9 | 12 | 15 | 18 | 21 | 24 | 27 | |
| 4 | | 8 | 12 | 16 | 20 | 24 | 28 | 32 | 36 | |
| 5 | | 10 | 15 | 20 | 25 | 30 | 35 | 40 | 45 | |
| 6 | | 12 | 18 | 24 | 30 | 36 | 42 | 48 | 54 | |
| 7 | | 14 | 21 | 28 | 35 | 42 | 49 | 56 | 63 | |
| 8 | | 16 | 24 | 32 | 40 | 48 | 56 | 64 | 72 | |
| 9 | | 18 | 27 | 36 | 45 | 54 | 63 | 72 | 81 | |
| 10 | | | | | | | | | | |

If the **squares,** such as three 3s and six 6s, seem easy tor emember, you can **eliminate another 6 facts.**

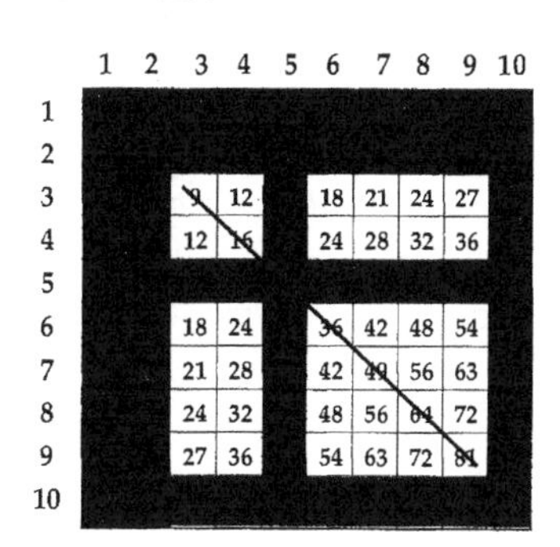

| | 1 | 2 | 3 | 4 | 5 | 6 | 7 | 8 | 9 | 10 |
|---|---|---|---|---|---|---|---|---|---|---|
| 1 | | | | | | | | | | |
| 2 | | | | | | | | | | |
| 3 | | | 9 | 12 | | 18 | 21 | 24 | 27 | |
| 4 | | | 12 | 16 | | 24 | 28 | 32 | 36 | |
| 5 | | | | | | | | | | |
| 6 | | | 18 | 24 | | 36 | 42 | 48 | 54 | |
| 7 | | | 21 | 28 | | 42 | 49 | 56 | 63 | |
| 8 | | | 24 | 32 | | 48 | 56 | 64 | 72 | |
| 9 | | | 27 | 36 | | 54 | 63 | 72 | 81 | |
| 10 | | | | | | | | | | |

That leaves only 30 facts to memorize. However, we still have duplicates like 3 x 4 and 4 x 3; so we can cut 30 in half, **eliminating 15 more.**

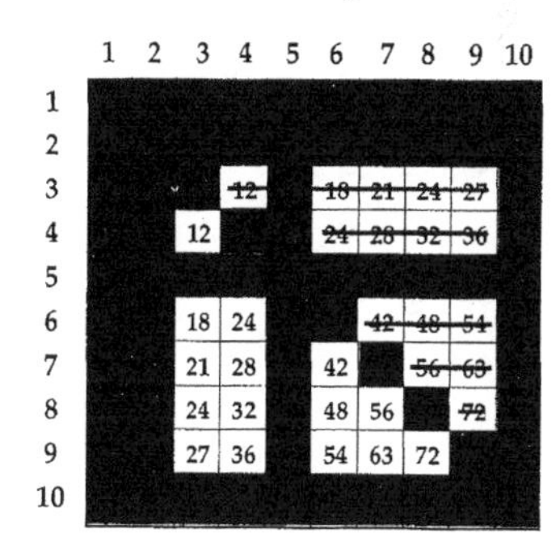

| | 1 | 2 | 3 | 4 | 5 | 6 | 7 | 8 | 9 | 10 |
|---|---|---|---|---|---|---|---|---|---|---|
| 1 | | | | | | | | | | |
| 2 | | | | | | | | | | |
| 3 | | | | 12 | | 18 | 21 | 24 | 27 | |
| 4 | | | 12 | | | 24 | 28 | 32 | 36 | |
| 5 | | | | | | | | | | |
| 6 | | | 18 | 24 | | | 42 | 48 | 54 | |
| 7 | | | 21 | 28 | | 42 | | 56 | 63 | |
| 8 | | | 24 | 32 | | 48 | 56 | | 72 | |
| 9 | | | 27 | 36 | | 54 | 63 | 72 | | |
| 10 | | | | | | | | | | |

How many **"difficult" facts** are left to memorize? **100 – 36 –28 – 6 – 15 = only ???**

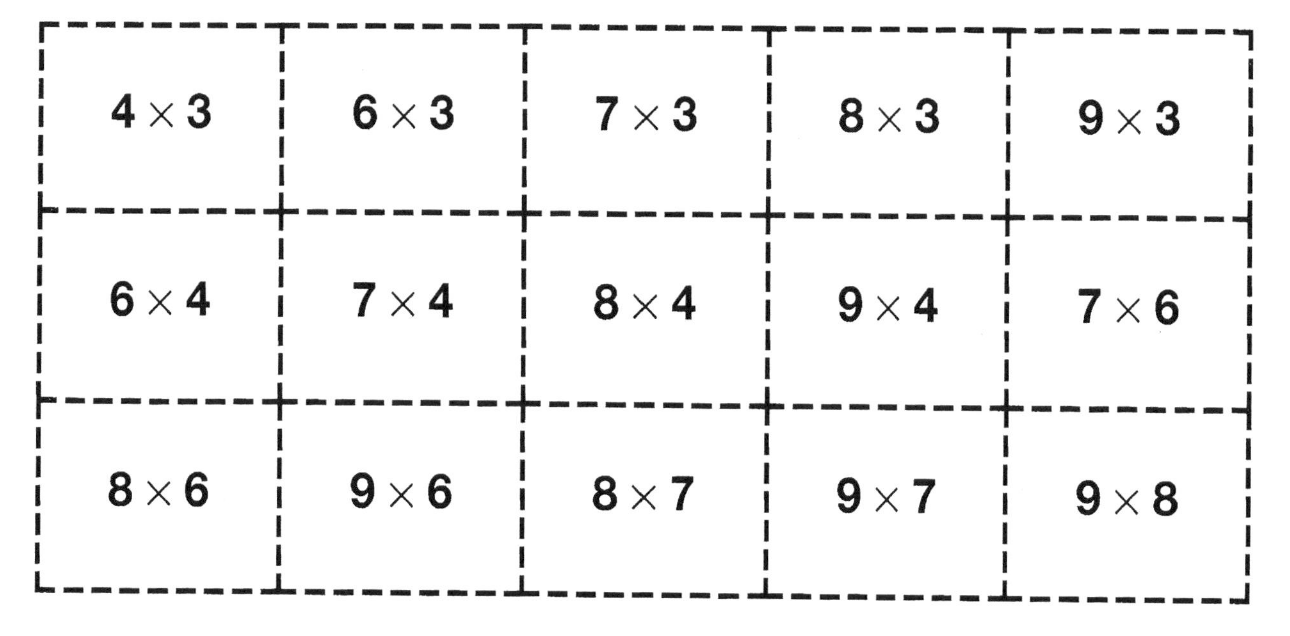

| | | | | |
|---|---|---|---|---|
| 4 × 3 | 6 × 3 | 7 × 3 | 8 × 3 | 9 × 3 |
| 6 × 4 | 7 × 4 | 8 × 4 | 9 × 4 | 7 × 6 |
| 8 × 6 | 9 × 6 | 8 × 7 | 9 × 7 | 9 × 8 |

# Matrix of Games and Sponges

G = Games S = Sponges

| Type | Title | Topic | Page | Materials | Class | Groups | Pairs |
|---|---|---|---|---|---|---|---|
| S | **200-Chart Pieces** | Number Relationships | 62 | Markers; 200 Chart p. 144; Form p. 63 | ✓ | ✓ | |
| G | **99 and Out** | 2-place Subtraction | 105 | Number Cubes; Scratch Paper | | ✓ | ✓ |
| S | **Add It Up** | Mental Addition | 82 | Digit Cards; Form p. 83 | ✓ | ✓ | |
| S | **Addition Chains** | Addition Facts | 16 | Scratch Paper | ✓ | ✓ | ✓ |
| S | **Can You Make...?** | All Operations | 132 | 5 x 8 Cards; Form p. 133 | ✓ | ✓ | |
| G | **Coins Tic-Tac-Toe** | Mental Addition of Coins | 56 | Paper Clips; Markers; Gameboard p. 57 | | | ✓ |
| G | **Cover Up** | All Facts | 137 | Markers; Number Cubes; Gameboard p. 138 | | | ✓ |
| S | **Creating Target Numbers** | Place Value | 64 | Digit Cards; Form p. 65 | ✓ | ✓ | |
| G | **Deciding Digits** | Place Value/Number Sense | 72 | Digit Squares; Form p. 73 | | ✓ | ✓ |
| S | **Difference Patterns** | Subtraction Facts | 33 | Overhead Pens; Form p. 34 | ✓ | ✓ | |
| S | **Diffy** | Mental Subtraction | 99 | Forms pp. 100–101 | ✓ | ✓ | |
| S | **Disappearing Person** | Subtraction Facts | 32 | Chalkboard; Chalk; Eraser | ✓ | ✓ | |
| G | **Factors Pathway** | Multiplication Facts (3s, 4s, 5s) | 121 | Markers; Number Cubes; Gameboard pp. 122–123 | | | ✓ |
| G | **Fifty** | Mental Addition to 50 | 87 | Markers; Gameboard p. 88 | | | ✓ |
| S | **Finding Differences** | Mental Subtraction | 98 | Chalkboard or Overhead Projector | ✓ | ✓ | |
| G | **Four Sums-in-a-Row** | Addition Facts | 23 | Markers; Paper Clips; Gameboard p. 24 | | ✓ | ✓ |
| G | **Four-in-a-Row** | Multiplication Facts | 124 | Markers; Paper Clips; Gameboard p. 125 | | ✓ | ✓ |
| G | **Matching Sums** | Addition Facts | 25 | Number Cubes; Calculator; Form p. 26 | ✓ | ✓ | ✓ |
| S | **Name My Numbers** | Multiplication/Addition Facts | 116 | Chalkboard or Overhead Projector | ✓ | ✓ | |
| S | **Name the Combination** | Adding Coins | 49 | Overhead Coins; Form p. 50 | ✓ | ✓ | |
| G | **Place Value Paths** | Place Value | 69 | Digit Cards; Form pp. 70–71 | ✓ | ✓ | ✓ |
| G | **Race to Two Dollars** | Adding Nickels and Quarters | 54 | Markers; Number Cubes; Gameboard p. 55 | | | ✓ |
| S | **Rhythm Multiplication** | Multiplication Facts | 117 | | ✓ | ✓ | |
| S | **Seeking Sums** | Addition Facts | 14 | Digit Cards (Transparent Set); Form p. 15 | ✓ | ✓ | |
| S | **Signal Math** | All Facts | 130 | Markers; Form p. 131 | ✓ | ✓ | |
| G | **Subtracting to Zero** | Mental Subtraction | 40 | Markers; Gameboard p. 40 | | | ✓ |
| G | **Sum and Subtract** | Subtraction Facts | 38 | Markers; Number Cubes; Gameboard p. 39 | | | ✓ |
| G | **Target 20/Target 200** | 2-place/3-place Subtraction | 106 | Digit Squares; Forms pp. 107–108 | | ✓ | ✓ |
| G | **Target 80** | Mental Addition to 80 | 89 | Digit Squares (1–9); Form p. 90 | | | ✓ |
| S | **Tossing Sums** | Mental Addition | 80 | Form p. 81 | ✓ | ✓ | |
| G | **Uncover** | Addition Facts | 21 | Markers; Number Cubes; Gameboard p. 22 | | ✓ | |
| S | **Valuable Words** | Adding Quarters and Dimes | 48 | Chalkboard or Overhead Projector | ✓ | ✓ | |

# Addition Facts

**Assumptions** The addition facts have previously been taught and reviewed, emphasizing understanding. Concrete objects and visual models, such as ten frames and dominoes, have been used extensively. An attempt has been made to assist students to categorize the facts, in order to learn the few that are not recalled quickly. (See *Addition Facts Made Easy*, p. 10.)

## Section Overview and Suggestions

### Sponges

**Seeking Sums** pp. 14–15

**Addition Chains** pp. 16–17

These open-ended, whole-class, or small-group activities, reinforce practice of the addition facts.

### Skill Checks

**Just the Facts 1–6** pp. 18–20

The Skill Checks provide a way to help parents, students, and you to see students' improvement with the addition facts. Each page of *Just the Facts* may be copied and cut in half so that each check may be used at a different time. Remember to have all students respond to STOP, the number sense task, before solving the ten problems.

### Games

**Uncover** pp. 21–22

**Four Sums-in-a-Row** pp. 23–24

**Matching Sums** pp. 25–26

These open-ended, repeatable Games actively involve students in practicing many addition facts. *Uncover* provides easier and more difficult methods for determining your score (see "Tip"). *Matching Sums* promotes mental computation as students find the sum of three addends.

### Independent Activities

**Seeking Sums Practice** pp. 27–28

**Circling Sums** p. 29

**Matching Sums Practice** p. 30

These open-ended Independent Activities provide long-term practice. After becoming familiar with the *Seeking Sums* Sponge, students should succeed with *Seeking Sums Practice I.* The blank *Seeking Sums Practice II* form allows students to practice many more variations. *Circling Sums* allows student or teacher choice. Success with the challenging *Matching Sums Practice* activities requires a good understanding of the directions from the corresponding Game (p. 25).

# Seeking Sums

**Topic:** Addition Facts

**Object:** Combine selected amounts to equal a target sum

**Groups:** Whole class or small group

*Tip* *For students needing to begin with easier facts, use only the digits 1–6 and find sums through 12.*

### Materials

- transparency of Digit Cards, p. 146
- transparency of *Seeking Sums* recording sheet, p. 15

### Directions

**1.** Leader draws four transparent digit cards and displays the numbers on the recording sheet. Using any of the four displayed numbers, players identify ways to make the sums 1 through 18.

*Example:* If 2, 3, 5, and 6 are displayed, 5 could be made by combining 2 and 3 or by using the 5 card alone.

**2.** As students identify solutions, the leader records these solutions (see illustration). After a solution is given, the leader should encourage players to seek additional solutions for the same sum.

### Making Connections

Promote reflection and make mathematical connections by asking:

- Were any sums not possible? If so, why not?
- Which sums could be made more than one way? Are these numbers similar?

# Seeking Sums

## Recording Sheet

| 1 | 2 | 3 | 4 | 5 | 6 |
|---|---|---|---|---|---|
| 7 | 8 | 9 | 10 | 11 | 12 |
| 13 | 14 | 15 | 16 | 17 | 18 |

# Addition Chains

**Topic:** Addition Facts and Patterns

**Object:** Add until a repeating pattern appears

**Groups:** Whole class as pair players or small group

### Materials

- scratch paper

### Directions

1. Leader uses two single digits, such as 3 and 4, to demonstrate how this activity works.
2. Students add the two digits and record only the one's place digit of the sum. Students continue adding the last two digits until the sequence of numbers begins to repeat.

   *Example:* 3 4 7 1 8 9 7 6 3 9 2 1 3 4

This pattern required 12 numbers before the pattern began to repeat.

3. Students work with a partner, use any two single digits, and record their addition chain.
4. When pairs complete a chain, have students share and compare their results.
5. Before concluding this activity, have students share their discoveries, highlighting interesting patterns.

### Making Connections

Promote reflection and make mathematical connections by asking:

- Which numbers generated shorter chains?
- What's the longest chain created?

# Addition Chains Recording Sheet

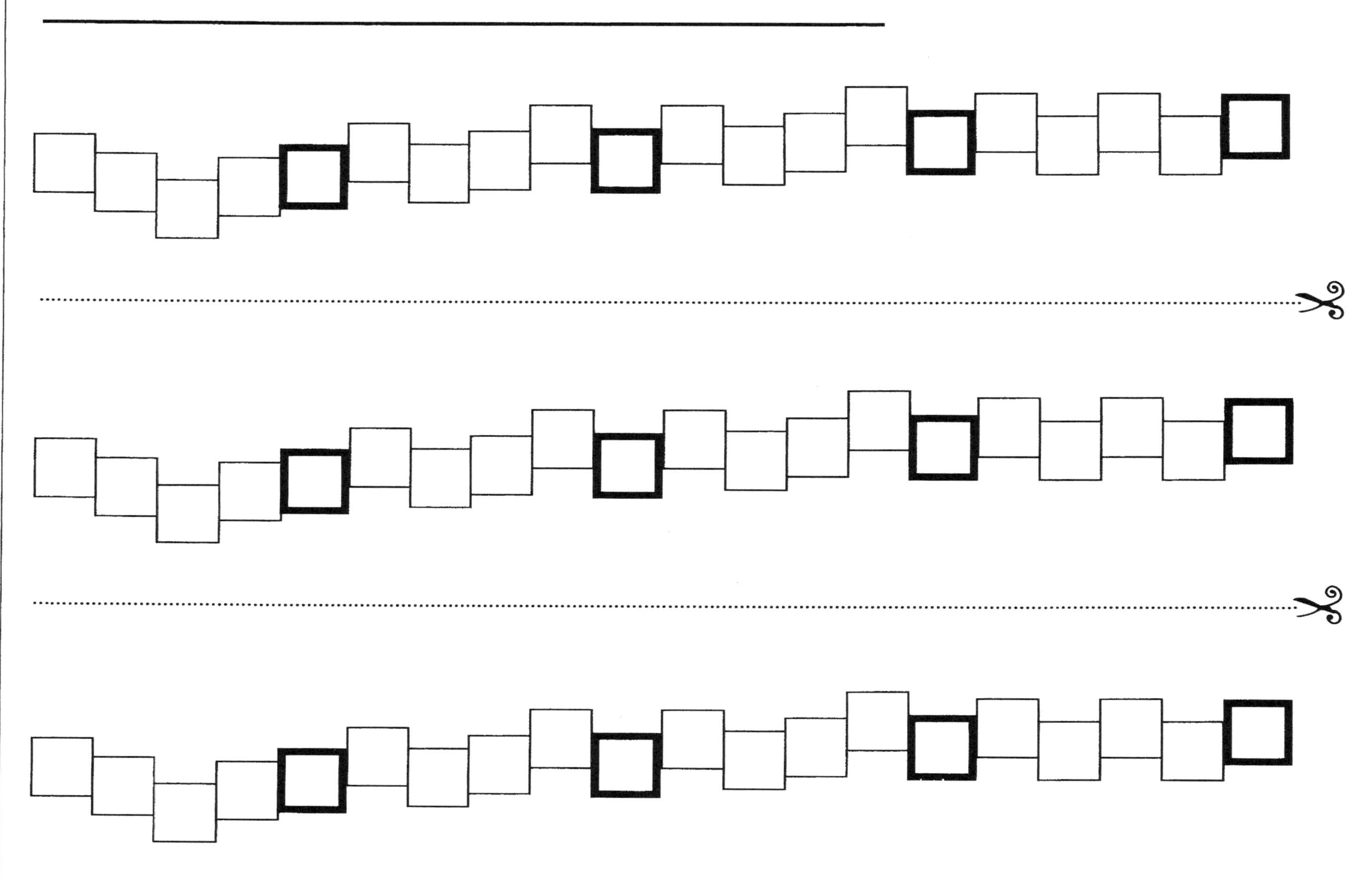

Date ____________ Name ____________________

# Just the Facts 1

**STOP** Don't start yet! Star two problems that may have even answers.

**1.** $\begin{array}{r} 2 \\ +6 \\ \hline \end{array}$ **2.** $\begin{array}{r} 4 \\ +8 \\ \hline \end{array}$ **3.** $\begin{array}{r} 9 \\ +7 \\ \hline \end{array}$ **4.** $\begin{array}{r} 8 \\ +8 \\ \hline \end{array}$

**5.** $3 + 5 =$ _____ **6.** $6 + 5 =$ _____ **7.** $8 + 7 =$ _____

**8.** $3 + 4 + 6 =$ _____ **9.** $4 + 5 + 6 =$ _____ **10.** $(6 + 4) + (5 + 2) =$ _____

**Go On** Write three facts that equal 14.

Date ____________ Name ____________________

# Just the Facts 2

**STOP** Don't start yet! Star two problems that may have answers less than 10.

**1.** $\begin{array}{r} 4 \\ +3 \\ \hline \end{array}$ **2.** $\begin{array}{r} 3 \\ +9 \\ \hline \end{array}$ **3.** $\begin{array}{r} 7 \\ +7 \\ \hline \end{array}$ **4.** $\begin{array}{r} 9 \\ +9 \\ \hline \end{array}$

**5.** $7 + 2 =$ _____ **6.** $4 + 7 =$ _____ **7.** $9 + 5 =$ _____

**8.** $6 + 3 + 6 =$ _____ **9.** $5 + 4 + 7 =$ _____ **10.** $(3 + 3) + (7 + 2) =$ _____

**Go On** What number is missing? 1, 4, 7, _____, 13, 16

Date ________________ Name ________________________

# Just the Facts 3

Don't start yet! Star two problems that may have an odd answer.

**1.** $\begin{array}{r} 5 \\ +4 \\ \hline \end{array}$ **2.** $\begin{array}{r} 9 \\ +3 \\ \hline \end{array}$ **3.** $\begin{array}{r} 7 \\ +8 \\ \hline \end{array}$ **4.** $\begin{array}{r} 5 \\ +9 \\ \hline \end{array}$

**5.** $7 + 3 =$ ____ **6.** $2 + 9 =$ ____ **7.** $8 + 9 =$ ____

**8.** $3 + 5 + 6 =$ ____ **9.** $3 + 4 + 2 =$ ____ **10.** $(6 + 4) + (2 + 4) =$ ____

**Go On** What numbers come next? 1, 3, 5, 7, ____, ____, ____

Date ________________ Name ________________________

# Just the Facts 4

Don't start yet! Star a problem that may have an answer larger than 15.

**1.** $\begin{array}{r} 2 \\ +7 \\ \hline \end{array}$ **2.** $\begin{array}{r} 6 \\ +5 \\ \hline \end{array}$ **3.** $\begin{array}{r} 9 \\ +4 \\ \hline \end{array}$ **4.** $\begin{array}{r} 5 \\ +8 \\ \hline \end{array}$

**5.** $6 + 4 =$ ____ **6.** $3 + 8 =$ ____ **7.** $6 + 9 =$ ____

**8.** $4 + 5 + 2 =$ ____ **9.** $2 + 7 + 4 =$ ____ **10.** $(4 + 5) + (2 + 6) =$ ____

**Go On** Write three facts that equal 12.

Date ____________ Name ____________________

# Just the Facts 5

**STOP** Don't start yet! Star a problem that may have an odd answer.

**1.** $4 + 4$

**2.** $3 + 8$

**3.** $9 + 6$

**4.** $8 + 5$

**5.** $5 + 2 =$ ____

**6.** $6 + 6 =$ ____

**7.** $8 + 8 =$ ____

**8.** $5 + 4 + 5 =$ ____

**9.** $6 + 2 + 8 =$ ____

**10.** $(4 + 3) + (6 + 4) =$ ____

**Go On** What other number fits? Please explain your answer.

| 12 | 8 |
|---|---|
| 14 | 16 |

Date ____________ Name ____________________

# Just the Facts 6

**STOP** Don't start yet! Star a problem that will have one of the smallest answers.

**1.** $3 + 6$

**2.** $4 + 7$

**3.** $9 + 8$

**4.** $8 + 6$

**5.** $9 + 1 =$ ____

**6.** $7 + 5 =$ ____

**7.** $4 + 9 =$ ____

**8.** $2 + 6 + 4 =$ ____

**9.** $6 + 3 + 6 =$ ____

**10.** $(3 + 6) + (2 + 4) =$ ____

**Go On** What numbers come next? 2, 5, 8, ____, ____, ____

# Uncover

**Topic:** Addition Facts

**Object:** Pick up greatest number of markers

**Groups:** Pair players or 2 players

### Materials for each group

- *Uncover* gameboard, p. 22
- 2 number cubes (1–6)
- 12 transparent markers for each pair

***Tip*** *As students gain skill and confidence, have them total the numerical value of the uncovered numbers to determine their score. Winners have lower scores.*

### Directions

1. To begin, pairs place markers on each numbered space along both number strips.
2. The first pair rolls the number cubes and adds the numbers on the number cubes. The pair can uncover the sum or any combination of addends that equals the rolled sum.

   *Example:* If 2 and 4 are rolled, the pair can uncover 6 or any combination that makes 6, such as 1 + 5, 1 + 2 + 3, or 2 + 4.
3. Pairs alternate turns, rolling number cubes and uncovering sums or addends from their individual number strips.
4. When a pair can no longer use the "covered" numbers to make a sum or combination, play stops for that pair. When both pairs stop, the game ends.
5. The pair who picks up the most markers wins.

### Making Connections

Promote reflection and make mathematical connections by asking:

- Which sums did you prefer to roll? Why?
- What strategies helped you uncover more markers?

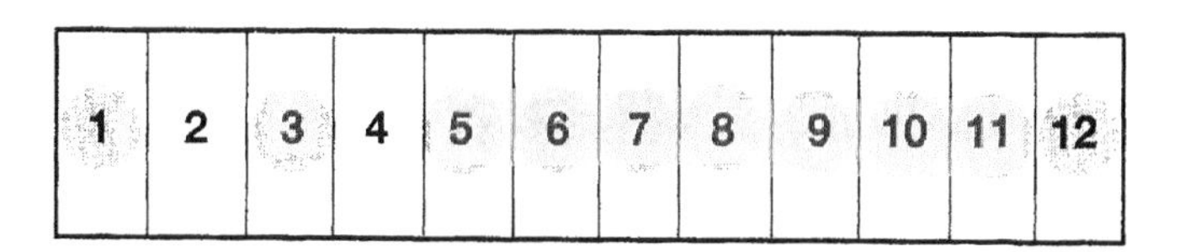

# Uncover

| | |
|---|---|
| 1 | 12 |
| 2 | 11 |
| 3 | 10 |
| 4 | 9 |
| 5 | 8 |
| 6 | 7 |
| 7 | 6 |
| 8 | 5 |
| 9 | 4 |
| 10 | 3 |
| 11 | 2 |
| 12 | 1 |

# Four Sums-in-a-Row

**Topic:** Addition Facts

**Object:** Cover four numbers in a row

**Groups:** 2 pair players

*Tip* *For players feeling insecure with the facts, allow three in a row to win.*

### Materials for each group

- *Four Sums-in-a-Row* gameboard, p. 24
- 2 paper clips
- different markers for each pair

### Directions

1. The first pair places two paper clips at the bottom of the gameboard, indicating two addends. The pair then adds the two numbers and places a marker on the resulting sum.
2. The other pair moves *only one* of the paper clips to a new addend. Then this pair adds the two indicated numbers and places a marker on that sum. (It is permissible to have two paper clips on the same addend.)
3. Pairs continue alternating turns moving one paper clip each time, adding the numbers, stating the fact, and placing markers on the gameboard.
4. The first pair to have four markers in a row horizontally, vertically, or diagonally is the winner.

### Making Connections

Promote reflection and make mathematical connections by asking:

- Was it difficult to block your opponent? Why or why not?
- What strategies helped you line up your markers in a row?

| | | | | |
|---|---|---|---|---|
| 10 | 14 | 8 | 17 | 13 |
| 5 | 12 | 16 | 15 | 9 |
| 18 | 17 | 11 | 6 | 12 |
| 7 | 4 | 13 | 9 | 16 |
| 11 | 15 | 18 | 14 | 10 |

1 2 3 4 5 6 7 8 9

# Four Sums-in-a-Row

| | | | | |
|---|---|---|---|---|
| 10 | 14 | 8 | 17 | 13 |
| 5 | 12 | 16 | 15 | 9 |
| 18 | 17 | 11 | 6 | 12 |
| 7 | 4 | 13 | 9 | 16 |
| 11 | 15 | 18 | 14 | 10 |

1 2 3 4 5 6 7 8 9

# Matching Sums

*Tip* *As students gain competence, use 1–9 digit cards to identify numbers for cells.*

**Topic:** Addition Facts

**Object:** Create matching sums

**Groups:** Whole class as pair players or small group

### Materials for each group

- Number Cube (1–6)
- *Matching Sums* recording sheet, p. 26
- calculator (for determining score)

### Directions

1. Leader rolls the number cube and calls out the number rolled.
2. Each pair writes the number in one of the nine cells on a recording sheet. Once a number is recorded, it cannot be changed.
3. Leader continues rolling the number cube, and pairs enter the rolled number in the same nine-cell grid.
4. After nine numbers have been called and recorded, pairs add their numbers and write the sums in the circles adjacent to each row, column, and diagonal. Each pair should have eight sums.
5. Sums that have no matches are eliminated (crossed out). Only matching sums are totaled to determine each pair's score. (Access to calculators seems appropriate.)

   *Example:*

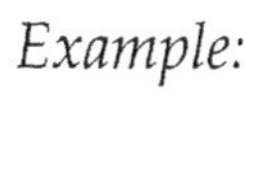

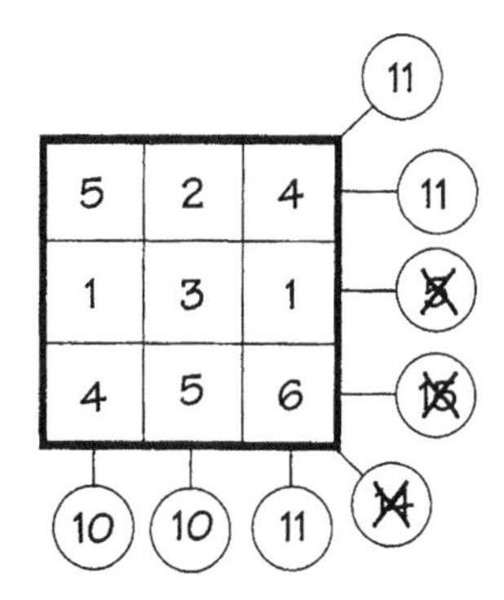


6. The pairs with the highest totals are the winners.

### Making Connections

Promote reflection and make mathematical connections by asking:

- What strategy helped you make matches?
- When you play this again, what will you do differently?

# Matching Sums

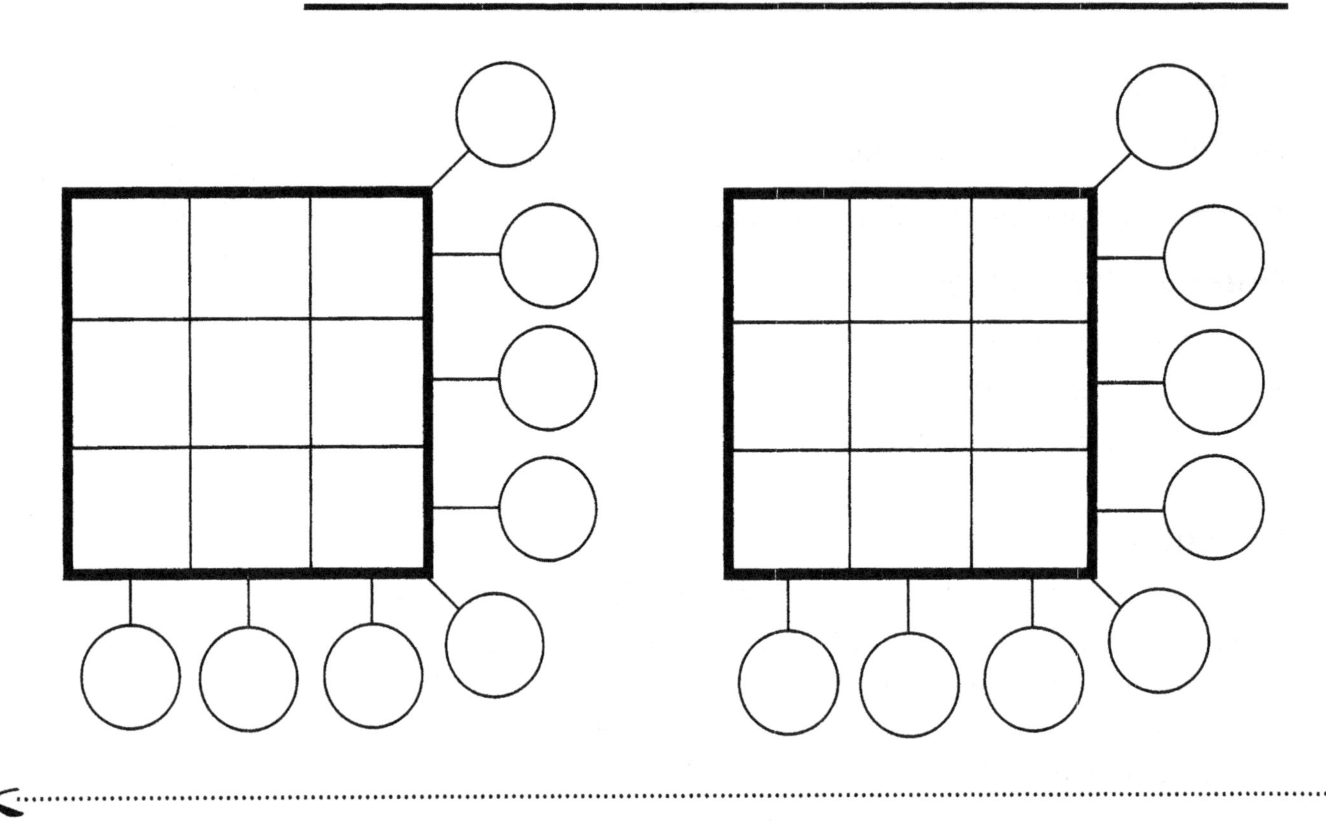

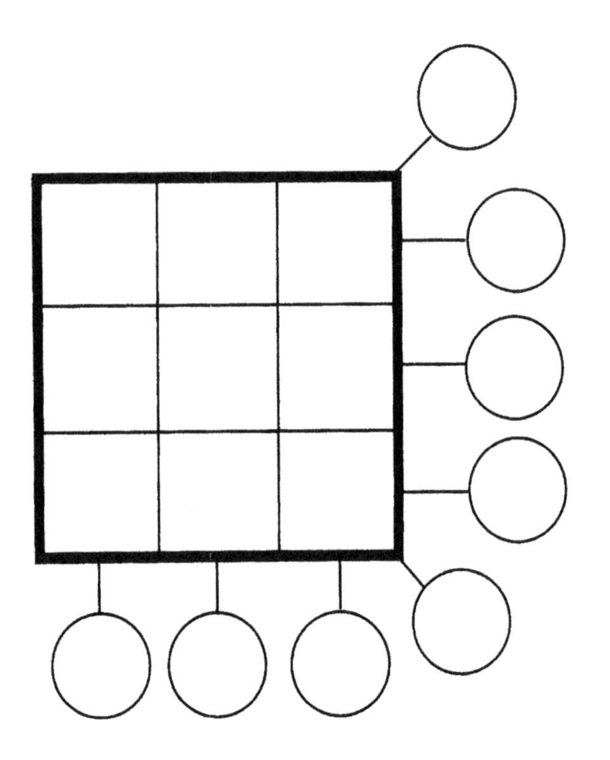

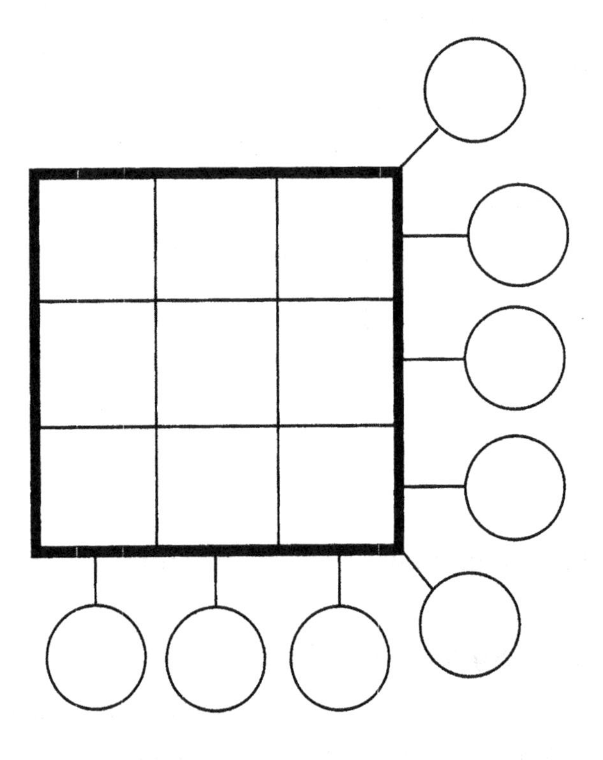

Date ________________ Name ________________________

# Seeking Sums Practice I

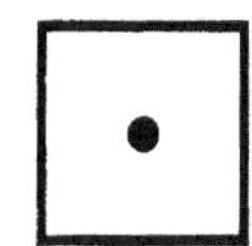
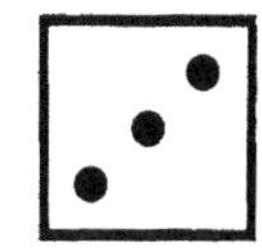
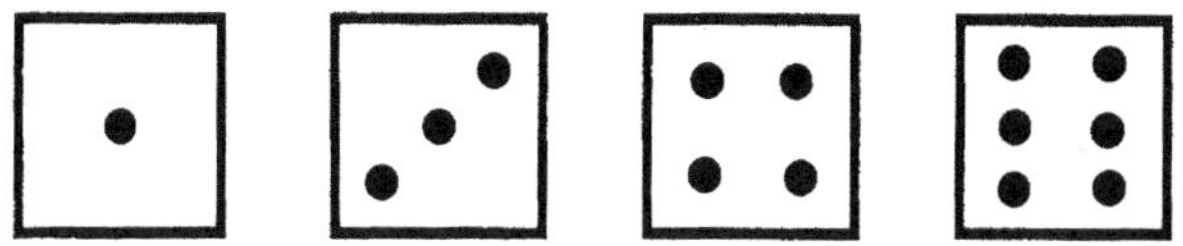

1 ____ ____ ____

Which of the sums below can be shown using the dot patterns above?
If you find a way, record your solution.

| | | |
|---|---|---|
| 6 ____________ | 9 ____________ | 12 ____________ |
| 7 ____________ | 10 ____________ | 13 ____________ |
| 8 ____________ | 11 ____________ | 14 ____________ |

---

| 1 | 3 | 5 | 7 |
|---|---|---|---|

Which of the sums below can be shown using the numbers above?
If you find a way, record your solution.

| | |
|---|---|
| 6 ________________ | 11 ________________ |
| 7 ________________ | 12 ________________ |
| 8 ________________ | 13 ________________ |
| 9 ________________ | 14 ________________ |
| 10 ________________ | 15 ________________ |

Date ____________ Name ____________________

# Seeking Sums Practice II

Before seeking sums, write a single digit in each box.

Which of the sums below can be shown using the numbers above?
If you find a way, record your solution.

| | | |
|---|---|---|
| 6 ________ | 9 ________ | 12 ________ |
| 7 ________ | 10 ________ | 13 ________ |
| 8 ________ | 11 ________ | 14 ________ |

---

Before seeking sums, write a single digit in each box.

Which of the sums below can be shown using the numbers above?
If you find a way, record your solution.

| | |
|---|---|
| 6 ____________ | 11 ____________ |
| 7 ____________ | 12 ____________ |
| 8 ____________ | 13 ____________ |
| 9 ____________ | 14 ____________ |
| 10 ____________ | 15 ____________ |

Date ____________ Name ____________

# Circling Sums

Circle any two numbers that add up to a [ ]

Circle sums of 8.

| | | |
|---|---|---|
| 2 + 6 | 4 + 4 | 3 + 5 |
| 1 | 5 | 2 + 3 |
| | | 7 + 6 |

| | | |
|---|---|---|
| sum of 10 | sum of 13 | even sum less than 10 |
| sum of 12 | sum of 14 | sum greater than 14 |

| | | | | | | | |
|---|---|---|---|---|---|---|---|
| 6 | 4 | 2 | 9 | 1 | 8 | 2 | 7 |
| 3 | 5 | 8 | 3 | 7 | 6 | 5 | 9 |
| 4 | 7 | 9 | 2 | 5 | 3 | 4 | 1 |
| 2 | 6 | 4 | 5 | 2 | 6 | 3 | 8 |
| 7 | 5 | 3 | 9 | 6 | 7 | 2 | 4 |
| 6 | 2 | 5 | 7 | 3 | 8 | 4 | 5 |

Date ______________ Name ______________________

# Matching Sums Practice

Follow the directions for Matching Sums game (p. 25) to complete this activity.

**1.** Arrange these numbers using 1, 1, 2, 3, 3, 4, 4, 5, 6 to produce a score over 30.

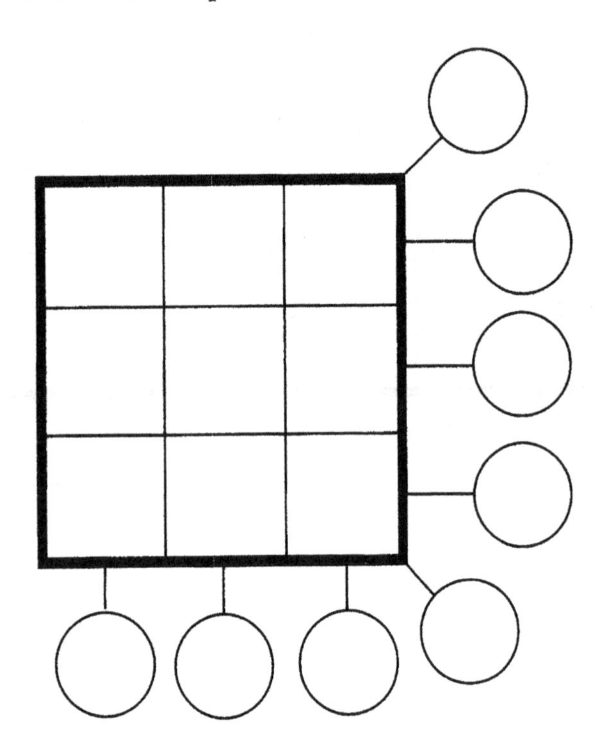

**2.** Arrange these numbers using 1, 2, 2, 3, 3, 4, 4, 5, 6 to produce a score over 35.

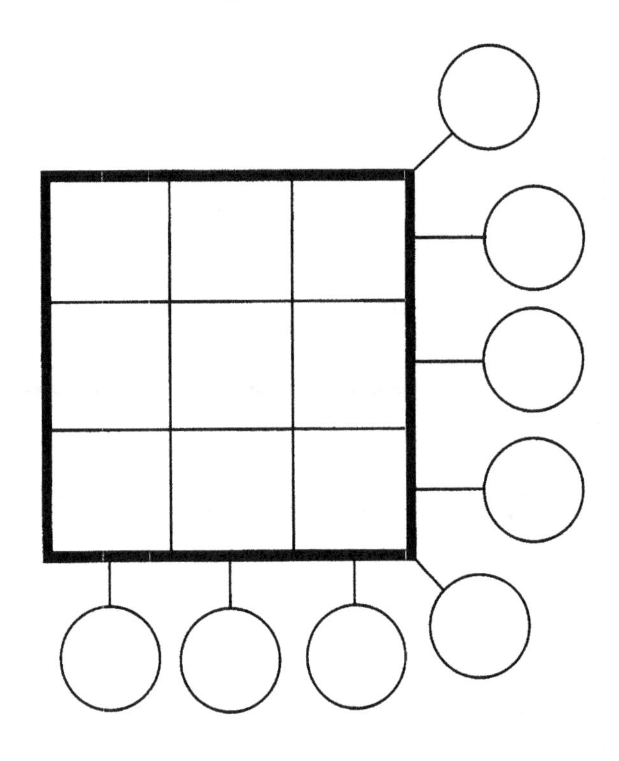

**3.** Arrange these numbers using 1, 1, 2, 2, 3, 4, 4, 5, 6 to produce a score over 40.

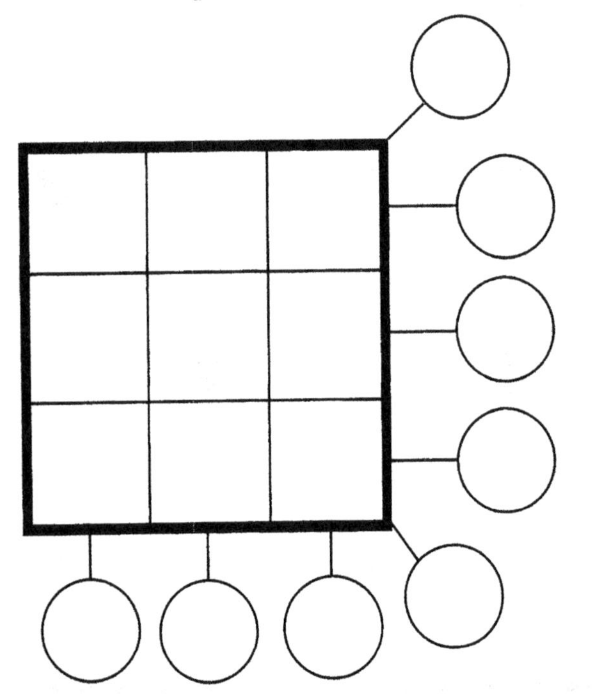

**4.** Try for the highest possible score using 1, 2, 2, 3, 3, 4, 5, 5, 6.

Score _______

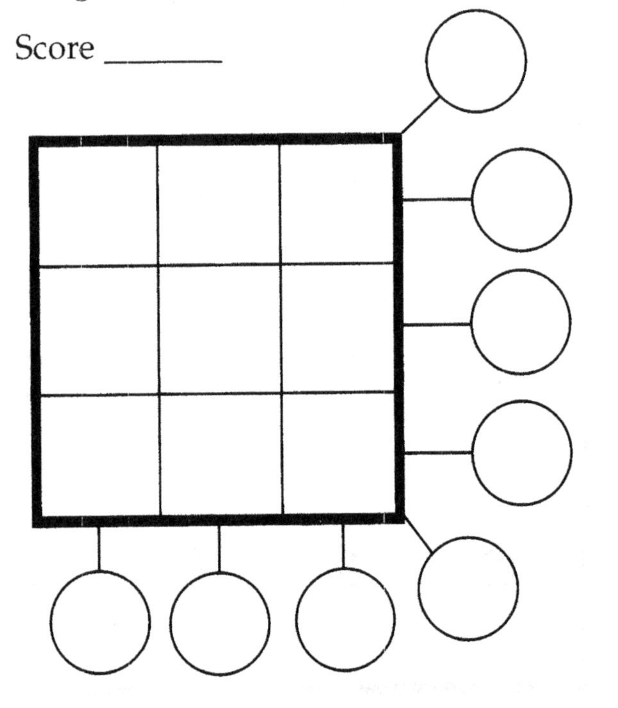

# Subtraction Facts

**Assumptions** The subtraction facts have previously been taught and reviewed, emphasizing understanding. Concrete objects and visual models, such as coins and ten frames, have been used extensively. An attempt has been made to assist students to categorize the facts, in order to learn the few that are not recalled quickly. (See *Addition Facts Made Easy*, p. 10.)

## Section Overview and Suggestions

### Sponges

**Disappearing Person** p. 32

**Difference Patterns** pp. 33–34

These open-ended, whole-class, or small-group activities reinforce practice of the subtraction facts.

### Skill Checks

**What's the Difference?** 1–6 pp. 35–37

These provide a way for parents, students, and you to see students' improvement with the subtraction facts. Each page of *What's the Difference?* may be copied and cut in half so that each check may be used at a different time. Remember to have all students respond to STOP, the number sense task, before solving the ten problems.

### Games

**Sum and Subtract** pp. 38–39

**Subtracting to Zero** p. 40

These open-ended and repeatable Games actively involve students in practicing many subtraction facts. Both Games promote mental computation as strategic thinking skills are enhanced.

### Independent Activities

**Tic-Tac-Toe Subtract** pp. 41–42

**What's Left?** pp. 43–44

**Subtraction Squares** pp. 45–46

*Tic-Tac-Toe Subtract* and *What's Left?* require students to independently practice either the easier or more difficult subtraction facts to solve inviting puzzles. Teachers find students enjoy creating their own *What's Left?* puzzles for others to solve. The easier and more challenging *Subtraction Squares* provide lots of facts practice with ways to self-check. Use the blank *Subtraction Squares* worksheet, p. 151, with student-authored puzzles to provide additional independent practice.

# Disappearing Person

**Topic:** Subtraction Facts

**Object:** Erase body parts by creating and solving subtraction equations

**Groups:** Whole class or small group

### Materials

- chalkboard and chalk
- chalk eraser

*Tip* *Numbers written inside the body parts can be varied according to the range of student abilities. With younger students, you could fill the parts with 2s, 3s, and 4s only.*

### Directions

1. Leader draws a person with numbered body parts (similar to illustration) on the chalkboard. Numbers 2 through 9 work best.
2. Students take turns describing subtraction facts or subtraction situations that equal a number found inside a body part.
3. Leader calls on other students (or hands them a chalk eraser) to state the subtraction equation, identify the difference, and erase a body part containing the difference.

   *Example:* Student: "What's the difference between 12 and 8?"

   Responder with eraser: "12 minus 8 equals 4." (Responder erases the left hand.)

   Student: "What's left when you subtract 9 from 16?"

   Responder: "16 minus 9 equals 7." (Responder erases the top of the hat.)

# Difference Patterns

**Topic:** Subtraction Facts

**Object:** Create subtraction sequences

**Groups:** Whole class or small group

### Materials

- transparency of *Difference Patterns,* p. 34
- overhead pens

*Tip To easily reuse transparency for a new descending pattern, use a blank transparency on top of the* Difference Patterns *transparency.*

### Directions

**1.** Leader thinks of a number to subtract from 20 and draws an arrowed line from 20 to the resulting difference.

*Example:* 20 to 17

**2.** Students take turns volunteering to continue the descending pattern by subtracting the same amount, 3.

*Example:* Student draws an arrowed line from 17 to 14.

**3.** Volunteers continue drawing arrowed lines until the path ends at 0, or until no other possibilities exist. Arrowed lines may go in any direction and may cross.

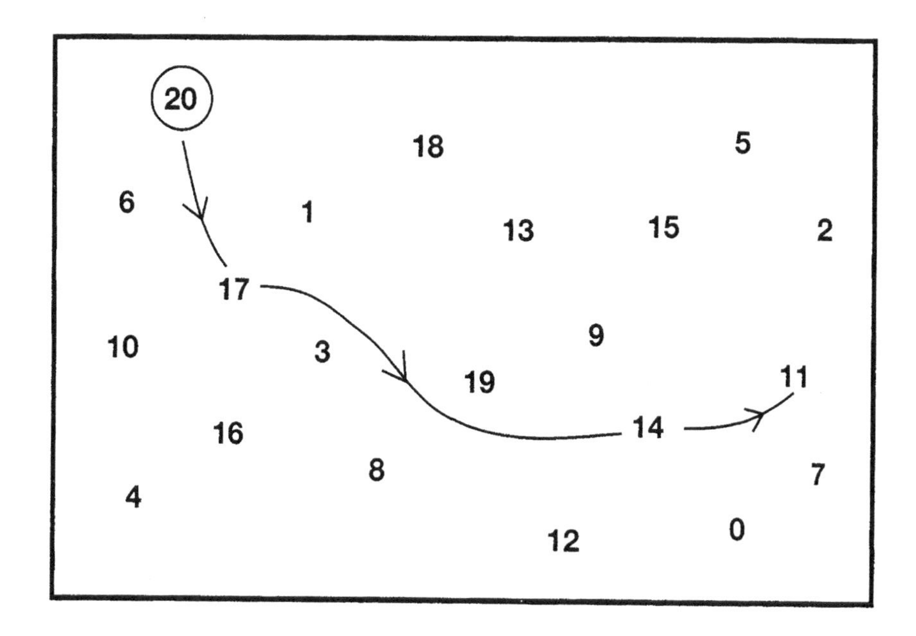

# Difference Patterns

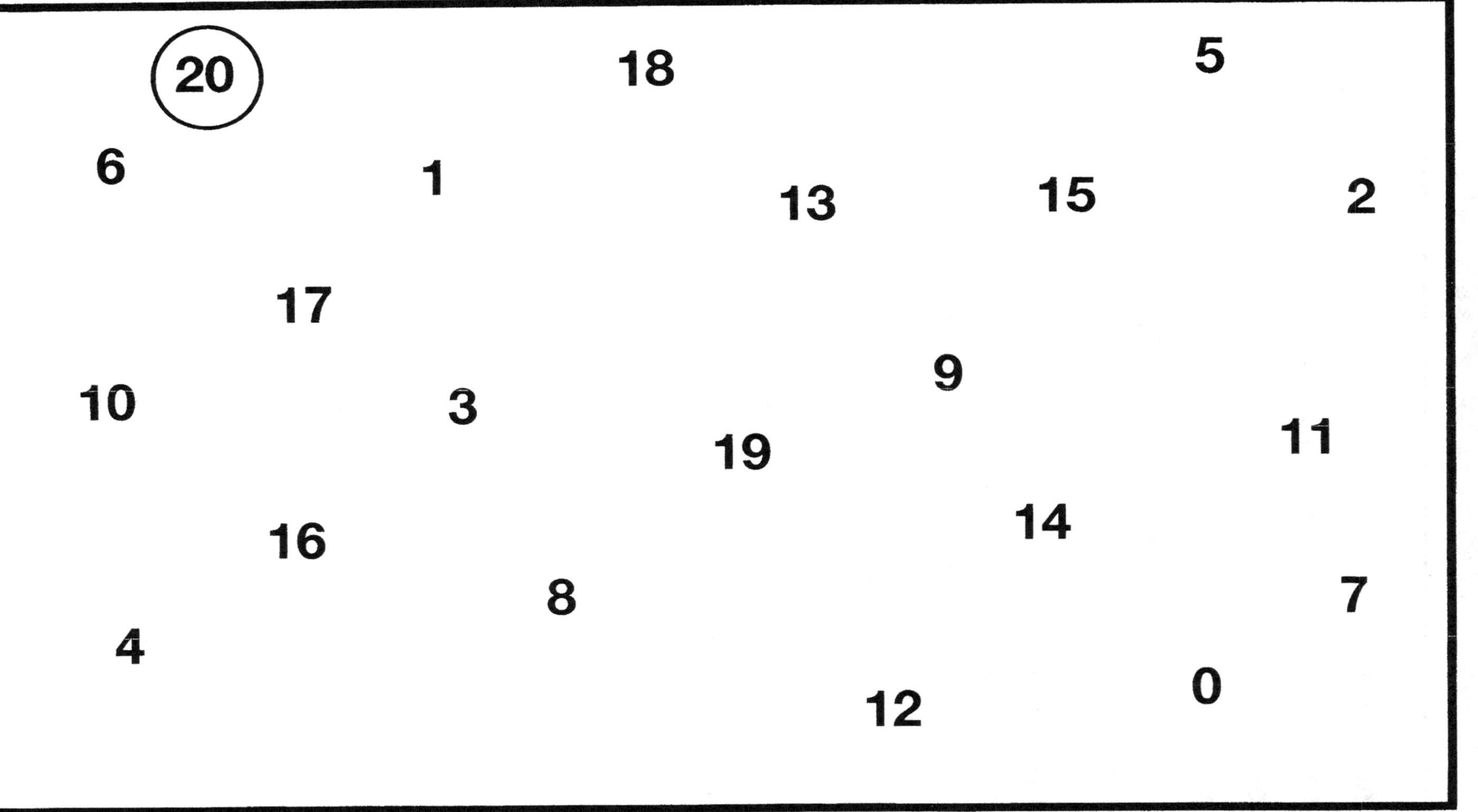

Date ____________ Name ____________________

# What's the Difference? 1

Don't start yet! Star two problems that may have odd answers.

**1.** 8 – 5 = ____ **2.** 10 – 4 = ____

**3.** 12 – 7 = ____ **4.** 14 – 6 = ____

**5.** 9 – 3 = ____ **6.** 11 – 4 = ____ **7.** 15 – 6 = ____ **8.** 18 – 9 = ____

**9.** (12 – 3) – 5 = ____ **10.** (15 – 4) – 6 = ____

**Go On** What numbers come next? 20, 15, 10, ____ , ____

Date ____________ Name ____________________

# What's the Difference? 2

Don't start yet! Star the problem in Row 2 that will have the larger answer.

**1.** 9 – 4 = ____ **2.** 11 – 6 = ____

**3.** 12 – 6 = ____ **4.** 16 – 9 = ____

**5.** 8 – 5 = ____ **6.** 10 – 7 = ____ **7.** 14 – 8 = ____ **8.** 16 – 7 = ____

**9.** (11 – 2) – 6 = ____ **10.** (15 – 3) – 7 = ____

**Go On** What number is missing? 18, 15, 12, ____ , 6, 3

Date ____________ Name ____________________

# What's the Difference? 3

**STOP** Don't start yet! Star the problems in Row 3 that may have even answers.

**1.** $7 - 3 =$ ____ **2.** $10 - 6 =$ ____

**3.** $12 - 5 =$ ____ **4.** $15 - 8 =$ ____

**5.** $\begin{array}{r} 9 \\ -6 \\ \hline \end{array}$ **6.** $\begin{array}{r} 11 \\ -3 \\ \hline \end{array}$ **7.** $\begin{array}{r} 14 \\ -9 \\ \hline \end{array}$ **8.** $\begin{array}{r} 16 \\ -8 \\ \hline \end{array}$

**9.** $(13 - 5) - 2 =$ ____ **10.** $(17 - 4) - 8 =$ ____

**Go On** Give three subtraction facts that equal 4.

---

Date ____________ Name ____________________

# What's the Difference? 4

**STOP** Don't start yet! Star the problem in Row 3 that will have the larger answer.

**1.** $9 - 5 =$ ____ **2.** $10 - 3 =$ ____

**3.** $12 - 6 =$ ____ **4.** $14 - 5 =$ ____

**5.** $\begin{array}{r} 8 \\ -3 \\ \hline \end{array}$ **6.** $\begin{array}{r} 11 \\ -7 \\ \hline \end{array}$ **7.** $\begin{array}{r} 13 \\ -6 \\ \hline \end{array}$ **8.** $\begin{array}{r} 15 \\ -7 \\ \hline \end{array}$

**9.** $(11 - 4) - 2 =$ ____ **10.** $(16 - 5) - 4 =$ ____

**Go On** What numbers come next? 17, 14, 11, ____ , ____

Date ____________ Name ____________

# What's the Difference? 5

Don't start yet! Star two problems that may have answers less than 5.

**1.** 8 – 6 = ____ **2.** 11 – 5 = ____

**3.** 12 – 4 = ____ **4.** 15 – 9 = ____

**5.** $\begin{array}{r} 9 \\ -5 \\ \hline \end{array}$ **6.** $\begin{array}{r} 10 \\ -3 \\ \hline \end{array}$ **7.** $\begin{array}{r} 14 \\ -7 \\ \hline \end{array}$ **8.** $\begin{array}{r} 17 \\ -9 \\ \hline \end{array}$

**9.** (12 – 5) – 3 = ____ **10.** (18 – 6) – 6 = ____

**Go On** What number fits? Please explain your answer.

| 12 – 7 | 8 – 3 |
|---|---|
| 11 – 6 | 10 – ? |

Date ____________ Name ____________

# What's the Difference? 6

Don't start yet! Star the problems in Row 3 that may have odd answers.

**1.** 9 – 3 = ____ **2.** 12 – 8 = ____

**3.** 10 – 6 = ____ **4.** 16 – 8 = ____

**5.** $\begin{array}{r} 8 \\ -2 \\ \hline \end{array}$ **6.** $\begin{array}{r} 11 \\ -7 \\ \hline \end{array}$ **7.** $\begin{array}{r} 13 \\ -6 \\ \hline \end{array}$ **8.** $\begin{array}{r} 15 \\ -8 \\ \hline \end{array}$

**9.** (12 – 4) – 3 = ____ **10.** (16 – 5) – 4 = ____

**Go On** What number is missing? 20, 16, 12, ____, 4

# Sum and Subtract

**Topic:** Subtraction Facts

**Object:** Cover 3 in a row with your markers

**Groups:** 2 pair players

*Tip* *If the game is played at home, require adult players to get four in a row.*

### Materials for each group

- *Sum and Subtract* gameboard, p. 39
- markers (different kind for each pair)
- 2 Number Cubes (1–6)
- special Number Cube (4–9), p. 149

### Directions

1. The first pair rolls three number cubes. The pair decides which two number cubes to add. The pair then subtracts the third number cube from the sum, states the equations, and places a marker on the resulting difference.
2. Pairs alternate turns—rolling number cubes, stating equations, and placing markers on the gameboard.
3. The first pair to have three markers in a row horizontally, vertically, or diagonally wins.

### Making Connections

Promote reflection and make mathematical connections by asking:

- What strategies helped you line up your markers in a row?

# Sum and Subtract

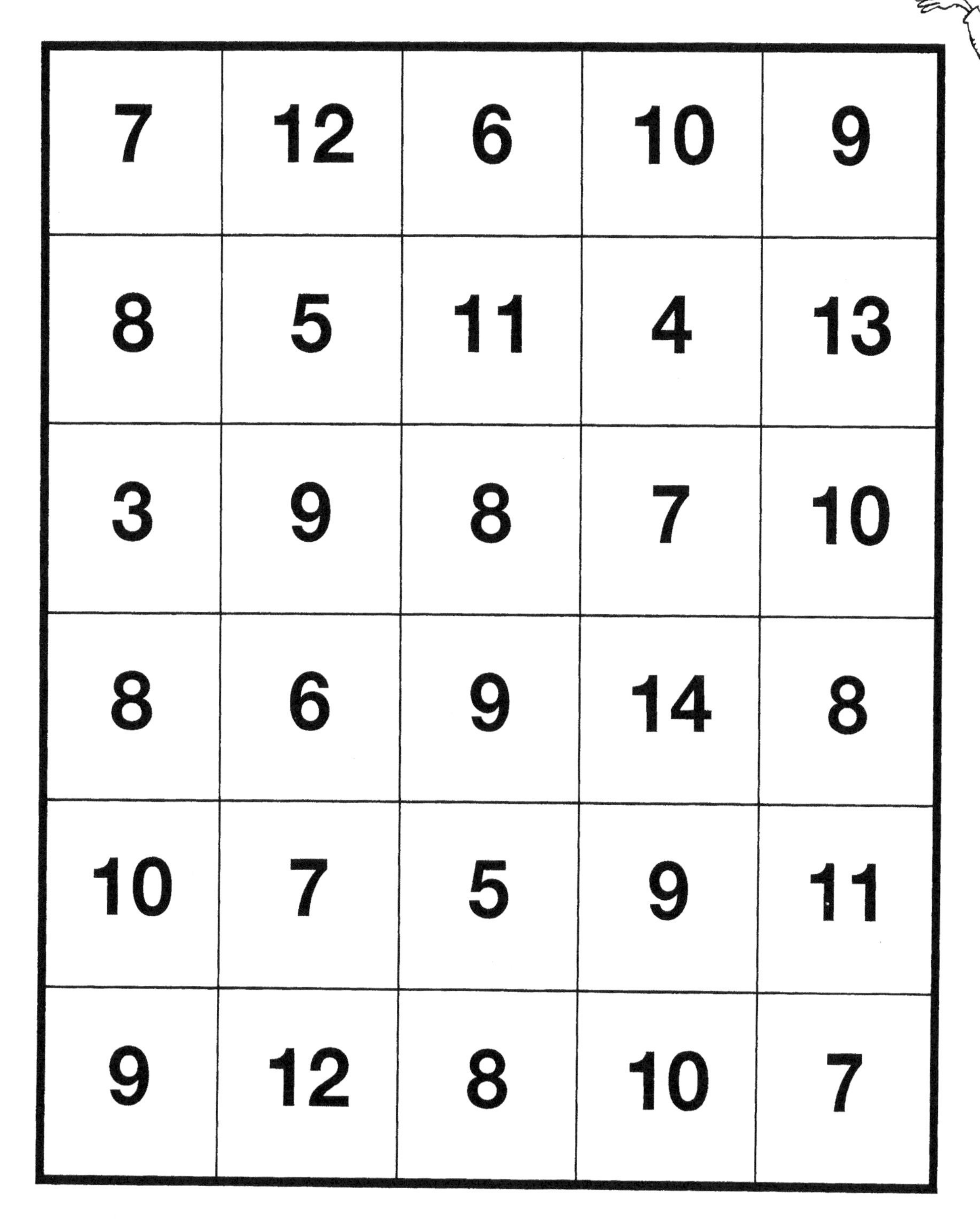

| 7 | 12 | 6 | 10 | 9 |
|---|---|---|---|---|
| 8 | 5 | 11 | 4 | 13 |
| 3 | 9 | 8 | 7 | 10 |
| 8 | 6 | 9 | 14 | 8 |
| 10 | 7 | 5 | 9 | 11 |
| 9 | 12 | 8 | 10 | 7 |

# Subtracting to Zero

**Topic:** Mental Subtraction of Facts

**Object:** Subtract to zero or close

**Groups:** Pair players or 2 players

**Materials for each group**

- *Subtracting to Zero* gameboard (below)
- 15 markers

*Tips* *Encourage students to play additional rounds to see patterns and discover winning strategies. Remove one column of choices, to require more strategic thinking.*

**Directions**

1. Leader picks a beginning number between 15 and 20.
2. Pairs alternate turns by placing one counter on uncovered numbers and stating the new difference.

   *Example:* If 3 and 2 are covered and the beginning number is 16, then the current difference is 11. If the next pair covers 2, the new difference is 9.

3. The pair stating zero or the smallest difference wins.

| | | | | |
|---|---|---|---|---|
| 3 | 3 | 3 | 3 | 3 |
| 2 | 2 | 2 | 2 | 2 |
| 1 | 1 | 1 | 1 | 1 |

**Making Connections**

Promote reflection and make mathematical connections by asking:

- What strategy helped you get close to zero?

*Acknowledgment: This activity is adapted from "Target Addition" in FAMILY MATH, ©Regents, University of California, with permission of the authors Jean Kerr Stenmark, Virginia Thompson, and Ruth Cossey.*

Date ____________ Name ____________

# Tic-Tac-Toe Subtract I

Solve each problem. For each puzzle find the three problems in a row that have the same answer. Draw a line to show the only possible tic-tac-toe for each puzzle.

**1.**

| | | |
|---|---|---|
| 6 – 3 = | 9 – 5 = | 10 – 6 = |
| 10 – 7 = | 12 – 9 = | 11 – 8 = |
| 11 – 6 = | 12 – 5 = | 11 – 4 = |

**2.**

| | | |
|---|---|---|
| 11 – 6 = | 12 – 4 = | 10 – 6 = |
| 10 – 7 = | 11 – 4 = | 9 – 5 = |
| 9 – 3 = | 12 – 6 = | 10 – 4 = |

**3.**

| | | |
|---|---|---|
| 8 – 4 = | 10 – 6 = | 12 – 6 = |
| 10 – 2 = | 12 – 8 = | 11 – 5 = |
| 9 – 5 = | 10 – 3 = | 11 – 7 = |

**4.**

| | | |
|---|---|---|
| 8 – 3 = | 11 – 8 = | 10 – 5 = |
| 10 – 4 = | 11 – 5 = | 12 – 7 = |
| 10 – 7 = | 12 – 3 = | 9 – 4 = |

Date ____________ Name ____________________

# Tic-Tac-Toe Subtract II

Solve each problem. For each puzzle find the three problems in a row that have the same answer. Draw a line to show the only possible tic-tac-toe for each puzzle.

**1.**

| | | |
|---|---|---|
| 15 – 7 = | 14 – 5 = | 16 – 7 = |
| 11 – 6 = | 17 – 9 = | 13 – 6 = |
| 14 – 7 = | 13 – 9 = | 13 – 5 = |

**2.**

| | | |
|---|---|---|
| 17 – 8 = | 12 – 9 = | 11 – 5 = |
| 15 – 9 = | 14 – 8 = | 13 – 7 = |
| 13 – 8 = | 16 – 8 = | 11 – 4 = |

**3.**

| | | |
|---|---|---|
| 13 – 7 = | 15 – 9 = | 16 – 9 = |
| 13 – 6 = | 12 – 5 = | 11 – 3 = |
| 15 – 8 = | 12 – 4 = | 14 – 6 = |

**4.** Complete this Tic-Tac-Toe Subtract puzzle so that it only works *one* way.

| | | |
|---|---|---|
| 11 – 7 = | 18 – 9 = | 13 – 8 = |
| 13 – 9 = | 12 – 8 = | |
| 13 – 7 = | | |

Date ____________ Name ____________________

# What's Left? I

To find what's left, cross out the answers to each clue in the square at the right.

**1.** It's not **10 – 2** or **11 – 5.**
It's not **12 – 3** or **10 – 7.**
It's not **7 – 2** or **8 – 4.**
It's not an odd number.

What's left? ________

| 9 | 8 | 7 |
|---|---|---|
| 6 | 5 | 4 |
| 3 | 2 | 1 |

**2.** It's not **10 – 8** or **11 – 7.**
It's not **11 – 2** or **6 – 5.**
It's not **9 – 3** or **12 – 5.**
It's not greater than 4.

What's left? ________

| 9 | 8 | 7 |
|---|---|---|
| 6 | 5 | 4 |
| 3 | 2 | 1 |

**3.** It's not **10 – 4** or **12 – 9.**
It's not **11 – 3** or **8 – 7.**
It's not **8 – 3** or **12 – 3.**
It's not an even number.

What's left? ________

| 9 | 8 | 7 |
|---|---|---|
| 6 | 5 | 4 |
| 3 | 2 | 1 |

Trivia: The number left in Puzzle #3 equals the number of bones in a giraffe's neck.

Date ______________ Name ______________________

# What's Left? II

To find what's left, cross out the answers to each clue in the square at the right.

**1.** It's not **11 – 7** or **13 – 8**.
It's not **12 – 9** or **13 – 7**.
It's not **11 – 4** or **8 – 7**.
It's not an even number.

What's left? ________

| 9 | 8 | 7 |
|---|---|---|
| 6 | 5 | 4 |
| 3 | 2 | 1 |

**2.** It's not **12 – 8** or **15 – 5**.
It's not **14 – 8** or **12 – 3**.
It's not **14 – 7** or **12 – 4**.
It's not an odd number.

What's left? ________

| 12 | 11 | 10 |
|---|---|---|
| 9 | 8 | 7 |
| 6 | 5 | 4 |

**3.** It's not **12 – 5** or **11 – 9**.
It's not **13 – 9** or **11 – 3**.
It's not **11 – 5** or **15 – 6**.
It's not an odd number.

What's left? ________

| 10 | 9 | 8 |
|---|---|---|
| 7 | 6 | 5 |
| 4 | 3 | 2 |

Trivia: The number left in Puzzle #3 equals the number of legs on a lobster.

Date ____________ Name ____________________

# Subtraction Squares

Subtract each row and column to fill in the missing numbers.

Sample

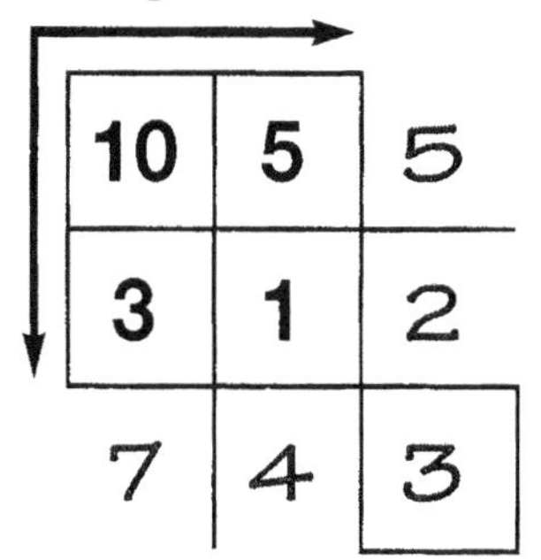


| 11 | 4 | |
|---|---|---|
| 5 | 3 | |
| | | |

| 12 | 3 | |
|---|---|---|
| 6 | 0 | |
| | | |

| 12 | 5 | |
|---|---|---|
| 4 | 2 | |
| | | |

| 12 | 3 | |
|---|---|---|
| 5 | 1 | |
| | | |

| 13 | 5 | |
|---|---|---|
| 6 | 3 | |
| | | |

| 13 | 8 | |
|---|---|---|
| 7 | 2 | |
| | | |

| 14 | 9 | |
|---|---|---|
| 7 | 3 | |
| | | |

| 15 | 7 | |
|---|---|---|
| 6 | 2 | |
| | | |

| 16 | 9 | |
|---|---|---|
| 8 | 3 | |
| | | |

| 17 | 8 | |
|---|---|---|
| 9 | 4 | |
| | | |

| 18 | 9 | |
|---|---|---|
| 10 | 6 | |
| | | |

Date ______________ Name ______________________

# Subtraction Squares Challenge

Fill in the missing numbers. The first problem provides helpful clues.

Sample

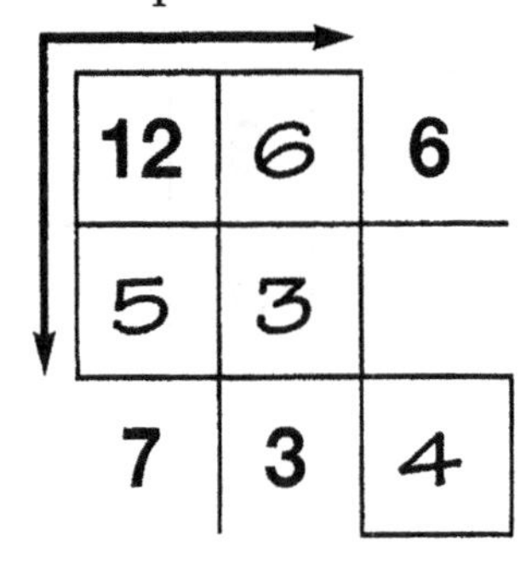


| 11 | | 5 |
|---|---|---|
| | 2 | |
| 8 | | 4 |

| 12 | | 5 |
|---|---|---|
| 4 | | 2 |
| | 5 | |

| 13 | | 8 |
|---|---|---|
| | 2 | |
| 9 | | 6 |

| 14 | | 6 |
|---|---|---|
| | | |
| 7 | | 1 |

| 13 | 6 | |
|---|---|---|
| | | |
| 4 | | 3 |

| 14 | | 8 |
|---|---|---|
| | 4 | |
| 5 | | |

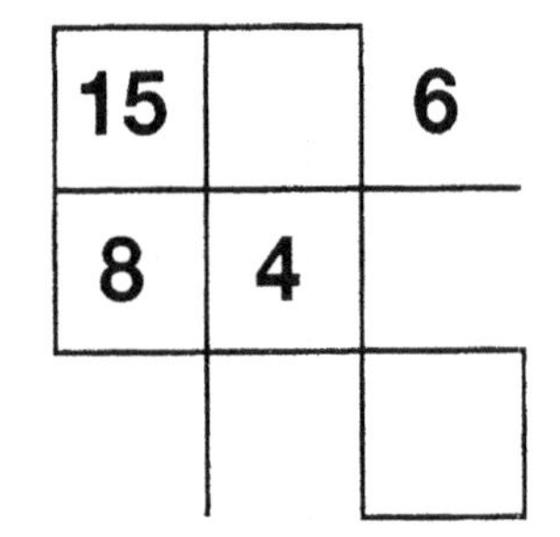


| | 8 | 8 |
|---|---|---|
| | | |
| 9 | | 6 |

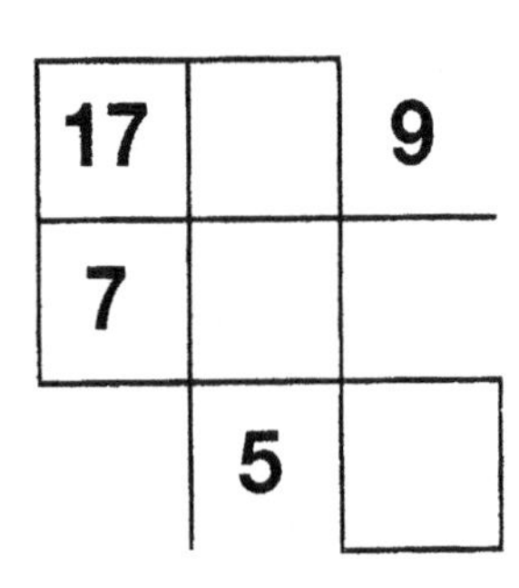


Create two squares for classmates to solve. Be sure you have enough clues.

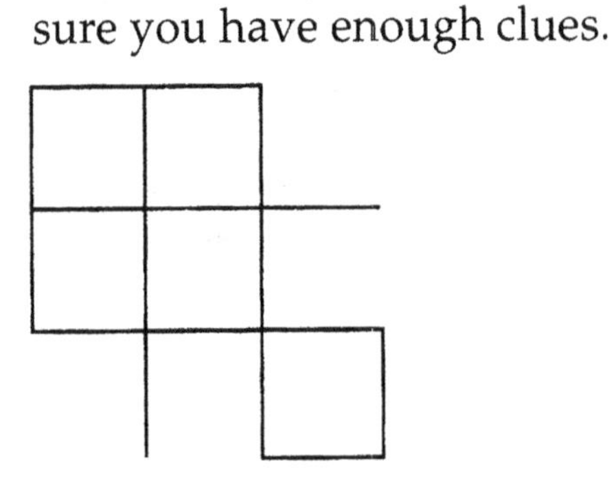

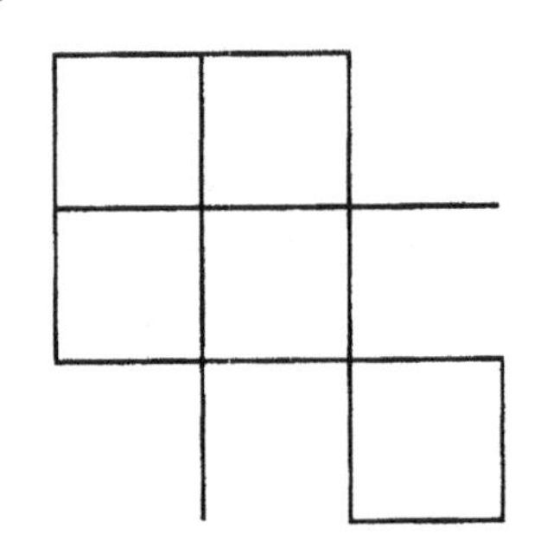

## Questions

What mathematics was practiced?

What patterns did you notice?

# Money

**Assumptions** Money concepts have been taught for understanding, with an effort to enhance number sense. Concrete and visual models, such as coins and play money, have been used extensively. Students have practiced finding the value of many coin combinations.

## Section Overview and Suggestions

### Sponges

**Valuable Words** p. 48

**Name the Combination** pp. 49–50

These open-ended, repeatable warm-ups require mental combining of coin values. *Valuable Words* is a familiar activity that provides many extensions for long-term use. *Name the Combinations* has varying levels of difficulty.

### Skill Checks

**Making Cents 1–3** pp. 51–53

The Skill Checks provide a way for parents, students, and you to see students' improvement in working with money. Remember to have all students respond to STOP, the number sense task, before solving the ten problems.

### Games

**Race to Two Dollars** pp. 54–55

**Coins Tic-Tac-Toe** pp. 56–57

*Race to Two Dollars* requires students to make appropriate money exchanges. By playing the *Race to Zero* variation (see "Tips"), students practice making change. Adequate exposure to *Name the Combination* (p. 49) should ensure student success with the challenging *Coins Tic-Tac-Toe* Game that requires strategic thinking. *Race to Two Dollars* and *Coins Tic-Tac-Toe* are engaging Games that families will enjoy playing repeatedly.

### Independent Activities

**Coin Combinations** p. 58

**Find the Combination** p. 59

**Vending Machine Math** p. 60

*Coin Combinations* and *Find the Combination* showcase skills students developed while experiencing *Name the Combinations* and *Coins Tic-Tac-Toe.* After listing two solutions for *Coin Combinations,* students could work with a partner to find as many different combinations as possible for each problem. *Coin Combinations* prepares students for the more challenging *Find the Combination* activity. *Coin Combinations* and *Find the Combination* could easily be modified to provide additional practice. *Vending Machine Math* presents a real-life situation that requires students to make change.

# Valuable Words

**Topic:** Adding Quarters and Dimes

**Object:** Determine value of words and names

**Groups:** Whole class or small group

### Materials

- chalkboard or overhead projector

### Directions

1. Leader displays some words with corresponding values:

   | | | |
   |---|---|---|
   | to = 35¢ | bet = 45¢ | beat = 70¢ |
   | be = 35¢ | best = 55¢ | boat = 70¢ |

2. Leader asks students, "What pattern has been followed for assigning values to these words?" After analyzing the listing, students suggest possible rules.
3. After determining the rule (consonants = 10¢ and vowels = 25¢), students determine and compare the values of their first names.
4. As leader gives additional words, students determine each word's value.
5. Next, students take a group of words, such as color words, and order them by their value.
6. Students work with a partner to find sample words worth 35¢, 55¢, 60¢, 65¢, 70¢, and 75¢. (A class collection for each value might be gathered and displayed.)
7. The leader shares the following information about a "secret word."

   My word is worth ________ ¢. My word begins with ________ and means ________. What's my word?

8. Students partner to create additional "Valuable Word Riddles" and pose them to the class.

### Making Connections

Promote reflection and make mathematical connections by asking:

- What word values are more common?
- What word values are difficult to make?
- Are most people's first names worth more or less than their last names?

# Name the Combination

**Topic:** Mental Adding of Coins

**Object:** Determine exact coin combinations

**Groups:** Whole class or small group

*Tip* *This recording form is easier to handle if you cut the rows apart to create movable strips for each coin combination template.*

### Materials

- transparency of *Name the Combination* form, p. 50 (See Tip.)
- overhead set of coins
- play coins for students (optional)

### Directions

1. Leader displays the top section of the *Name the Combination* form. Students identify the value of each coin that is recorded on each corresponding price tag.
2. Leader selects and displays one of the coin templates from the *Name the Combination* form. Leader states and records one possible total value.

   *Example:* The leader selects the first template. "What 3 coins equal 21¢?"

   When the combination is identified, it is displayed with transparent coins by the responder or the leader. Other possible totals using 3 coins: 7¢, 11¢, 12¢, 15¢, 16¢, 30¢, 31¢, 36¢, 40¢, 45¢, 55¢, 60¢, 75¢.

3. Combinations requiring more coins are introduced as students are ready for a greater challenge:

   Some possible totals using 4 coins: 8¢, 12¢, 16¢, 17¢, 20¢, 22¢, 25¢, 35¢, 40¢, 55¢, 70¢

   Some possible totals using 5 coins: 21¢, 23¢, 25¢, 38¢, 41¢, 42¢, 50¢, 56¢, 65¢, 80¢, 95¢

   Some possible totals using 6 coins: 10¢, 18¢, 26¢, 30¢, 33¢, 35¢, 45¢, 50¢, 55¢, 60¢, 78¢

### Making Connections

Promote reflection and make mathematical connections by asking:

- What strategies helped you find solutions?
- Which totals allowed more than one solution?

# Name the Combination

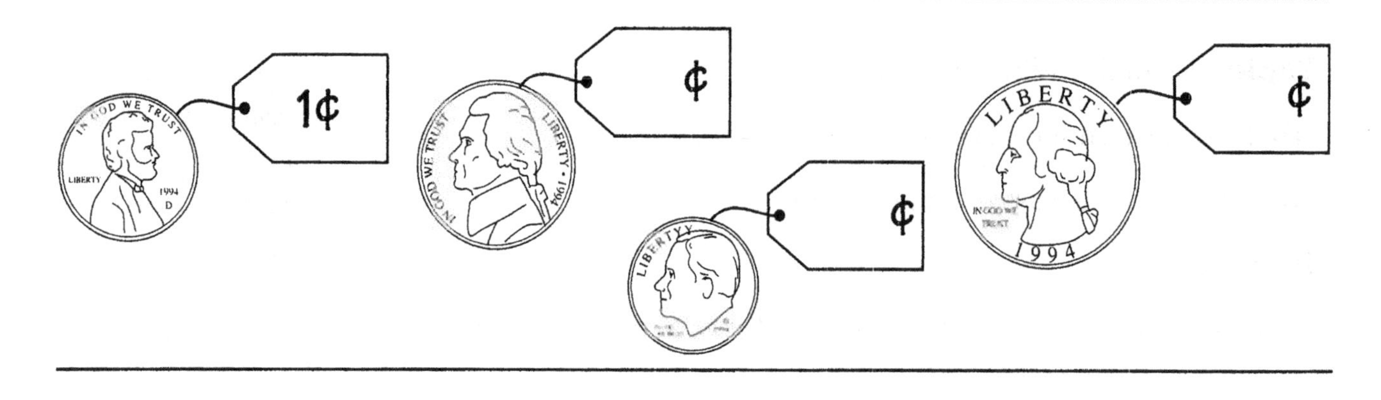


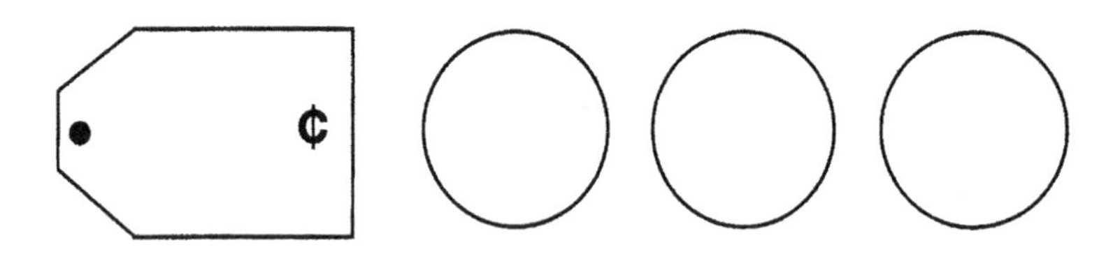


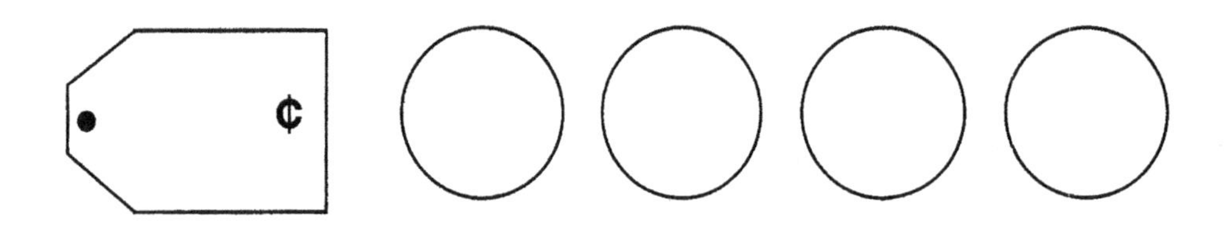


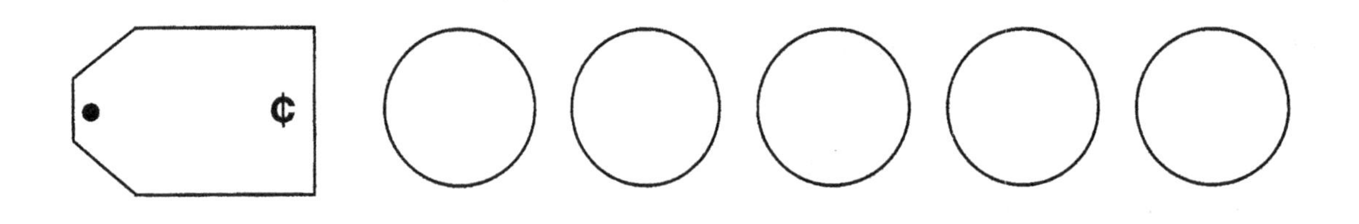


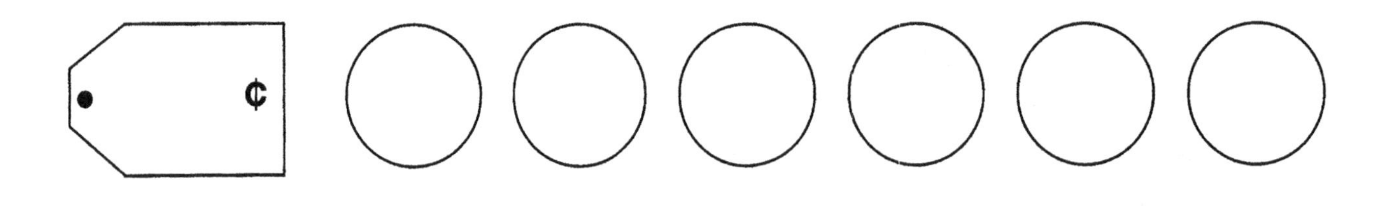


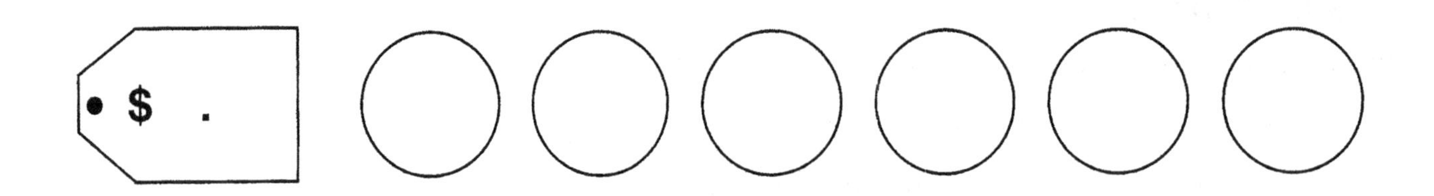

Date ______________ Name ______________________

# Making Cents 1

STOP Don't start yet. Star problems 1, 2, or 3 if they will equal an odd amount.

**1.** 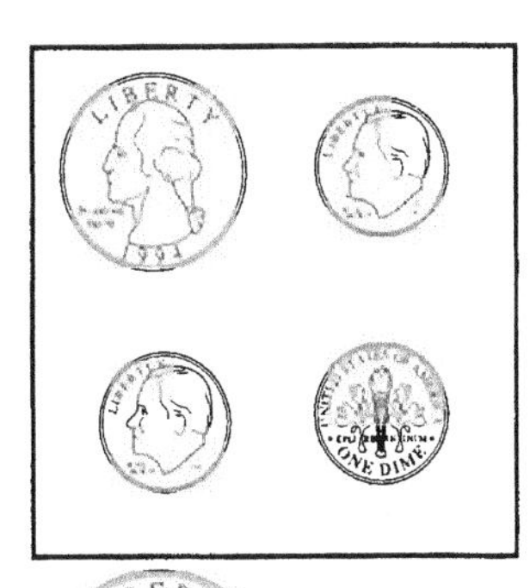 = ______ ¢

**2.** 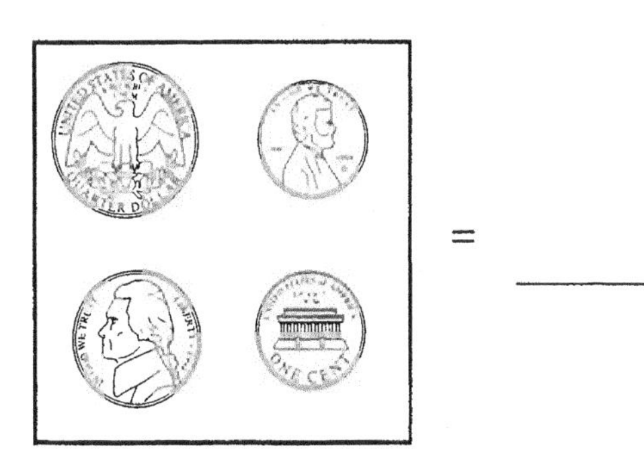 = ______ ¢

**3.**   + __________ = 60¢

**4.** Use 2 coins to make 35¢. __________ **5.** Use 3 coins to make 35¢. __________

**6.** Use 4 coins to make 80¢. ______________________

You have     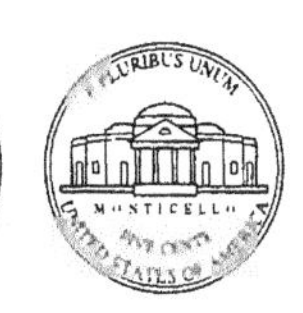 .

**7.** How can you make 20¢? ______________________

**8.** How can you make 40¢? ______________________

**9.** Use   to pay for a 35¢ item.

What coins might be your change? ______________________

**10.** Use    to pay for a 38¢ item.

What coins might be your change? ______________________

Which coin should you move so both sides equal the same amount?

   |   

Date ____________ Name ____________________

# Making Cents 2

**STOP** Don't start yet. Star problems 1, 2, or 3 if they will equal an even amount.

**1.**  = ______ ¢

**2.** 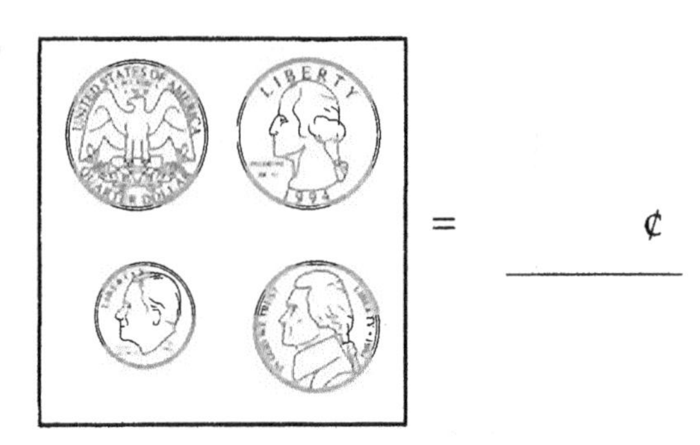 = ______ ¢

**3.**     + ____________ = 60¢

**4.** Use 2 coins to make 30¢. __________

**5.** Use 3 coins to make 51¢. __________

**6.** Use 4 coins to make 55¢. ____________________

You have     

**7.** How can you make 60¢? ______________________________

**8.** How can you make 45¢? ______________________________

**9.** Use   to pay for a 29¢ item.

What coins might be your change? ______________________________

**10.** Use    to pay for a 52¢ item.

What coins might be your change? ______________________________

Which coin should you move so both sides equal the same amount?

   |  

Date ______________ Name ______________________

# Making Cents 3

**STOP** Don't start yet. Star problems 1, 2, or 3 if they will equal an odd amount.

**1.**  = ______ ¢

**2.** 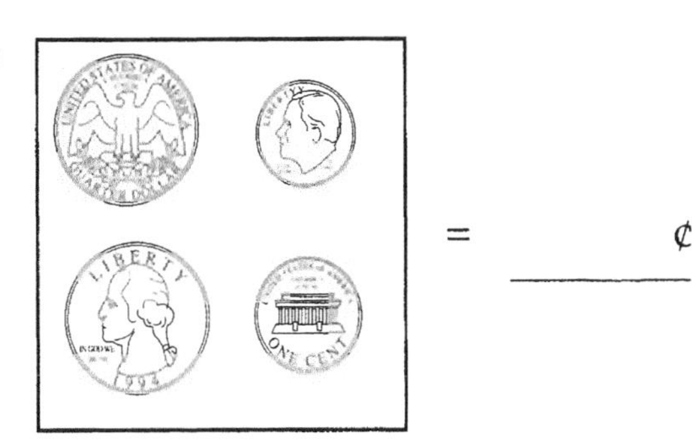 = ______ ¢

**3.**   + ________ = 75¢

**4.** Use 2 coins to make 50¢. ________

**5.** Use 3 coins to make 60¢. ________

**6.** Use 4 coins to make 65¢. ______________

You have     

**7.** How can you make 30¢? ______________________

**8.** How can you make 46¢? ______________________

**9.** Use   to pay for a 34¢ item.

What coins might be your change? ______________________

**10.** Use    to pay for a 52¢ item.

What coins might be your change? ______________________

Which coin should you move so both sides equal the same amount?

     |  

# Race to Two Dollars

**Topic:** Adding Nickels and Quarters

**Object:** Reach $2.00 or more

**Groups:** 2 players or pair players

### Materials for each group

- *Race to Two Dollars* gameboard, p. 55
- special Number Cube (3–5), p. 149
- 16 markers
- play coins, nickels and quarters (optional)

*Tips* *Some students find it helpful to record the number rolled and the accumulated total after each turn.*

*Reinforce subtraction and making change by reversing the rules. Begin with one dollar and four quarters and "Race to Zero."*

### Directions

1. The first player rolls the special Number Cube. The number rolled indicates the number of nickels awarded for that turn. The player displays the amount on his or her side of the gameboard by covering that many nickels.

2. The second player rolls and indicates the value of his or her roll on the appropriate side of the gameboard.
3. Players continue to alternate turns. After accumulating five nickels, a player must represent it as one quarter. After accumulating four quarters, a player must represent this as one dollar. That player is halfway to a winning round. Players win when they have accumulated two dollars. If players have the same number of turns, it is possible for both players to win.
4. Since exchanging coins is worthwhile to practice, encourage players to play additional rounds.

### Making Connections

Promote reflection and make mathematical connections by asking:

- How did you avoid confusion and exchange easily when you gathered more than five nickels?
- If you were to redesign the special number cube, how would you change it? Why?

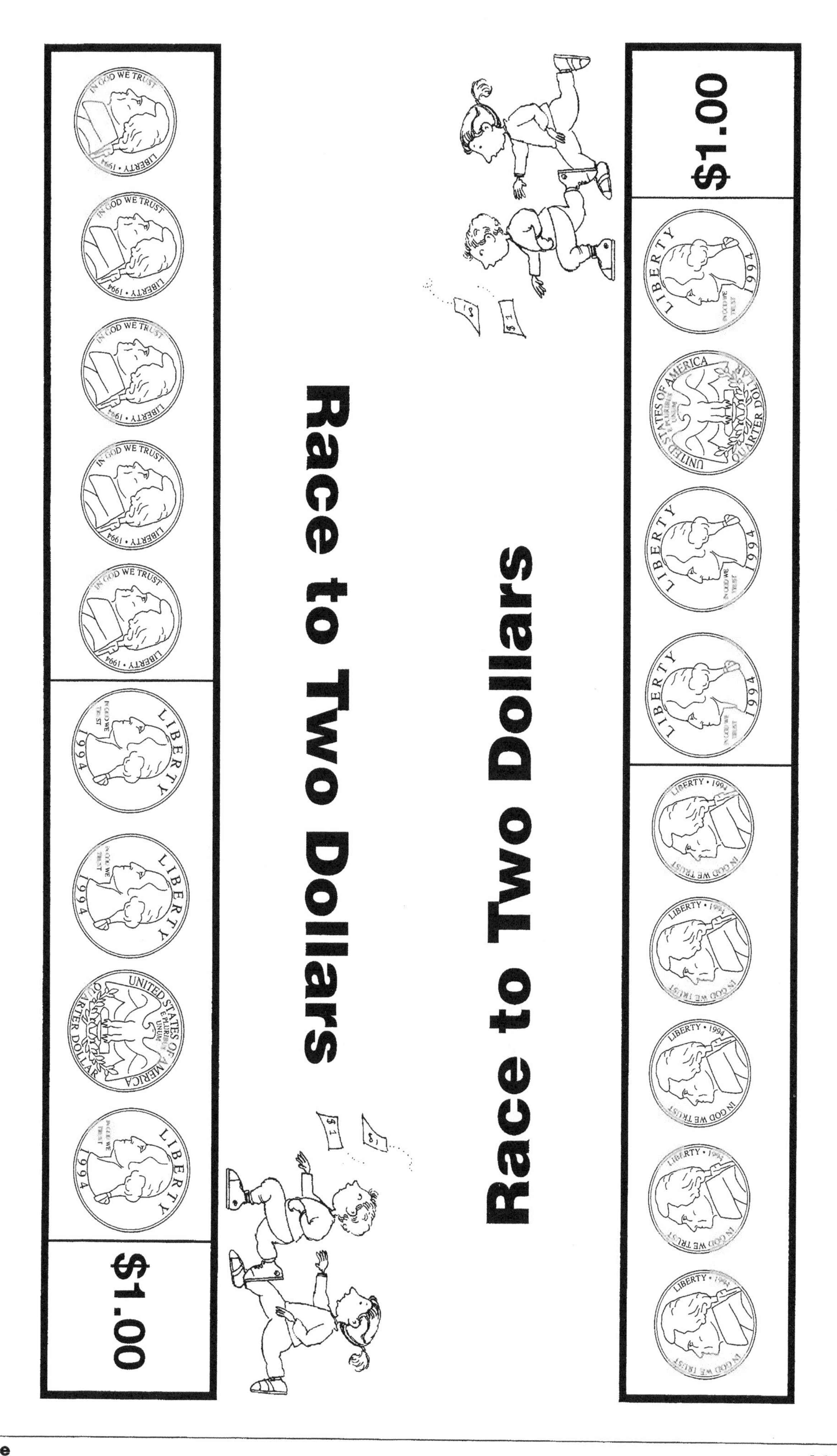
Race to Two Dollars
$1.00
Race to Two Dollars
$1.00

# Coins Tic-Tac-Toe

*Tip* *For players feeling insecure combining coins, allow three in a row to win.*

**Topic:** Mental Addition of Coins

**Object:** Cover four numbers in a row with your markers

**Groups:** 2 pair players

### Materials for each group

- *Coins Tic-Tac-Toe* gameboard, p. 57
- 4 paper clips (or transparent markers)
- markers (different kind for each pair)

### Directions

1. The first pair places four paper clips at the bottom of the gameboard, indicating four coins. The same pair combines the four coins and places a marker on the resulting total.
2. The other pair moves *only one* of the paper clips to a new coin. Next, this pair combines the four indicated coins and places a marker on that total.
3. Pairs continue alternating turns, moving one paper clip each time, totaling the coins, and placing markers on the gameboard.
4. The winner is the first pair to have four of its markers in a row horizontally, vertically, or diagonally.

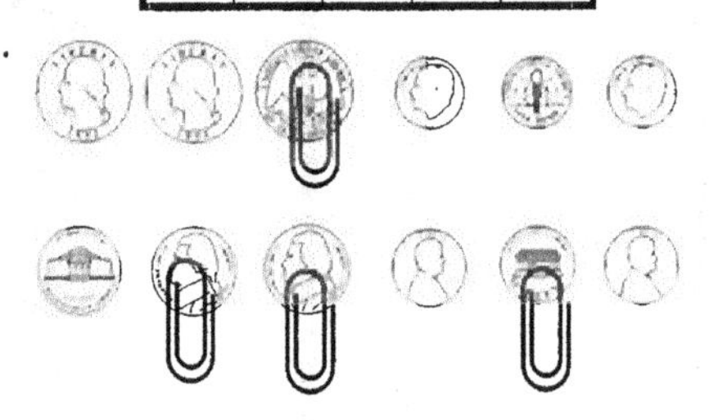

| | | | | |
|---|---|---|---|---|
| 85¢ | 31¢ | 52¢ | 21¢ | 76¢ |
| 50¢ | 17¢ | 70¢ | | 25¢ |
| 26¢ | 40¢ | 80¢ | 32¢ | 56¢ |
| 55¢ | 30¢ | 22¢ | 65¢ | 41¢ |
| 35¢ | 60¢ | 45¢ | 61¢ | 28¢ |

### Making Connections

Promote reflection and make mathematical connections by asking:

- What strategies helped you line up your markers in a row?

# Coins Tic-Tac-Toe

| | | | | |
|---|---|---|---|---|
| 85¢ | 31¢ | 52¢ | 21¢ | 76¢ |
| 50¢ | 17¢ | 70¢ | 36¢ | 25¢ |
| 26¢ | 40¢ | 80¢ | 32¢ | 56¢ |
| 55¢ | 30¢ | 22¢ | 65¢ | 41¢ |
| 35¢ | 60¢ | 45¢ | 61¢ | 28¢ |

Date ____________ Name ____________________

# Coin Combinations

Find two different combinations and their total values to fit each description.

**1.**

| 4 coins Worth more than 25¢, less than 40¢ | |
|---|---|
| | |

**2.**

| 4 coins Worth more than 40¢, less than 60¢ | |
|---|---|
| | |

**3.**

| 5 coins Worth more than 45¢, less than 60¢ | |
|---|---|
| | |

**4.**

| 5 coins Worth more than 75¢, less than 90¢ | |
|---|---|
| | |

**5.**

| 6 coins Worth more than 50¢, less than 60¢ | |
|---|---|
| | |

**6.**

| 6 coins Worth more than \$1.00, less than \$1.30 | |
|---|---|
| | |

Date ____________________ Name ________________________________

# Find the Combination

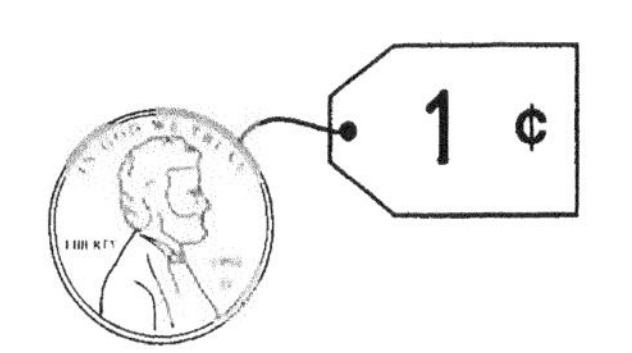

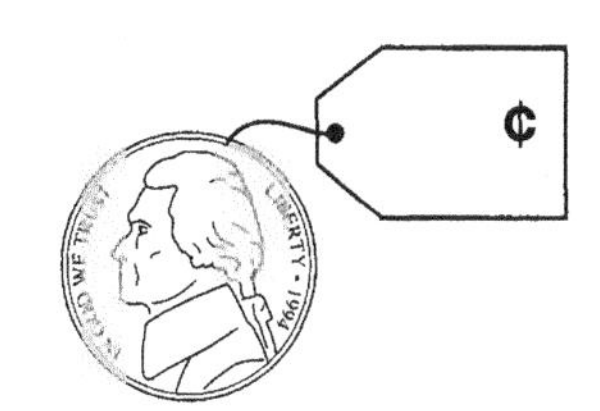

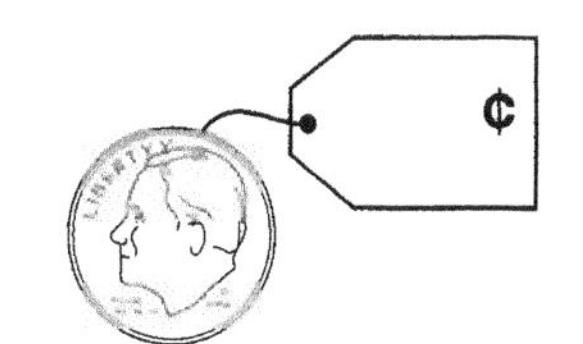

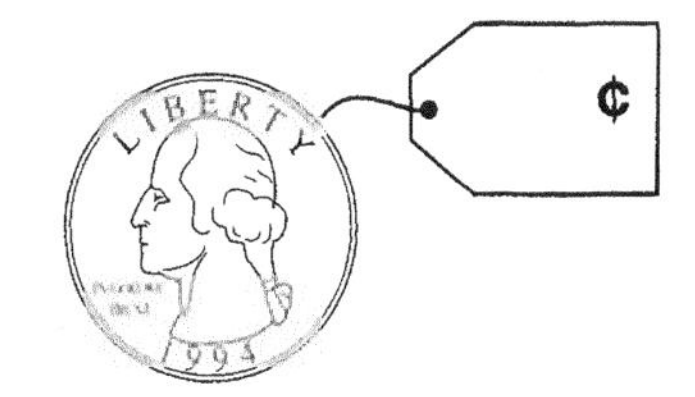


Find a coin combination to match the amount on the price tag. Use the exact number of coins indicated by the circles.

| Price | Coins | Price | Coins |
|---|---|---|---|
| 45¢ | (25¢) (10¢) (10¢) | 31¢ | ○ ○ ○ |
| 60¢ | ○ ○ ○ | 55¢ | ○ ○ ○ |
| 65¢ | ○ ○ ○ ○ | 32¢ | ○ ○ ○ ○ |
| 80¢ | ○ ○ ○ ○ | 50¢ | ○ ○ ○ ○ |
| 86¢ | ○ ○ ○ ○ ○ | 75¢ | ○ ○ ○ ○ ○ |
| 42¢ | ○ ○ ○ ○ ○ | 50¢ | ○ ○ ○ ○ ○ |
| 56¢ | ○ ○ ○ ○ ○ | 60¢ | ○ ○ ○ ○ ○ |
| 50¢ | ○ ○ ○ ○ ○ ○ | 75¢ | ○ ○ ○ ○ ○ ○ |
| $1.35 | ○ ○ ○ ○ ○ ○ | 95¢ | ○ ○ ○ ○ ○ ○ |
| $1.06 | ○ ○ ○ ○ ○ ○ | 66¢ | ○ ○ ○ ○ ○ ○ |

Date ____________ Name ____________________

# Vending Machine Math

How much change would you receive?

| | Coins Used | Change | | Coins Used | Change |
|---|---|---|---|---|---|
| **1.** **25¢** cookie | | ______ | **3.** **40¢** apple | | ______ |
| **2.** **35¢** crackers | | ______ | **4.** **50¢** brownie | | ______ |

You have only four quarters and one dime.
Determine which coins you would use to pay for each item and what change you would receive.

| Item | Coins Used | Change Received |
|---|---|---|
| **5.** **30¢** raisins | | |
| **6.** **45¢** fruit roll | | |
| **7.** **55¢** trail mix | | |
| **8.** **65¢** peanuts | | |
| **9.** **80¢** bottled water | | |
| **10.** **59¢** yogurt | | |
| **11.** **66¢** popcorn | | |
| **12.** **44¢** juice | | |



**Independent Activity**

# Place Value

**Assumptions** Place value concepts have been taught for understanding with an emphasis on developing number sense. Concrete and visual models such as beansticks, 100 and 200 charts, and money have been used extensively.

## Section Overview and Suggestions

Throughout this section number sense is promoted.

### Sponges

**200-Chart Pieces** pp. 62–63

**Creating Target Numbers** pp. 64–65

*200 Chart Pieces* reinforces the use of a valuable visual tool. Eventually students should solve these puzzles mentally without use of the 200 Chart. *Creating Target Numbers,* a warm-up students enjoy revisiting, develops number sense and strategic thinking.

### Skill Checks

**Place It Right** 1–6 pp. 66–68

The Skill Checks provide a way to help parents, students, and you see students' improvement with place value. Each page of *Place It Right* may be cut in half so that each check may be used at a different time. Remember to have all students respond to STOP before solving the ten problems.

### Games

**Place Value Paths** pp. 69–71

**Deciding Digits** pp. 72–73

*Place Value Paths* and *Deciding Digits* require planning ahead and the thoughtful arrangement of drawn digits. The additional open-ended *Place Value Paths* gameboard allows you to adjust the level of difficulty to meet your students' needs.

### Independent Activities

**What Numbers Are Missing?** pp. 74–75

**How Many Can You Make?** pp. 76–77

**What's My Number?** p. 78

Students confident with the *200-Chart Pieces* Sponge are ready for *What Numbers Are Missing?* Skill with *Creating Target Numbers* and *Deciding Digits* should ensure successful, active involvement with *How Many Can You Make?*, an ideal activity for repeated homework use. *What's My Number?* improves number sense and logical thinking. Student-created *What's My Number?* puzzles provide additional place value practice.

# 200-Chart Pieces

**Topic:** Number Relationships

**Object:** Determine unknown numbers by visualizing the 200 Chart

**Groups:** Whole class or small group

*Tip* *As students become competent, conduct this warm-up without use of the 200 Chart.*

### Materials

- transparent patterns cut from *200-Chart Pieces*, p. 63
- 200 Chart for each student, p. 144
- one marker for each student

### Directions

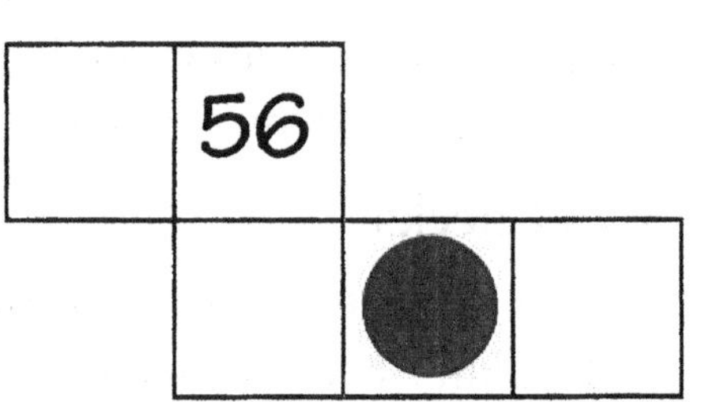


1. Leader displays one of the simpler 200-chart pieces and writes a number in one of the cells.
2. Next, the leader places a marker in one of the remaining empty cells.
3. Students try to determine what number belongs in the marked empty cell. They indicate their response by covering that number on their 200 Chart.
4. The leader continues to provide more challenging clues and the students identify the unknown numbers with their one marker and the 200 Chart.
5. As Sponge proceeds, students explain how they figured out the number. It's helpful to have different approaches shared.
6. Increase the difficulty by having students determine the answer before referring to the 200 Chart.

### Making Connections

Promote reflection and make mathematical connections by asking:

- What patterns have you noticed that help you identify the unknown number?

# 200-Chart Pieces

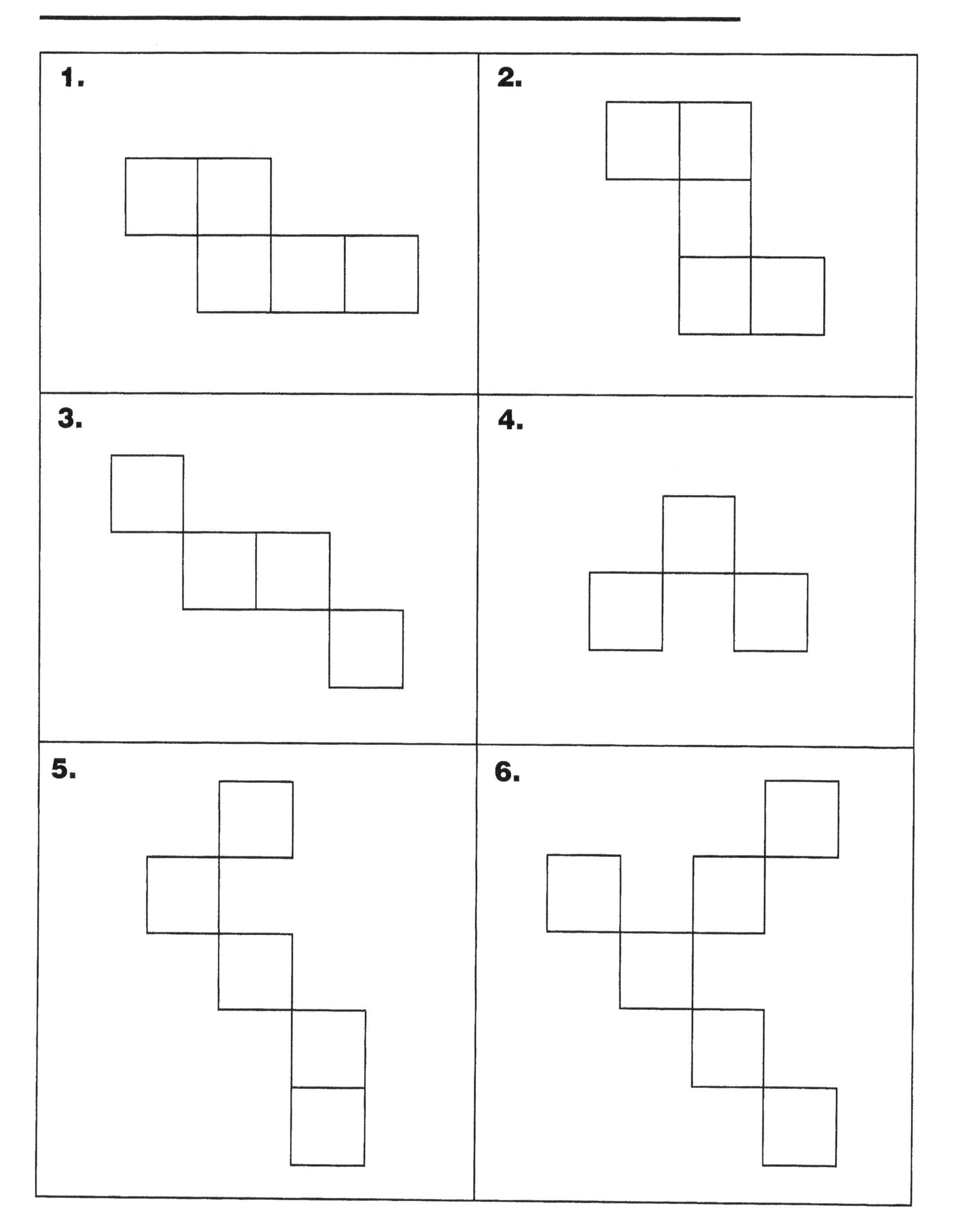

# Creating Target Numbers

**Topic:** Place Value

**Object:** Form 3-digit numbers to meet given criteria

**Groups:** Whole class or small group

### Materials

- 2 sets of Digit Cards, p. 146
- container for Digit Cards
- *Creating Target Numbers* recording sheet for each student, p. 65 (optional)

### Directions

1. Leader describes the criteria for the target numbers. (i.e., "Try to form the largest number, ... number closest to 700.") Leader then explains that four cards will be separately drawn and announced.
2. Leader draws one card and announces the digit. Each student records the digit in the 1s, 10s, or 100s place before the next digit is drawn. During each round, one drawn number may be discarded in the "reject box." Once a number is recorded it is not to be changed.
3. Leader continues to draw cards and announce digits until four digits have been drawn. After each digit card is announced, the leader makes sure it is recorded by each student before drawing a new digit card. (Drawn cards are not returned to the container until the end of the round.)
4. After four digits have been drawn and recorded, students compare their results to determine which numbers are the largest (or "closest to 700").
5. After students have an opportunity to play at least three rounds of this activity, students attempt to form 4-digit numbers using the second column's format. (Five digit cards are drawn for each round.)

### Making Connections

Promote reflection and make mathematical connections by asking:

- What procedures did you follow to place certain digits?
- What numbers appeared in your reject boxes? Please explain.

# Creating Target Numbers

30 or 300?

30 or 300?

Draw four digits from the container.

1. ____ ____ ____ ☐ Reject

2. ____ ____ ____ ☐ Reject

3. ____ ____ ____ ☐ Reject

4. ____ ____ ____ ☐ Reject

Draw five digits from the container.

1. ____ ____ ____ ____ ☐ Reject

2. ____ ____ ____ ____ ☐ Reject

3. ____ ____ ____ ____ ☐ Reject

4. ____ ____ ____ ____ ☐ Reject

Date ____________ Name ____________________

# Place It Right 1

**STOP** Don't start yet! Star a problem that may have an answer larger than 400.

Fill in the missing numbers from the 200 chart:

**1.** 33

**2.** 125

**3.** Order these numbers from smallest to largest: 142, 96, 157, 124 ____________

**4.** seventy-two ______ **5.** six hundred twelve ______ **6.** two tens less than 115______

Use 3, 4, and/or 5 to form:

**7.** even number between 48 and 60 ________ **8.** odd number greater than 50 ________

**9.** even number less than 50 ________ **10.** number between 400 and 450________

**Go On** What numbers come next? 372, 382, 392, _____ , _____ .

---

Date ____________ Name ____________________

# Place It Right 2

**STOP** Don't start yet! Star the problems in the third row that may have odd answers.

Fill in the missing numbers from the 200 chart:

**1.**

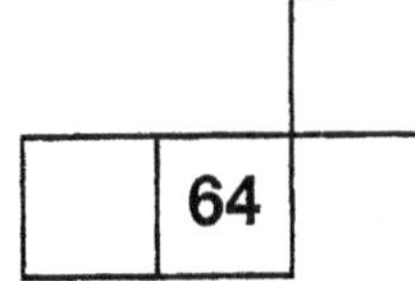


**2.**

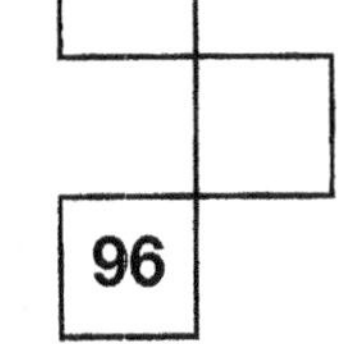


**3.** Order these numbers from smallest to largest: 91, 115, 188, 109 ____________

**4.** forty-five _____ **5.** three hundred seventy-nine _____ **6.** three tens more than 147_____

Use 2, 4, and/or 7 to form:

**7.** even number between 40 and 50 ________ **8.** odd number greater than 30 ________

**9.** even number less than 40 ________ **10.** even number between 400 and 500 ________

**Go On** Which is closest to 231? 220, 315, 240, or 195 ________ Please explain.

Date ____________ Name ____________

# Place It Right 3

**STOP** Don't solve yet! Star the problem in the third row that may have the smallest answer.

Fill in the missing numbers from the 200 chart:

**1.**

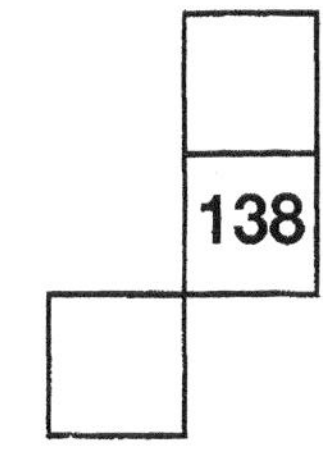


**2.**

75

**3.** Order these numbers from smallest to largest: 120, 84, 104, 99 ____________

**4.** sixty-three______ **5.** five hundred eighteen ______ **6.** two tens more than 92______

Use 5, 6, and/or 7 to form:

**7.** odd number between 70 and 80 ________ **8.** even number greater than 60________

**9.** odd number less than 60 ________ **10.** even number between 400 and 600 ________

**Go On** What other number fits? Please explain your answer.

146 140 142

---

Date ____________ Name ____________

# Place It Right 4

**STOP** Don't start yet! Star the problem that may have the largest answer.

Fill in the missing numbers from the 200 chart:

**1.**

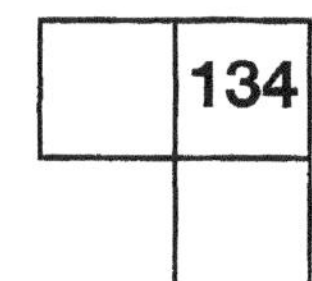


**2.**

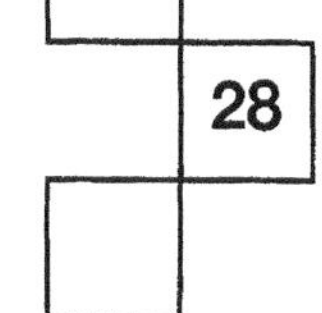


**3.** Order these numbers from smallest to largest: 127, 143, 136, 119 ____________

**4.** fifty-four ______ **5.** two hundred nine ______ **6.** three hundreds more than 210 ______

Use 1, 2, and/or 4 to form:

**7.** even number between 20 and 30 ________ **8.** odd number less than 30 ________

**9.** even number greater than 30________ **10.** even number between 200 and 400________

**Go On** What numbers come next? 133, 123, 113, ______, ______

Date ____________ Name ____________________

# Place It Right 5

STOP Don't start yet! Star two problems that may have answers greater than 500.

Fill in the missing numbers from the 200 chart:

**1.**

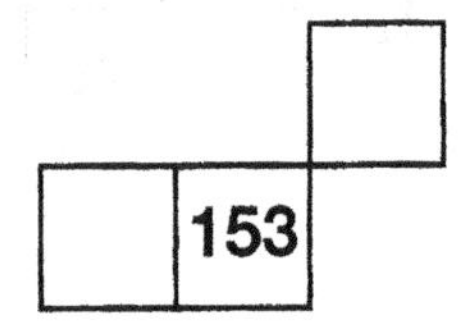


**2.**

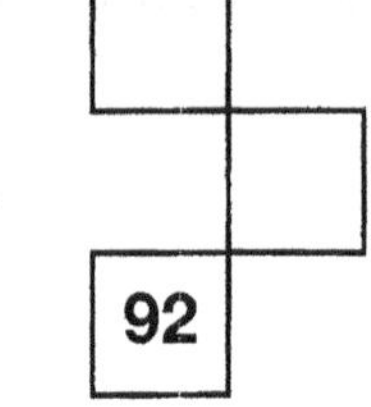


**3.** Order these numbers from smallest to largest: 152, 125, 149, 118 ____________

**4.** thirty-six ______ **5.** seven hundred fifty ______ **6.** two hundreds less than 425 ______

Use 4, 8, and/or 9 to form:

**7.** odd number between 80 and 90 ________ **8.** number greater than 95 ________

**9.** even number less than 80 ________ **10.** even number between 800 and 900 ________

**Go On** Which of the following numbers is closest to 327? 290, 334, 319, or 325 ________
Please explain your answer.

Date ____________ Name ____________________

# Place It Right 6

STOP Don't start yet! Star the problem in the third row that may have the largest answer.

Fill in the missing numbers from the 200 Chart:

**1.**

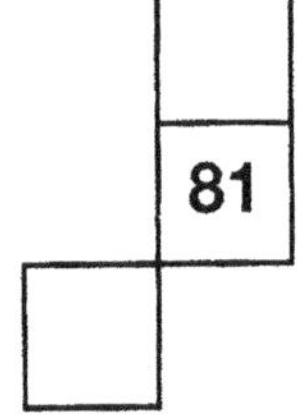


**2.**

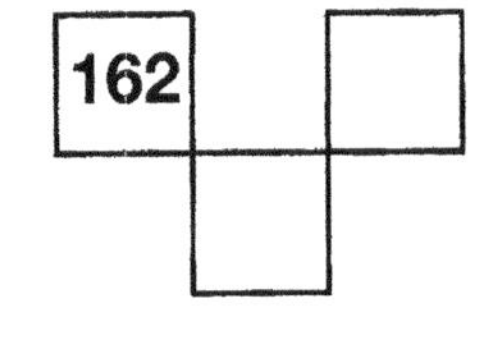


**3.** Order these numbers from smallest to largest: 143, 122, 113, 127 ____________

**4.** eighty-nine ______ **5.** four hundred ten ______ **6.** three tens more than 320 ______

Use 2, 6, and/or 7 to form:

**7.** odd number between 60 and 80 ________ **8.** number greater than 75 ________

**9.** even number less than 30 ________ **10.** even number between 200 and 500 ______

**Go On** What other number fits? Please explain your answer.

| 127 117 147 |
|---|

# Place Value Paths

**Topic:** Place Value and Number Sense

**Object:** Record numbers in an ascending sequence

**Groups:** Pair players in a small group

### Materials for each group

- 2 sets of Digit Cards, p. 146, or Digit Squares, p. 147
- *Place Value Paths A* recording sheet for each pair, p. 70

### Directions

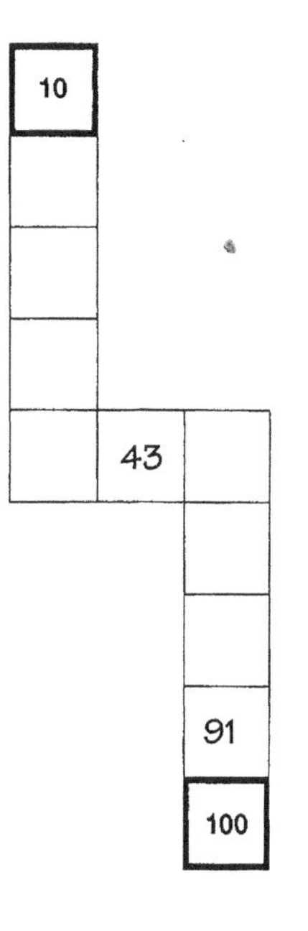


1. The two sets of Digit Cards are mixed together and stacked facedown. Each pair draws two cards and uses the drawn digits to form a 2-digit number. Keeping in mind where the created number fits between 10 and 100, each pair records the formed number in one of the cells along that pair's place value path. (Drawn cards are set aside.)
2. After each pair shares its decision and recording sheet with the other pair, the procedure is repeated. When the stack of cards is gone, remix and restack the discarded cards.
3. A pair loses a turn if the pair cannot form a 2-digit number that can be placed into one of the remaining cells.
4. Pairs follow this process until one pair correctly completes a place value path.

### Making Connections

Promote reflection and make mathematical connections by asking:

- How did you decide where to place your numbers?

*Tips* *This can be played as a whole-class activity with students individually deciding how to form and to place the 2-digit number from the drawn digits. Students compare their final results.*

*Extend this game to allow students to practice ordering 3-digit numbers. Players draw three Digit Cards and use* Place Value Paths B *recording sheet, p. 71. Beginning and ending numbers are determined by the leader, for example 100 and 1000, or 250 and 750.*

# Place Value Paths A

# Place Value Paths B

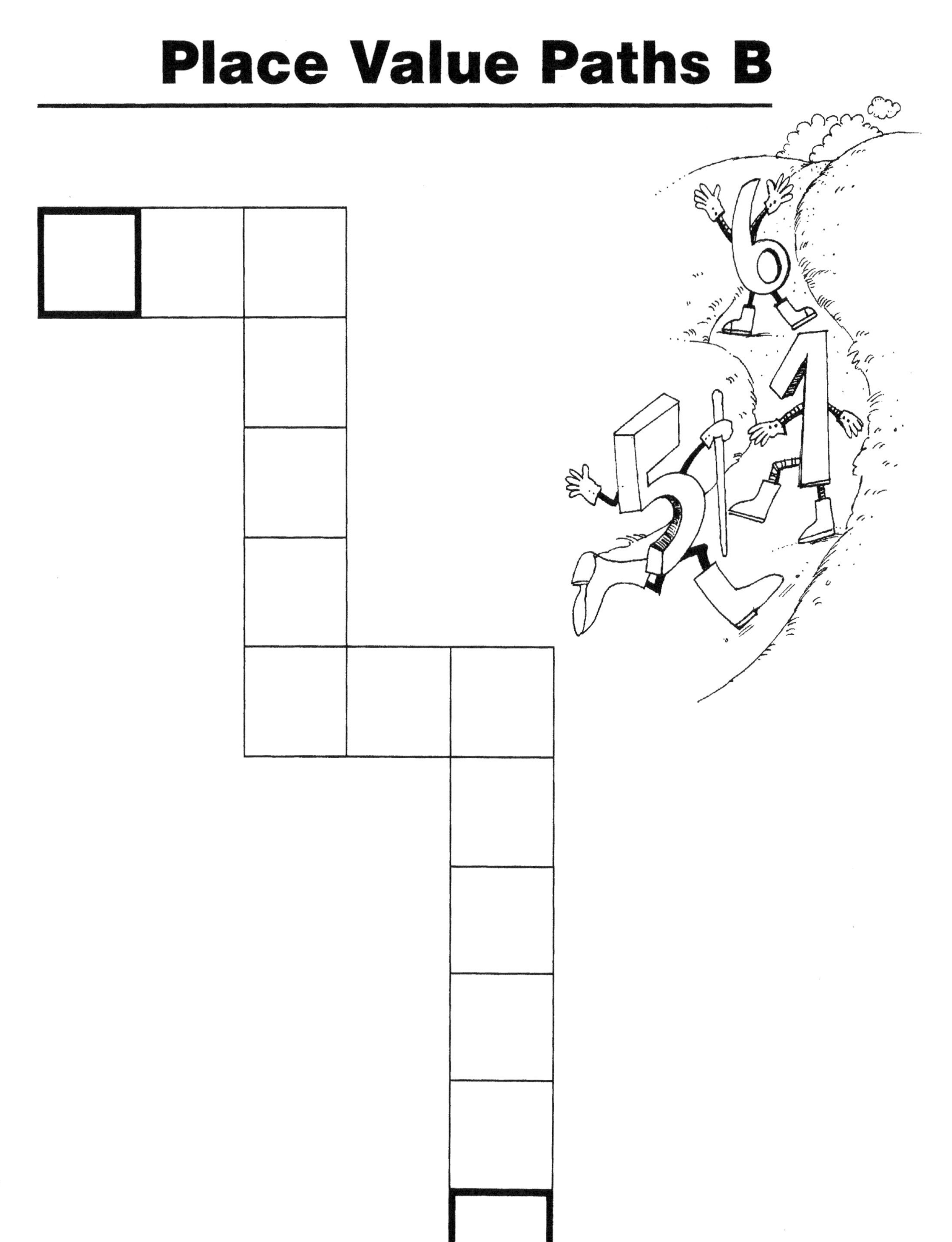

# Deciding Digits

**Topic:** Place Value and Number Sense

**Object:** Form as many qualifying numbers as possible

**Groups:** Pair players in small group

*Tip If desired, promote informal understanding of probability by allowing the use of only one set of Digit Squares for each round.*

### Materials for each group

- Digit Squares (2 sets per pair), p. 147
- containers for Digit Squares
- *Deciding Digits* recording sheet for each pair, p. 73

### Directions

1. Leader randomly mixes and places the Digit Squares in a container.
2. The first pair draws one Digit Square, discusses, and places the drawn Digit Square on their recording sheet. Once a Digit Square is recorded, it cannot be moved.
3. The next pair follows the same procedure, taking care to place the digit appropriately. If a pair draws a digit that cannot be used, the Digit Square is set aside.
4. Pairs continue alternating turns for Round One until each pair draws ten Digit Squares.
5. Pairs compare their recording sheets to see which pair formed the most qualifying numbers.
6. For Round Two, pairs return all Digit Squares to the containers and repeat this entire procedure.

### Making Connections

Promote reflection and make mathematical connections by asking:

- How did you decide where to place your Digit Squares?
- Which numbers were more difficult to place?

# Deciding Digits

## Recording Sheet

### Round 1

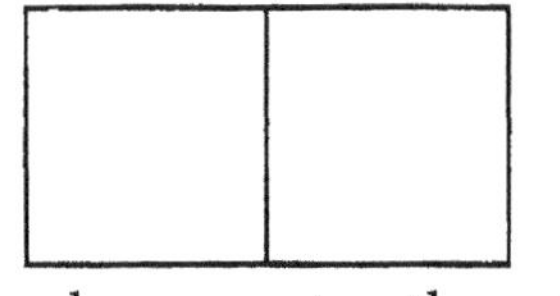

number greater than 45

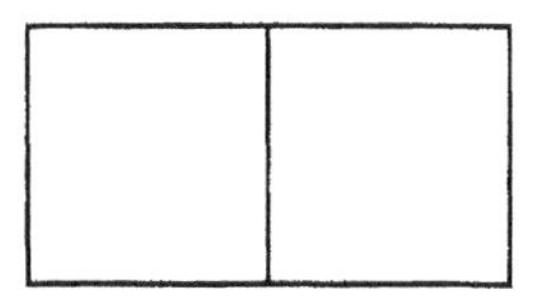

odd number

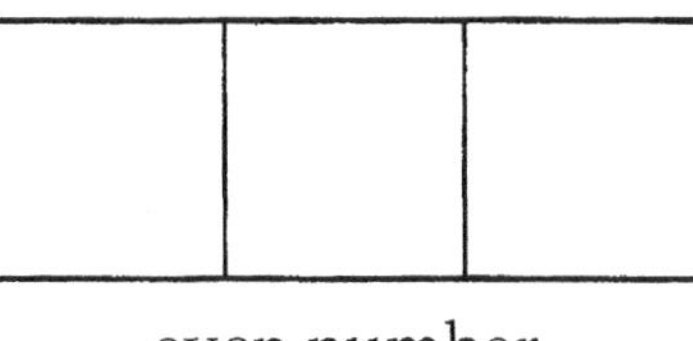

even number

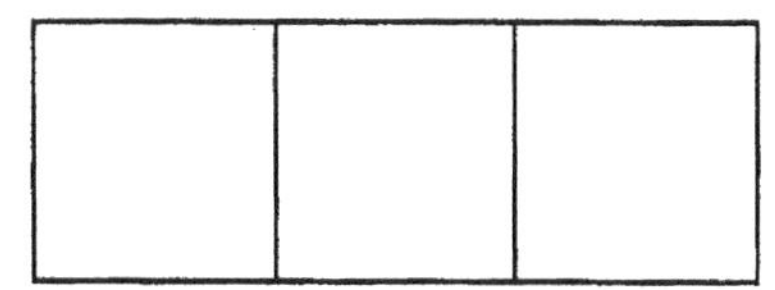

number less than 350

### Round 2

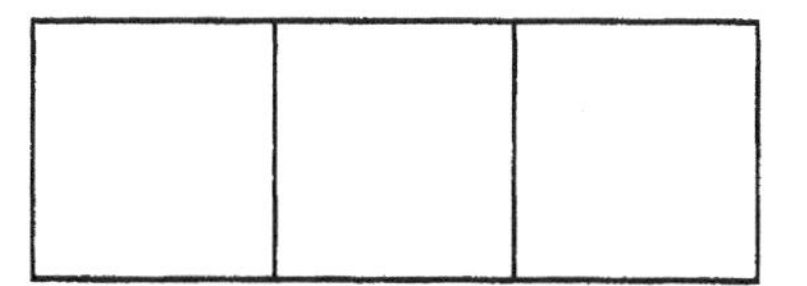

number between 400 and 700

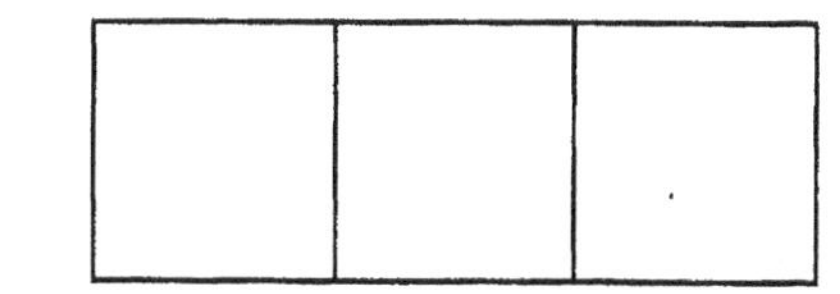

odd number greater than 650

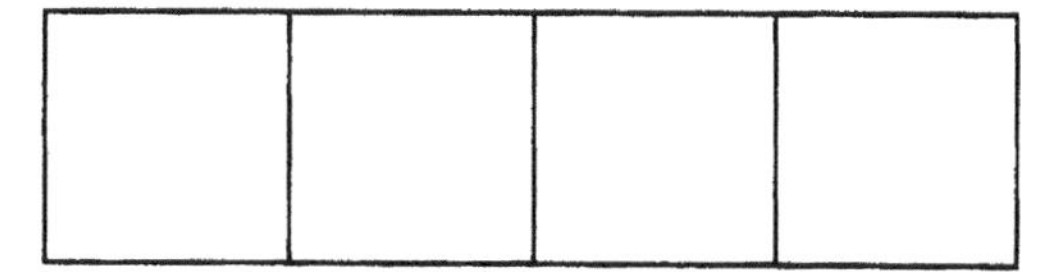

even number less than 5000

Date ____________ Name ____________________

# What Numbers Are Missing? I

Each of these is a piece cut from a 200 chart. Fill in the missing numbers.

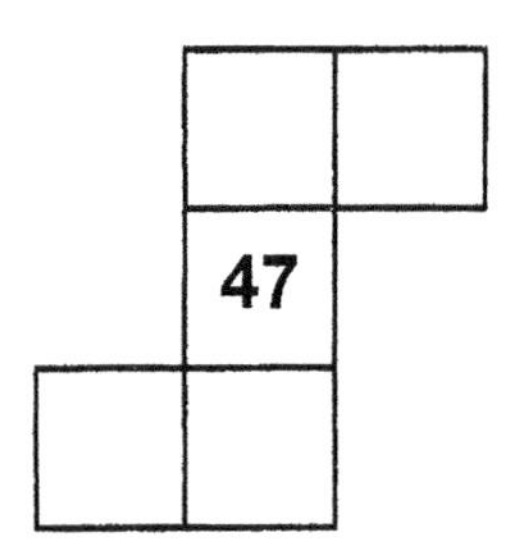


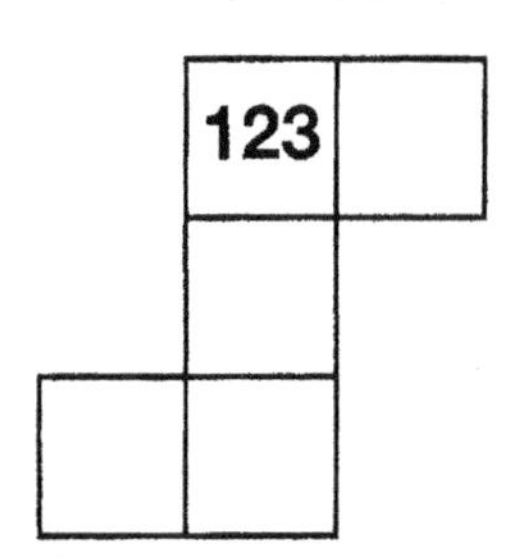


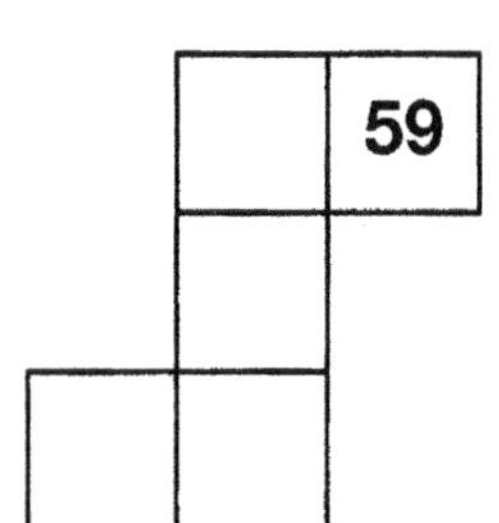


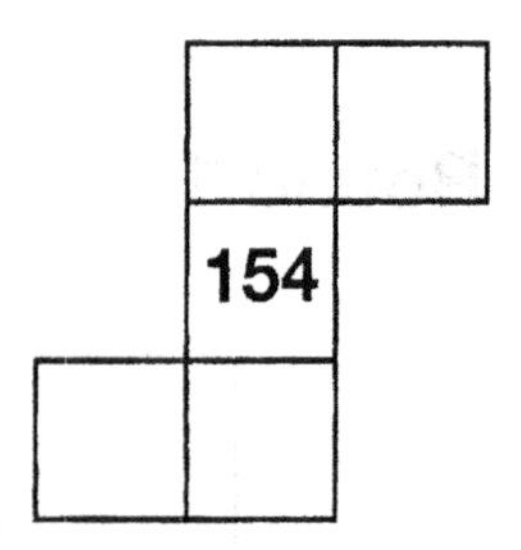


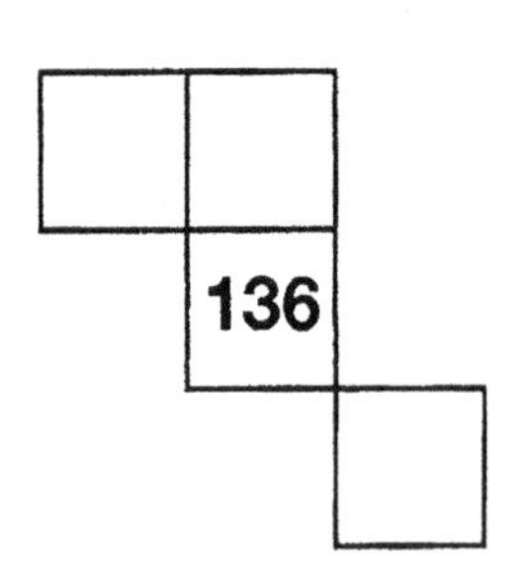


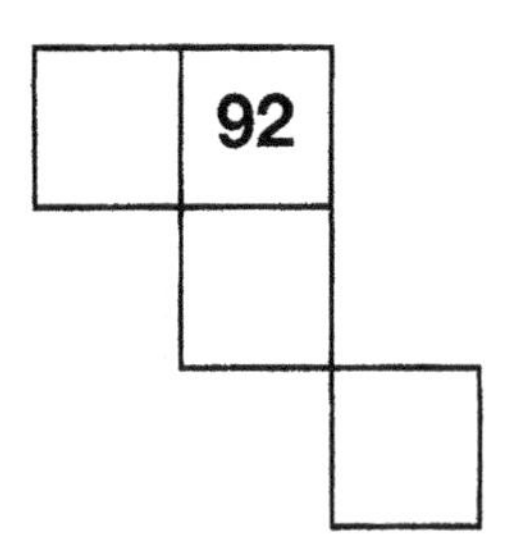


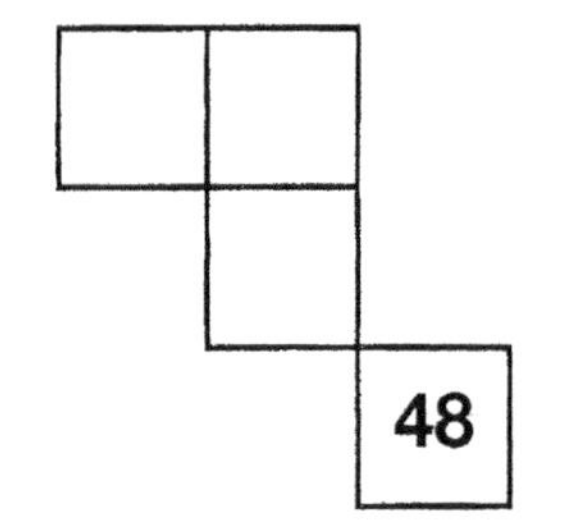


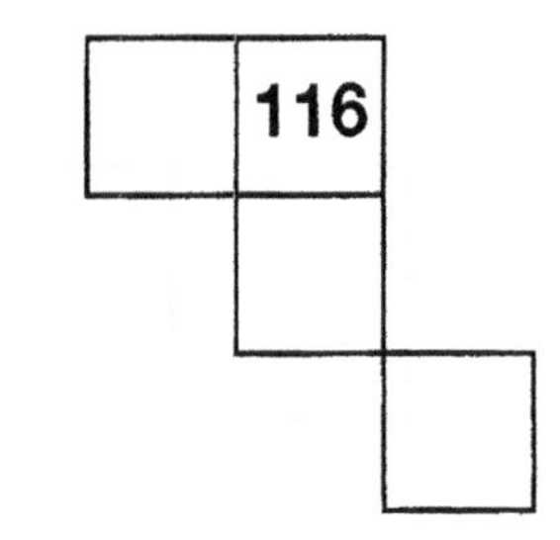


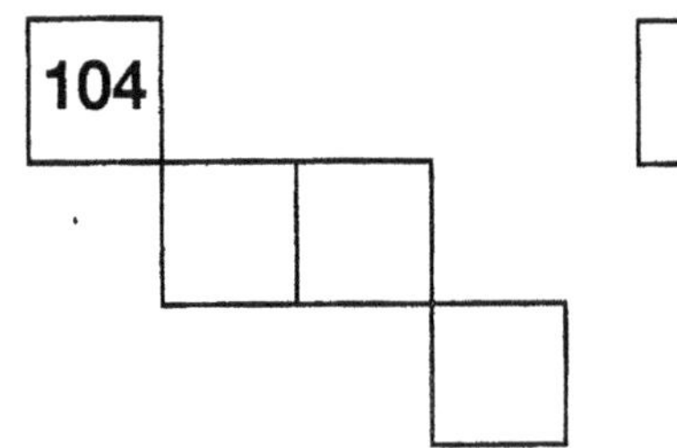


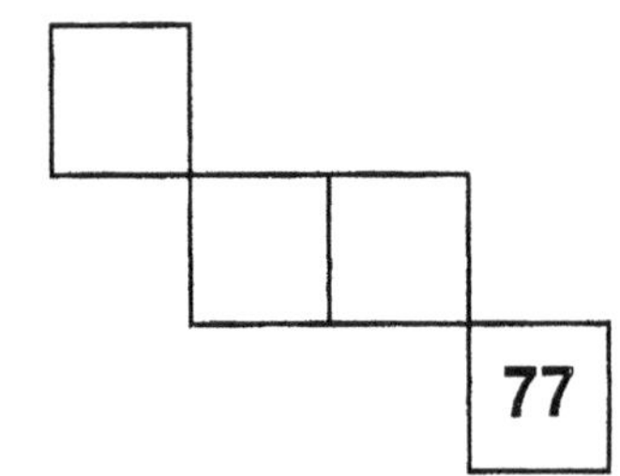


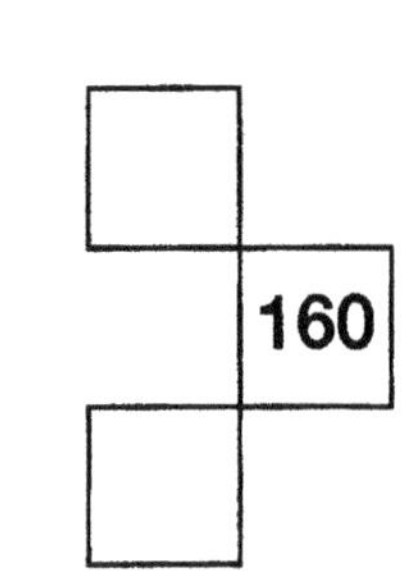


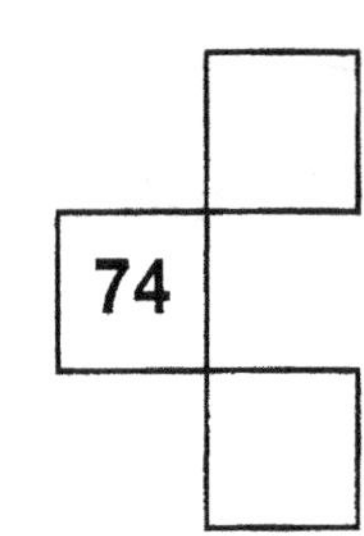


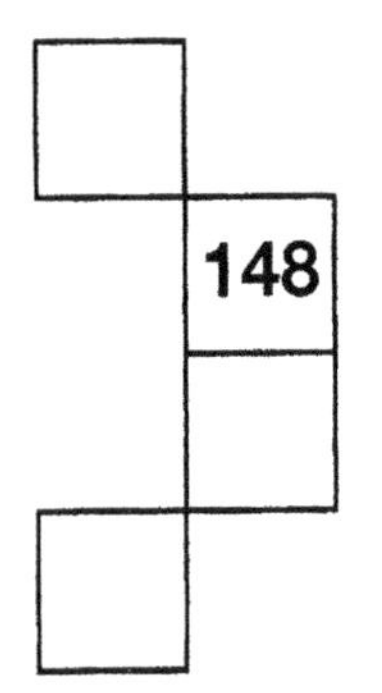


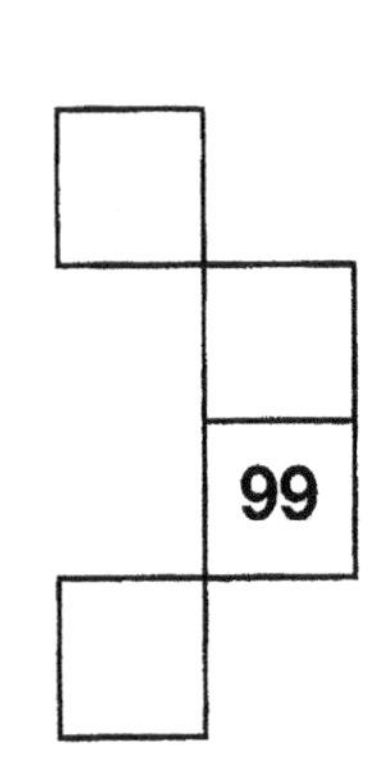


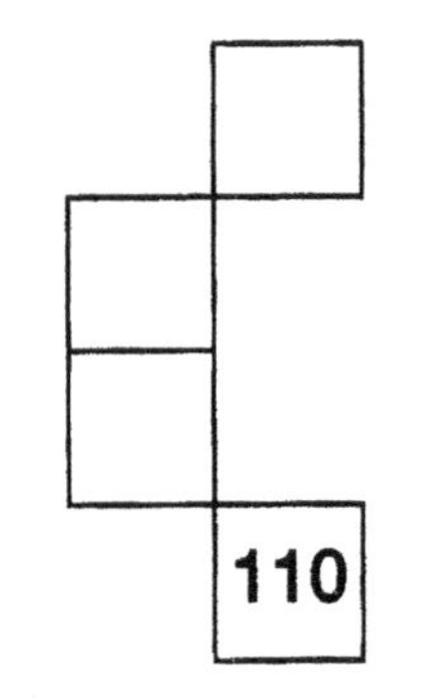


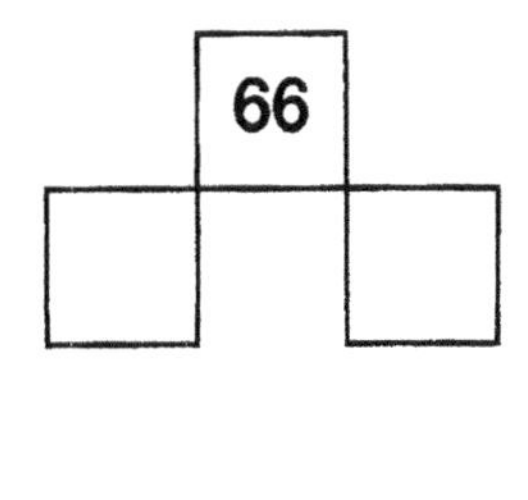


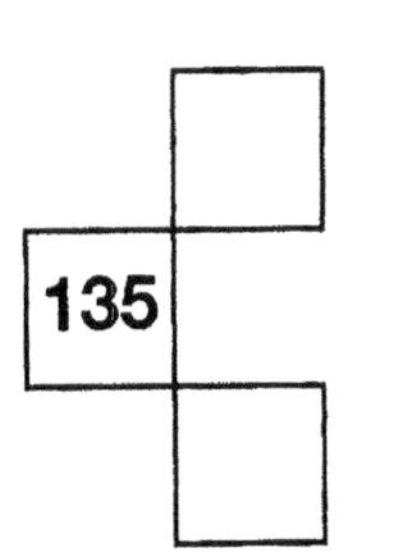


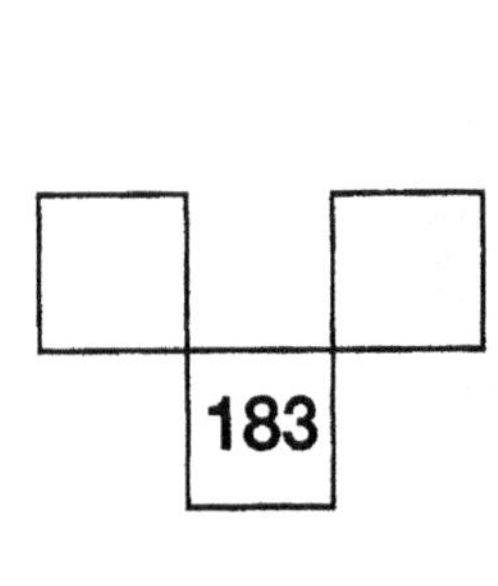


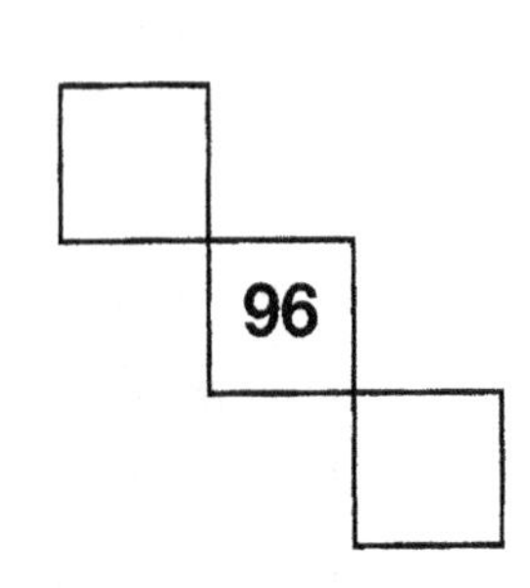


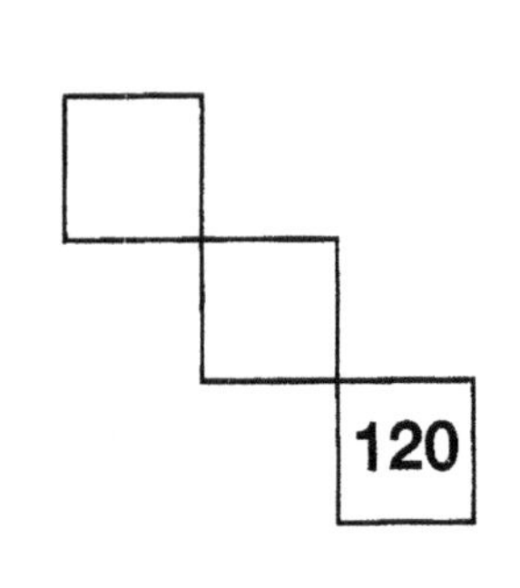

Date ____________ Name ____________________

# What Numbers Are Missing? II

Each of these is a piece cut from a 200 chart. Fill in the missing numbers.

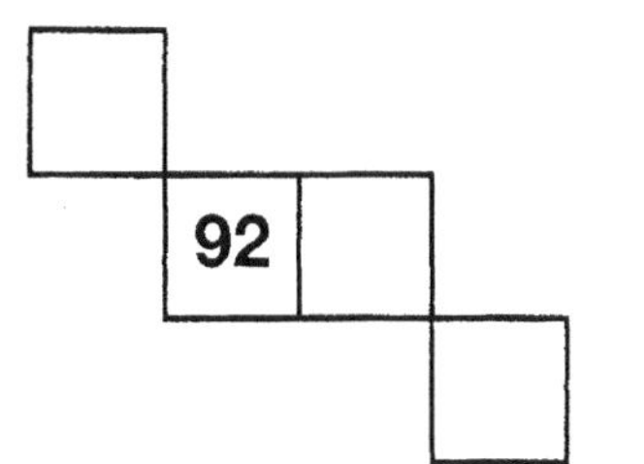

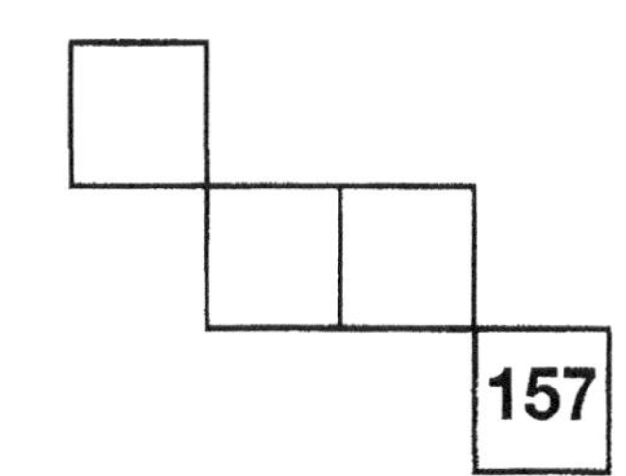

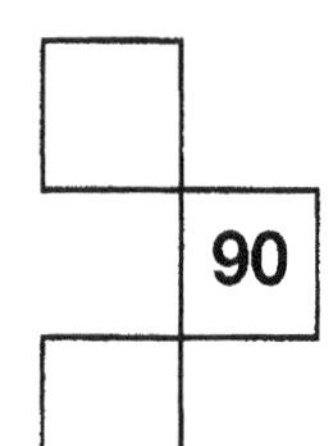

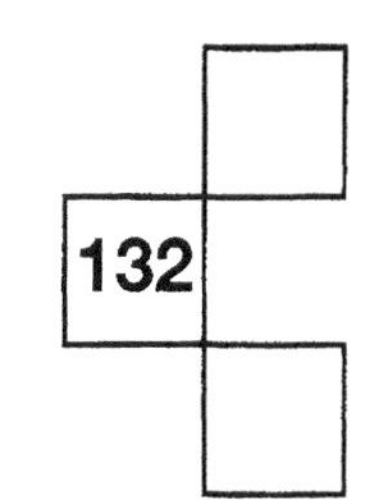


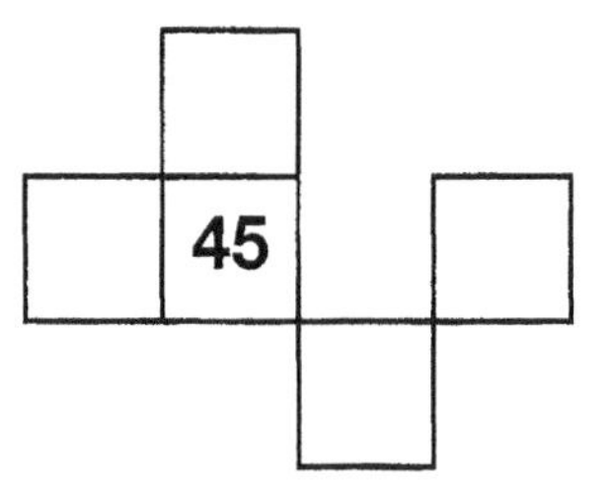

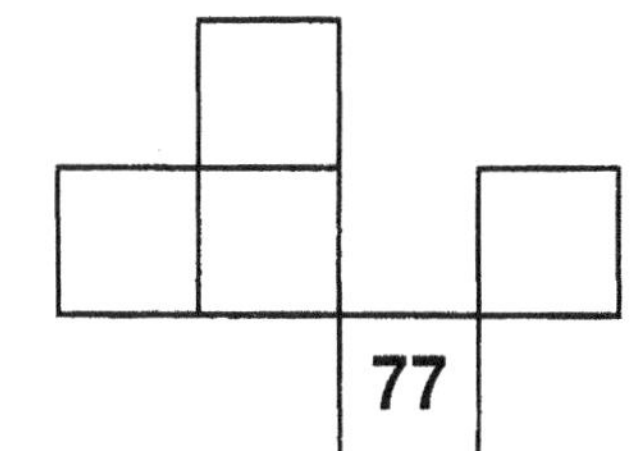

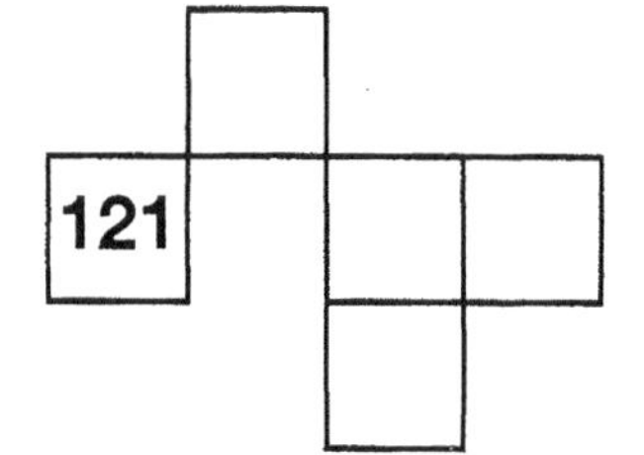

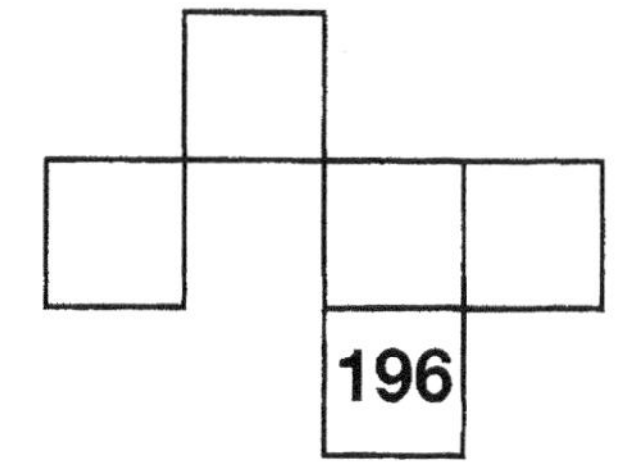


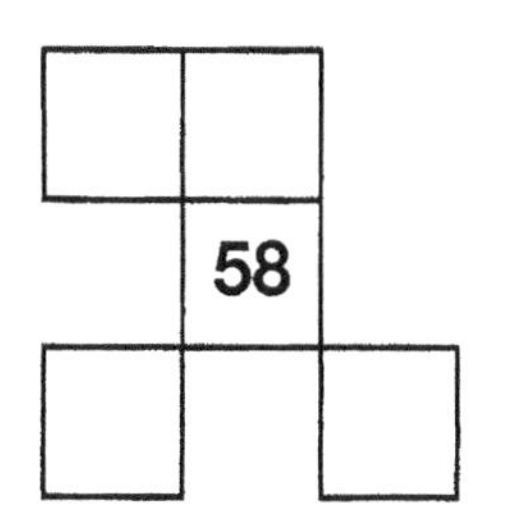

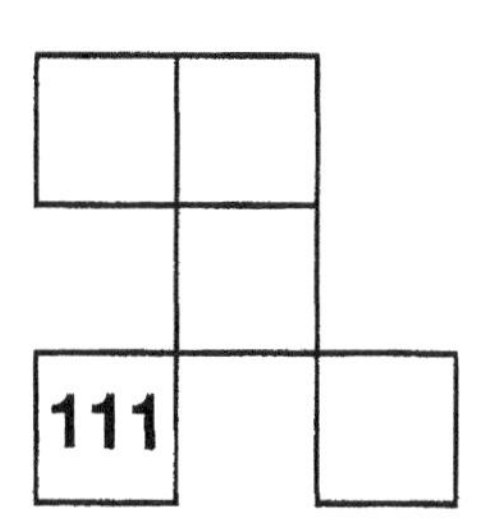

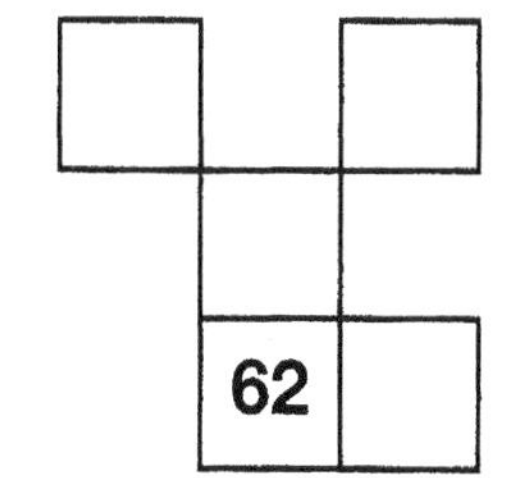

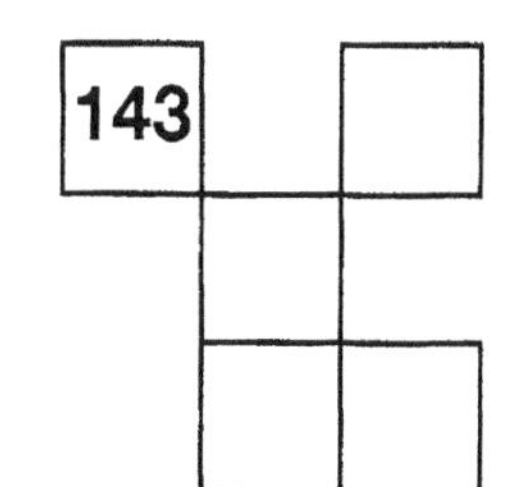


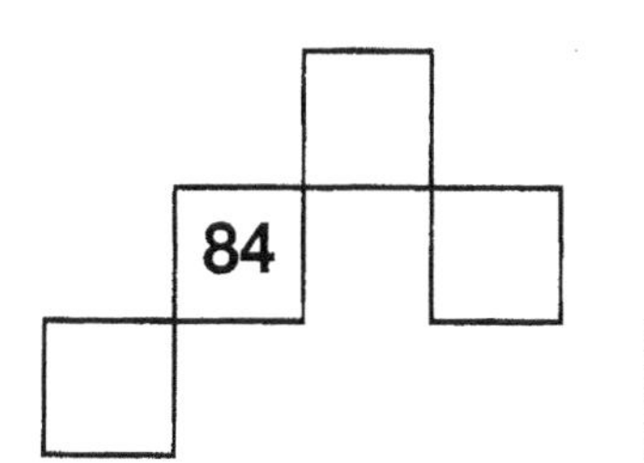

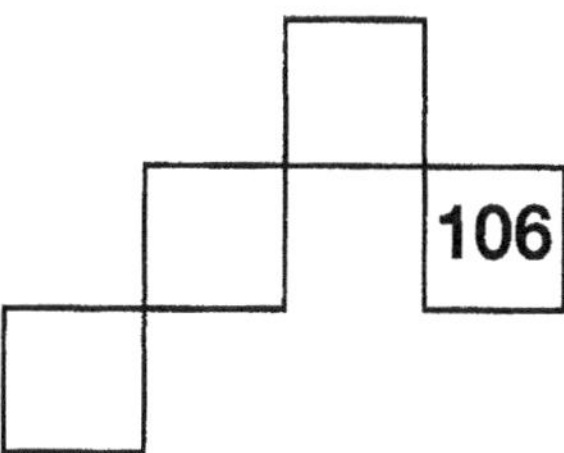

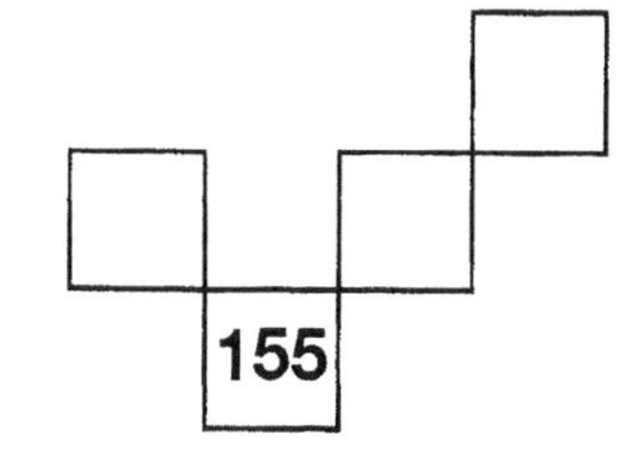

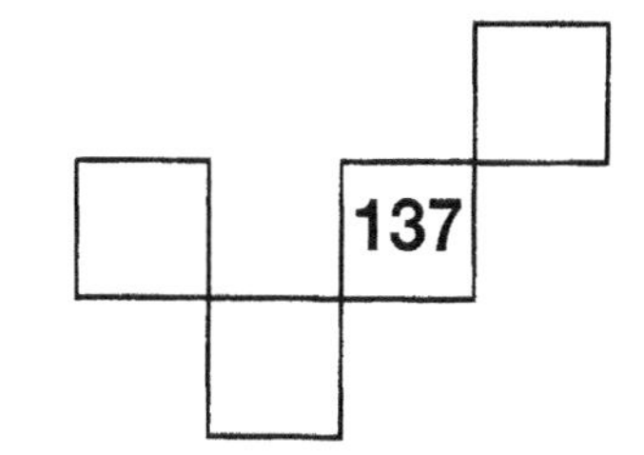


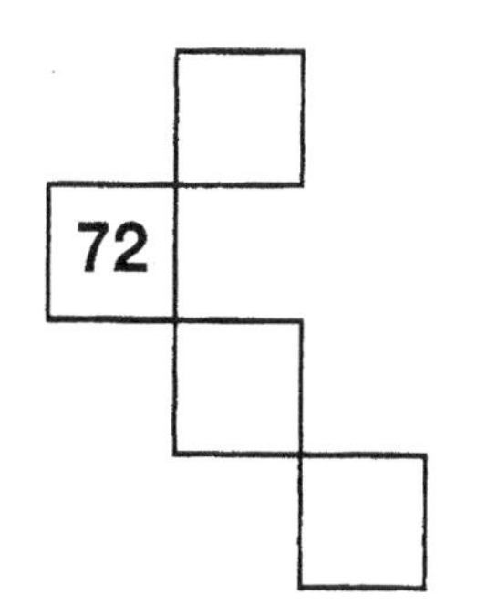

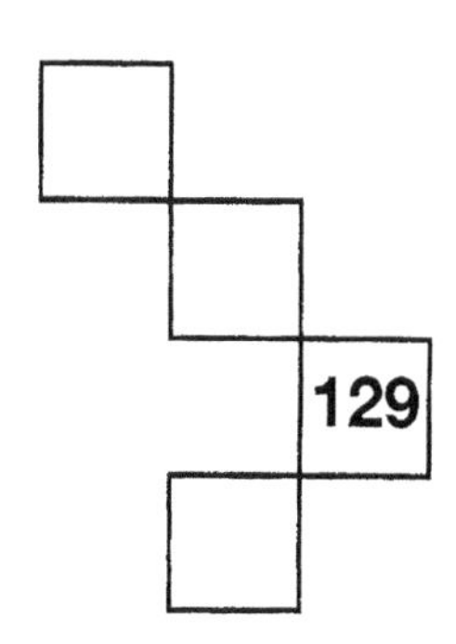

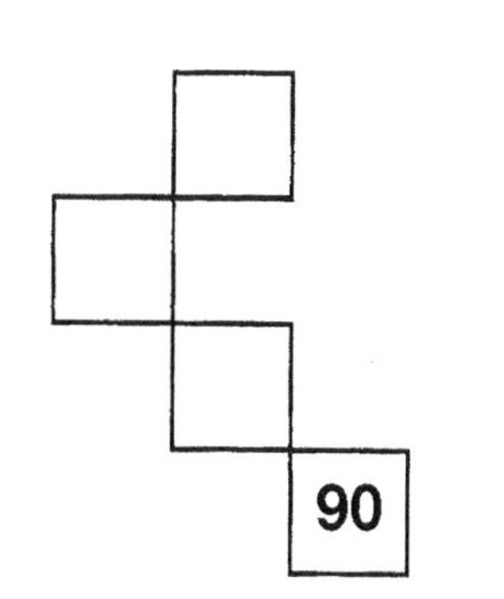

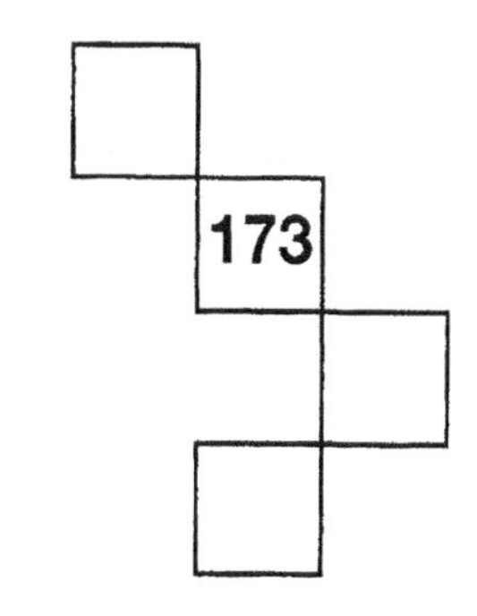

Date ____________ Name ____________________

# How Many Can You Make? I

Draw three cards. Use two of the three cards to form each number.

| even number | number between 20 and 45 | greater than 50 | less than 60 |
|---|---|---|---|

Shuffle cards. Draw three new cards. Use two of the three cards to form each number.

| odd number | number between 26 and 73 | greater than 60 | less than 45 |
|---|---|---|---|

Shuffle cards. Draw three new cards. Use two of the three cards to form each number.

| even number | number between 50 and 85 | greater than 45 | less than 30 |
|---|---|---|---|

Shuffle cards. Draw four new cards. Use three of the four cards to form each number.

| number between 600 and 950 | greater than 500 | less than 400 |
|---|---|---|

| 0 | 1 | 2 | 3 | 4 | 5 | 6 | 7 | 8 | 9 |
|---|---|---|---|---|---|---|---|---|---|

Date ____________ Name ____________________

# How Many Can You Make? II

Draw four cards. Use three of the four cards to form each number.

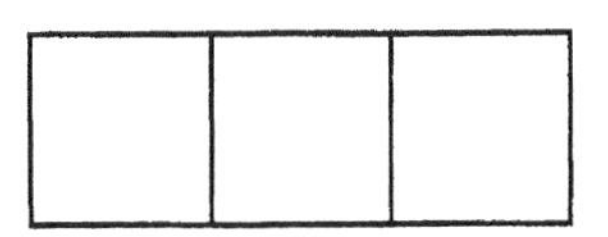
number between 200 and 500

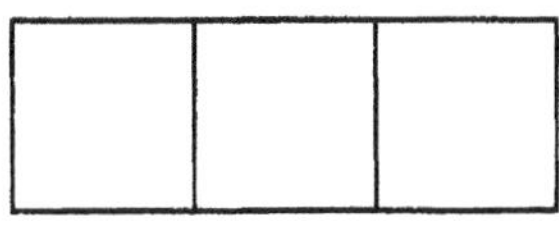
greater than 620

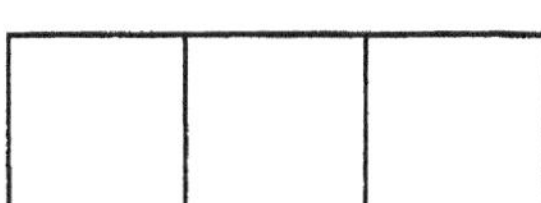
less than 775

Shuffle cards. Draw four new cards. Use three of the four cards to form each number.

number between 310 and 850

greater than 470

less than 650

Shuffle cards. Draw five new cards. Use four of the five cards to form each number.

number between 2500 and 6500

greater than 5800

less than 5100

Shuffle cards. Draw five new cards. Use four of the five cards to form each number.

number between 3900 and 7900

greater than 3520

less than 6750

| 0 | 1 | 2 | 3 | 4 | 5 | 6 | 7 | 8 | 9 |
|---|---|---|---|---|---|---|---|---|---|

Date ________________ Name ____________________________

# What's My Number?

## Use 2, 4, and 5

**1.** My number is more than 300.
The ten's place is worth 50.

My number is ______________.

**2.** My other number is even.
My number is less than 300.

My number is ______________.

## Use 3, 5, and 8

**3.** My number is an even number.
My number is more than 400.

My number is ______________.

**4.** My other number is odd.
My number is the largest possible number.

My number is ______________.

## Use 0, 4, and 7

**5.** My number is more than 600.
My ten's place is worth 40.

My number is ______________.

**6.** My other number is odd.
My number is more than 300.

My number is ______________.

## Use 1, 4, and 9

**7.** My number is more than 300.
The ten's place is worth more than 50.

My number is ______________.

**8.** My other number is more than 500.
My number is an even number.

My number is ______________.

| 0 | 1 | 2 | 3 | 4 | 5 | 6 | 7 | 8 | 9 |
|---|---|---|---|---|---|---|---|---|---|

# Addition

**Assumptions** Students have successfully used addition to solve problems given in context. Since an effort has been made to develop number sense and operation sense, students have discovered more than one meaningful way to find sums. It is also assumed that the students have had repeated experiences to improve their abilities to mentally compute.

## Section Overview and Suggestions

Throughout this section the intentional focus on two-digit problems should improve students' ability to add mentally.

### Sponges

**Tossing Sums** pp. 80–81

**Add It Up** pp. 82–83

These whole-class or small-group warm-ups emphasize mental addition. Both Sponges are open-ended and very repeatable.

### Skill Checks

**Sum It Up 1–6** pp. 84–86

The Skill Checks provide a way to help parents, students, and you to see students' improvement with addition. Each page of *Sum It Up* may be cut in half so that each check may be used at a different time. Remember to have all students respond to STOP before solving the ten problems. The problems written horizontally encourage mental computation.

### Games

**Fifty** pp. 87–88

**Target 80** pp. 89–90

*Fifty* and *Target 80* require strategic thinking and much addition. Because both Games are repeatable and actively involve students in mental addition, parents will enjoy playing them several times with their children.

### Independent Activities

**Loop Addition** pp. 91–92

**Making Sums** pp. 93–94

**Estimating Sums** p. 95

**Linked Equations** p. 96

*Loop Addition* and *Making Sums* provide lots of independent practice with a variety of numbers. The second version of each of these Independent Activities provides a familiar format with more challenging sums. Some sums for *Loop Addition* can be made in more than one way. *Estimating Sums* and *Linked Equations* provide immediate feedback to students.

# Tossing Sums

**Topic:** Mental Addition

**Object:** Identify three addends that equal a given sum

**Groups:** Whole class or small group

### Materials

- transparency of *Tossing Sums,* p. 81
- prepared listing of possible sums for three specified numbers

*Tip* *Select more challenging addend combinations to enhance students' mental competence.*

### Directions

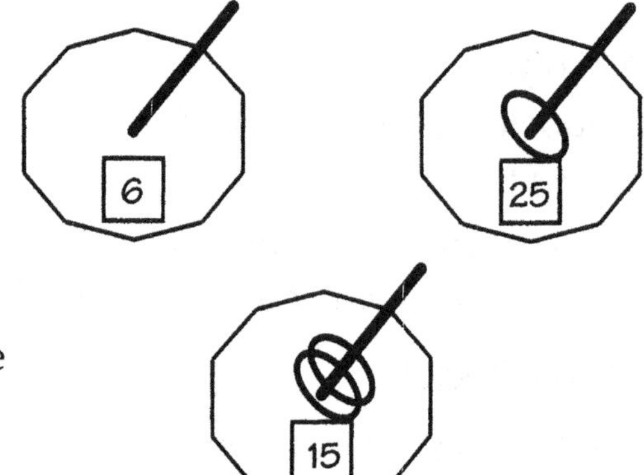


1. Leader records three numbers (addends) on the transparency.

   *Example:* 6 15 25

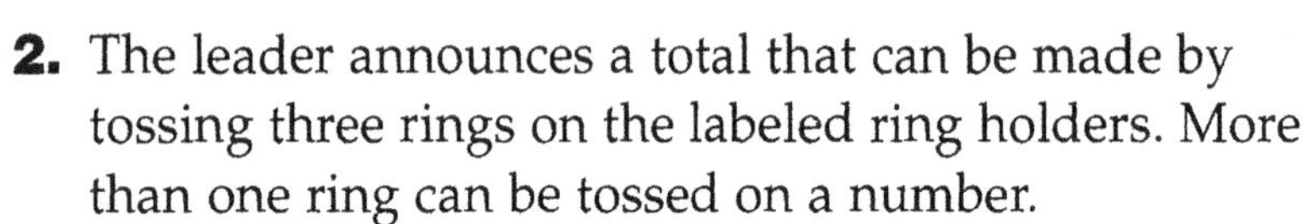

2. The leader announces a total that can be made by tossing three rings on the labeled ring holders. More than one ring can be tossed on a number.

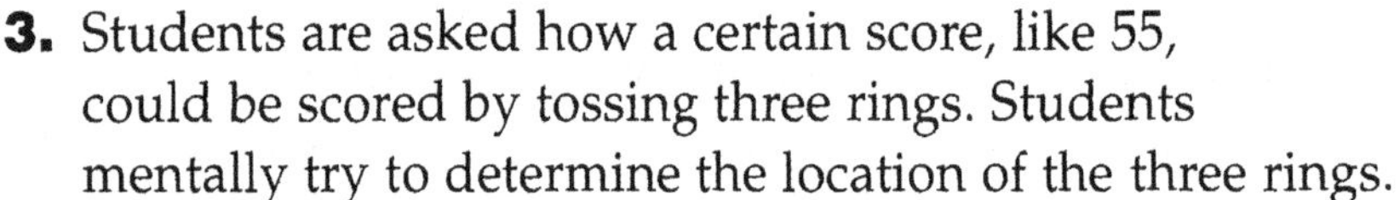

3. Students are asked how a certain score, like 55, could be scored by tossing three rings. Students mentally try to determine the location of the three rings.

   *Example Solution:* 15 + 15 + 25

   *Other possible scores using 6, 15, and 25 with three rings:* *18, 27, 36, 37, 45, 46, 56, 65, 75*

4. If it seems appropriate, use the same transparency but extend this activity to use four rings.

   *Some possible scores using 6, 15, and 25 with four rings:* *24, 33, 42, 43, 51, 52, 60, 61, 62, 70, 71, 80, 81, 90, 100*

   *An additional starter set: 8, 26, 32*

   *Some possible scores using 8, 26, and 32 with three rings:* *24, 42, 48, 60, 66, 72, 78, 84, 90, 96*

   *Some possible scores using 8, 26, and 32 with four rings:* 32, 50, 56, 68, 74, 80, 86, 92, 96, 104, 110, 116, 122, 128

### Making Connections

Promote reflection and make mathematical connections by asking:

- Which scores were easier to find? Please explain.
- What strategy helped you quickly find the addends?

# Tossing Sums

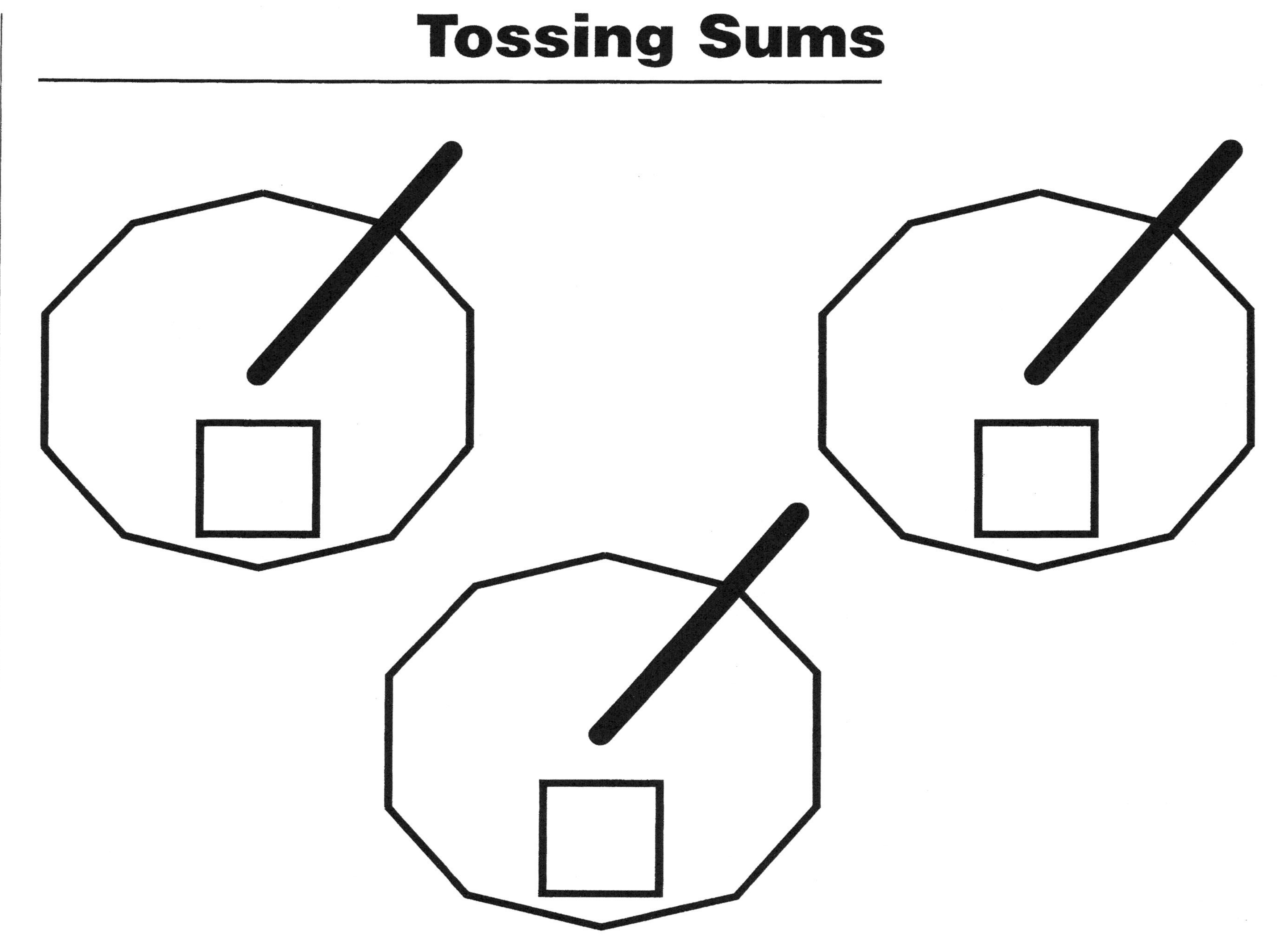

# Add It Up

**Topic:** Mental Addition

**Object:** Create addition problems that produce sums to meet given criteria

**Groups:** Whole class or small group

### Materials

- set of Digit Cards, p. 146
- container for Digit Cards
- transparency of *Add It Up* with forms cut apart, p. 83

*Tip If desired, leader can draw an additional Digit Card each round and students can discard one drawn number in a "reject box."*

### Directions

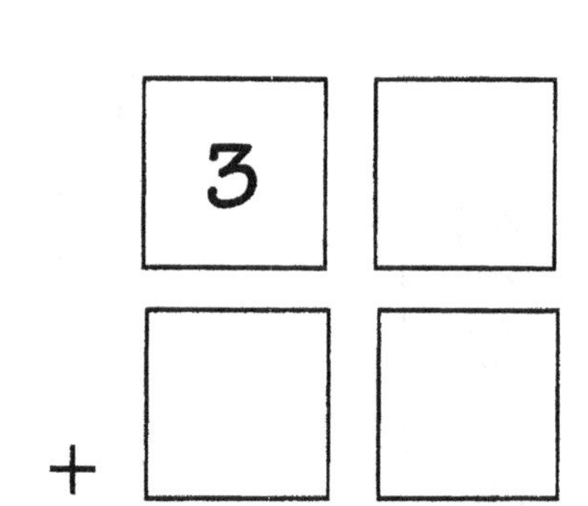


1. Leader describes the criteria for the desired sum.

   *Example:* Create an addition problem that produces a sum less than 100.

2. Leader displays the format (see illustration) for the addition problem that is copied by the students. Leader explains that four cards will be drawn one at a time and that the digits on them will be announced.
3. Leader draws the first card and announces the digit. Leader makes sure each student records the digit in one of the squares before leader draws the next card. Students may not change or move the recorded digits.
4. The leader follows this process until four cards are drawn. (Drawn cards are not returned to the container until the end of the round.)
5. After students have recorded the four digits, they complete their addition problems and determine which sums meet the given criteria.
6. Students continue to play additional rounds of this activity.

   *Possible criteria for future rounds:* Sum between 90 and 110; Odd-numbered sum greater than 100; Sum closest to 130; Largest sum; or Lowest sum.

7. If a more (or less) challenging addition problem format is used, p. 83, leader draws three, five, or six Digit Cards.

### Making Connections

Promote reflection and make mathematical connections by asking:

- How did you decide where to place certain digits?

# Add It Up

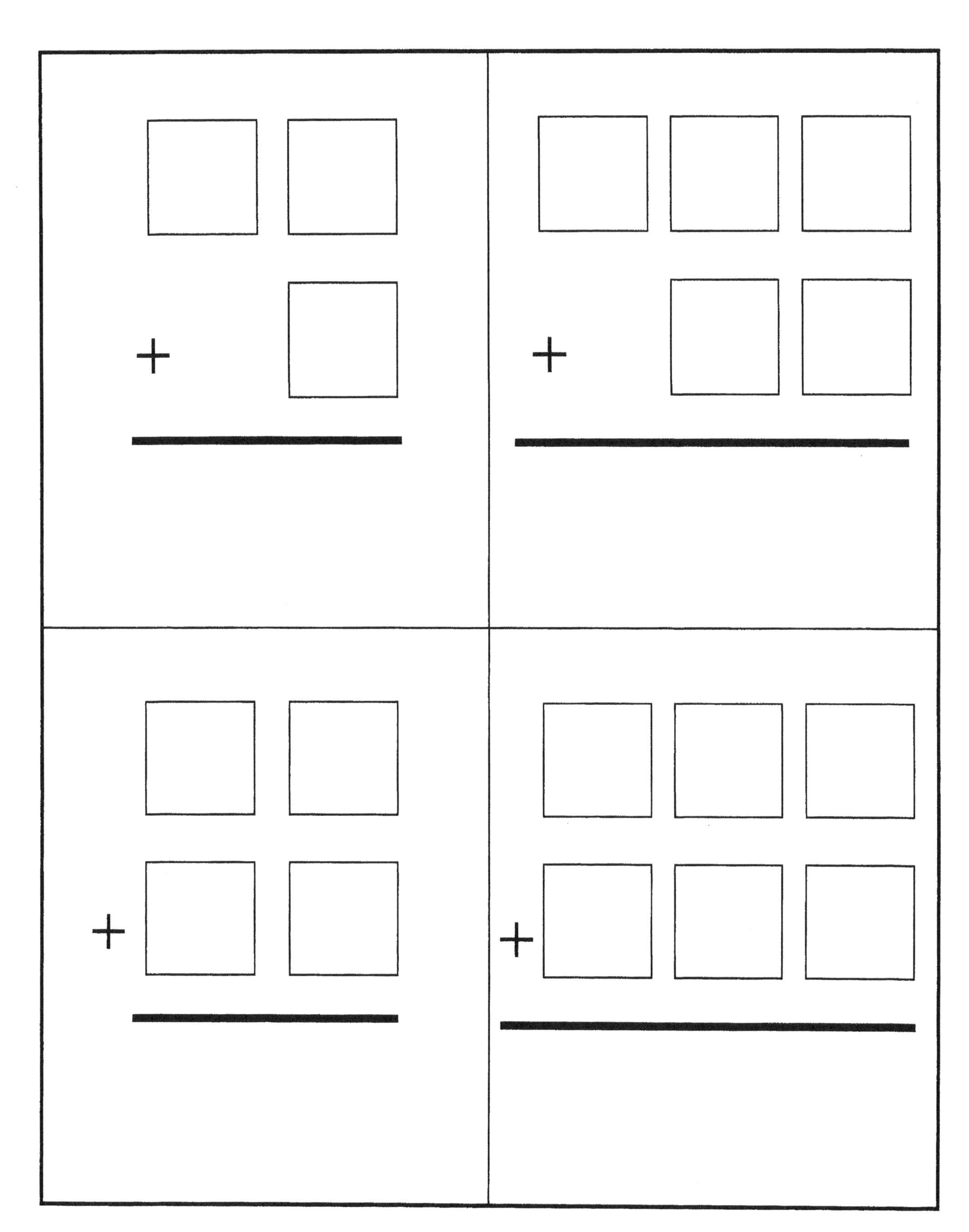

Date ____________ Name ____________________

# Sum It Up 1

**STOP** Don't start yet! Star three problems that may have even answers.

**1.** 25 + 8 = ________ **2.** 35 + 9 + 6 = ________ **3.** 16 + 95 = ________

**4.** 59 + 35 = ________ **5.** 136 + 14 = ________

**6.** 147 + 6

**7.** 37 + 27

**8.** 467 + 28

**9.** 364 + 485

**10.** 628 + 555

**Go On** What numbers come next? 353, 368, 383, 398, ______, ______

Date ____________ Name ____________________

# Sum It Up 2

**STOP** Don't start yet! Star two problems that may have answers under 60.

**1.** 37 + 5 = ________ **2.** 46 + 6 + 9 = ________ **3.** 36 + 18 = ________

**4.** 66 + 49 = ________ **5.** 127 + 33 = ________

**6.** 129 + 5

**7.** 75 + 16

**8.** 748 + 87

**9.** 264 + 927

**10.** 566 + 467

**Go On** Write another equation that fits. Please explain your answer.

135 + 15 =

133 + 17 =

128 + 22 =

Date ______________ Name ______________________

# Sum It Up 3

Don't start yet! Star the problem that will have the largest answer.

**1.** 36 + 7 = ________ **2.** 26 + 6 + 9 = ________ **3.** 47 + 18 = ________

**4.** 29 + 74 = ________ **5.** 152 + 28 = ________

**6.** 156 + 8

**7.** 56 + 35

**8.** 468 + 64

**9.** 257 + 546

**10.** 564 + 847

**Go On** Write three equations that equal 200.

Date ______________ Name ______________________

# Sum It Up 4

Don't start yet! Star two problems that may have answers between 60 and 100.

**1.** 44 + 8 = ________ **2.** 36 + 9 + 5 = ________ **3.** 56 + 17 = ________

**4.** 38 + 29 = ________ **5.** 137 + 13 = ________

**6.** 187 + 5

**7.** 54 + 28

**8.** 593 + 46

**9.** 366 + 536

**10.** 648 + 845

What number is missing? 159, 173, 187, ______, 215, 229

Date ____________ Name ____________

# Sum It Up 5

Don't start yet! Star the problem that may have the smallest answer.

**1.** 54 + 8 = ______ **2.** 34 + 8 + 6 = ______ **3.** 78 + 17 = ______

**4.** 27 + 69 = ______ **5.** 143 + 27 = ______

**6.** 165 + 8

**7.** 47 + 24

**8.** 568 + 33

**9.** 236 + 957

**10.** 684 + 746

What numbers come next? 245, 260, 275, 290, ______ , ______

Date ____________ Name ____________

# Sum It Up 6

STOP Don't start yet! Star the problems in the third row that may have odd answers.

**1.** 67 + 5 = ______ **2.** 23 + 8 + 6 = ______ **3.** 75 + 18 = ______

**4.** 59 + 76 = ______ **5.** 136 + 44 = ______

**6.** 176 + 9

**7.** 77 + 18

**8.** 384 + 38

**9.** 392 + 657

**10.** 648 + 776

Write three equations that equal 500.

# Fifty

**Topic:** Mental Addition to 50

**Object:** Reach the sum of 50 or above

**Groups:** 2 pair players or 2 players

### Materials for each group

- *Fifty* gameboard, p. 88
- 13 markers

### Directions

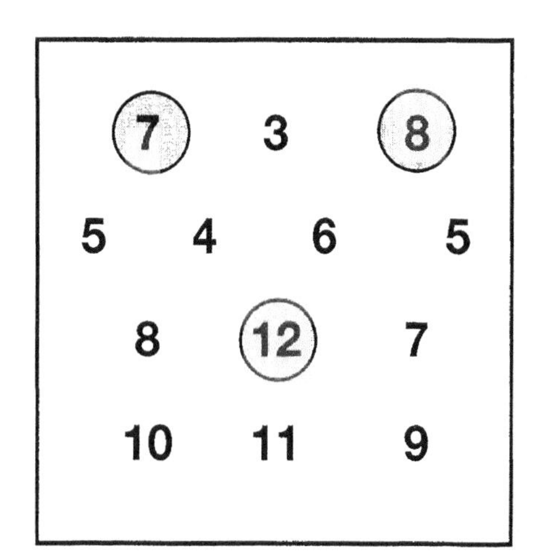


1. The first pair places a marker on any number and announces that number as the current total.
2. The other pair places a marker on any uncovered number, adds that number, and announces the new total. As totals are announced, they are checked by the other pair.
3. Pairs continue alternating turns, placing markers on the gameboard, and announcing the new totals.
4. A pair receives three points for reaching 50 exactly. For going over 50, the pair receives one point.
5. After several rounds, the points are totaled. The pair with the highest total wins.

### Making Connections

Promote reflection and make mathematical connections by asking:

- Did the winners of each round usually total exactly 50 or go beyond 50? How might this outcome be explained?
- What helped you keep track of the current totals?

# Fifty

7 3 8

5 4 6 5

8 12 7

10 11 9



Game

# Target 80

**Topic:** Mental Addition to 80

**Object:** Reach the sum of 80 or close

**Groups:** 2 pair players or 2 players

### Materials

- *Target 80* recording sheet for each pair, p. 90
- set of 1–9 Digit Squares (zero removed), p. 147
- container for the Digit Squares

### Directions

1. The first pair draws a hidden Digit Square and decides whether to put it in the tens place or the ones place. When recording a digit in the tens place, students should also record a zero in the ones place. Once a square is placed it cannot be changed.
2. The other pair follows the same procedure, drawing a Digit Square and placing it on that pair's recording sheet.
3. Pairs alternate turns by drawing and placing Digit Squares four more times.
4. After five Digit Squares are placed, each pair totals the results and records the difference between their total and 80.
5. The differences found in step 4 are the scores. The pair with the lower score wins.

### Making Connections

Promote reflection and make mathematical connections by asking:

- Why do you think the pair with the lower score wins?
- How did you decide where to place your digits?
- How would you play differently in future games?

***Tips*** *If students become confident playing this version, challenge them with higher target numbers. For example, have them draw six Digit Squares, and extend the target number to 100. The score sheet (right half of p. 90) allows players to record scores for multiple rounds.*

**Target 80**

| | | |
|---|---|---|
| Draw #1 | 2 | 0 |
| Draw #2 | | 4 |
| Draw #3 | | 8 |
| Draw #4 | 3 | 0 |
| Draw #5 | | |

**Target 80**
**Score Sheet**

Pair: Billy and Jose

| Our Total | Target Number | Our Score |
|---|---|---|
| 92 | 80 | 12 |
| 71 | 80 | 9 |
| | | |

# Target 80

| | | |
|---|---|---|
| Draw #1 | | |
| Draw #2 | | |
| Draw #3 | | |
| Draw #4 | | |
| Draw #5 | | |

______________
Total

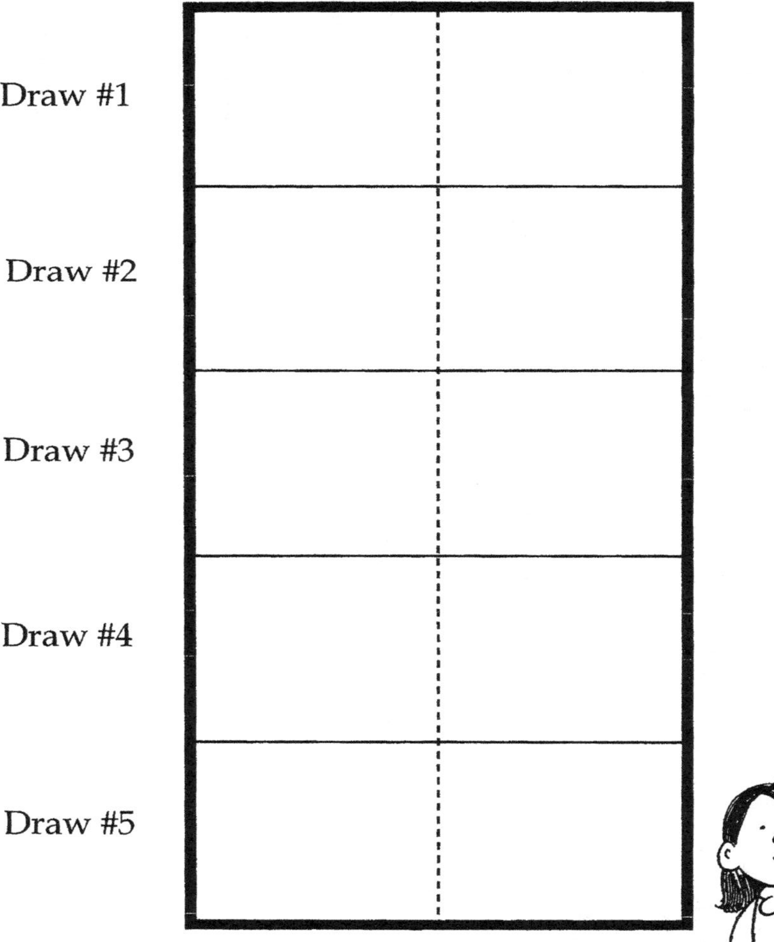


# Target 80
## Score Sheet

Pair: ______________

| Our Total | Target Number | Our Score |
|---|---|---|
| | **80** | |
| | | |
| | | |
| | | |
| | | |
| | | |
| | | |

Date ______________ Name ______________________

# Loop Addition I

Draw a loop around two groups of numbers to match the sum. See the example.

| Example<br>15 — 3 3 3 / 4 4 4<br>3 + 4 + 4 + 4 = 15 | 18 — 4 4 4 / 5 5 5 | 19 — 3 3 3 / 5 5 5 |
|---|---|---|
| 19 — 4 4 4 / 5 5 5 | 21 — 3 3 3 / 5 5 5 | 22 — 4 4 4 / 5 5 5 |
| 24 — 4 4 4 / 6 6 6 | 25 — 3 3 3 / 8 8 8 | 26 — 5 5 5 / 7 7 7 |

Draw a loop around one group of numbers to match the sum.

Example: **Sum = 16**

3

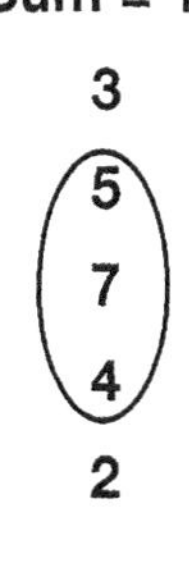


2

| Sum = 15 | Sum = 15 | Sum = 19 | Sum = 21 | Sum = 23 | Sum = 25 | Sum = 28 |
|---|---|---|---|---|---|---|
| 4 | 2 | 6 | 3 | 5 | 9 | 8 |
| 3 | 6 | 4 | 4 | 7 | 3 | 5 |
| 6 | 5 | 6 | 7 | 3 | 7 | 9 |
| 2 | 4 | 5 | 2 | 8 | 4 | 6 |
| 7 | 8 | 4 | 3 | 6 | 6 | 4 |
|  |  |  | 9 | 4 | 8 | 7 |

Date ____________ Name ____________________

# Loop Addition II

Draw a loop around two groups of numbers to match the sum. See the example.

| Example<br>19 — 4 4 4 4 / 5 5 5 5<br>4 + 5 + 5 + 5 = 19 | 30 — 4 4 4 4 / 9 9 9 9 | 27 — 3 3 3 3 / 7 7 7 7 |
|---|---|---|
| 32 — 6 6 6 6 / 7 7 7 7 | 36 — 5 5 5 5 / 7 7 7 7 | 36 — 3 3 3 3 / 8 8 8 8 |
| 38 — 6 6 6 6 / 8 8 8 8 | 39 — 6 6 6 6 / 9 9 9 9 | 46 — 7 7 7 7 / 9 9 9 9 |

Draw a loop around one group of numbers to match the sum.

Example: Sum = 16

3

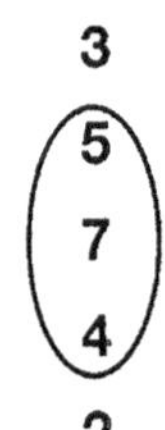

5
7
4

2

| Sum = 32 | Sum = 29 | Sum = 33 | Sum = 33 | Sum = 33 | Sum = 34 | Sum = 37 |
|---|---|---|---|---|---|---|
| 6 | 7 | 4 | 9 | 5 | 9 | 8 |
| 4 | 7 | 6 | 6 | 9 | 6 | 4 |
| 9 | 9 | 8 | 8 | 8 | 8 | 8 |
| 5 | 5 | 7 | 4 | 7 | 7 | 9 |
| 8 | 8 | 8 | 7 | 9 | 4 | 7 |
| 7 | 6 | 5 | 8 | 6 | 8 | 9 |

Date ____________ Name ____________

# Making Sums I

Use the numbers in the box to create correct addition problems.

| | |
|---|---|
| 15 | 16 |
| 20 | 22 |
| 28 | 40 |

____ + ____ = 37

____ + ____ = 55

____ + ____ = 68

____ + ____ = 43

____ + ____ + ____ = 82

____ + ____ + ____ = 65

____ + ____ = 50

____ + ____ = 38

____ + ____ = 44

____ + ____ = 31

---

Use the numbers in the box to create correct addition problems.

| | |
|---|---|
| 25 | 30 |
| 35 | 38 |
| 42 | 44 |
| 48 | 50 |

____ + ____ = 60

____ + ____ = 88

____ + ____ = 82

____ + ____ = 73

____ + ____ + ____ = 105

____ + ____ + ____ = 90

____ + ____ = 77

____ + ____ = 78

____ + ____ = 90

____ + ____ = 83

Date ______________ Name ______________________

# Making Sums II

Use the numbers in the box to create correct addition problems.

| | |
|---|---|
| 16 | 23 |
| 28 | 34 |
| 35 | 46 |

_____ + _____ = 39

_____ + _____ = 50

_____ + _____ = 51

_____ + _____ = 74

_____ + _____ = 69

_____ + _____ = 44

_____ + _____ = 62

_____ + _____ = 81

_____ + _____ + _____ = 67

_____ + _____ + _____ = 92

Use the numbers in the box to create correct addition problems.

| | |
|---|---|
| 17 | 24 |
| 35 | 38 |
| 42 | 57 |
| 60 | 66 |

_____ + _____ = 81

_____ + _____ = 74

_____ + _____ = 55

_____ + _____ = 99

_____ + _____ = 123

_____ + _____ = 66

_____ + _____ = 90

_____ + _____ = 98

_____ + _____ = 92

_____ + _____ + _____ = 126

Date ____________ Name ____________________

# Estimating Sums

Estimate each sum. Match your estimate with a letter in the box. Record the matching letter.

| | |
|---|---|
| 80 | A |
| 90 | B |
| 100 | I |
| 120 | K |
| 140 | R |
| 150 | S |
| 160 | T |
| 170 | Y |

**1.** 39 + 48 = ____

**2.** 99 + 69 = ____

**3.** 53 + 49 = ____

**4.** 75 + 83 = ____

**5.** 63 + 86 = ____

**6.** 27 + 59 = ____

**7.** 16 + 67 = ____

**8.** 64 + 75 = ____

**9.** 67 + 49 = ____

Answer the riddle by recording the letters in order below.

How can you recognize a dogwood tree?

____ ____   ____ ____ ____   ____ ____ ____ ____

Date ____________ Name ______________________

# Linked Equations

Find all the sums to complete the puzzle.

| 19 | + | 17 | = |  |  |  |  | 59 | + | 84 | = |  |
|---|---|---|---|---|---|---|---|---|---|---|---|---|
| + |  |  |  | + |  |  |  | + |  |  |  | + |
| 26 |  |  |  | 18 | + | 28 | = |  |  |  |  | 78 |
| = |  |  |  | = |  |  |  | = |  |  |  | = |
|  | + | 9 | = |  |  |  |  | 105 | + | 116 | = |  |
|  |  | + |  |  |  |  |  |  |  | + |  |  |
|  |  | 18 |  |  |  |  |  |  |  | 288 |  |  |
|  |  | = |  |  |  |  |  |  |  | = |  |  |
| 155 | + |  | = |  |  |  |  | 327 | + | 404 | = |  |
| + |  |  |  | + |  |  |  | + |  |  |  | + |
| 73 |  |  |  | 221 | + | 138 | = |  |  |  |  | 249 |
| = |  |  |  | = |  |  |  | = |  |  |  | = |
|  | + | 175 | + |  |  |  |  |  | + | 294 | = |  |

# Subtraction

**Assumptions** Students have successfully used subtraction to solve problems given in context. Since an effort has been made to develop number sense and operation sense, students have discovered more than one meaningful way to find differences. Students have had repeated experiences to improve their abilities to mentally compute.

## Section Overview and Suggestions

The use of two-digit problems throughout this section is intended to improve students' abilities to mentally subtract. It is appropriate to use calculators to check mental computation results.

### Sponges

**Finding Differences** p. 98

**Diffy** pp. 99–101

These whole-class or small-group warm-ups emphasize mental subtraction. *Diffy* is open-ended and very repeatable.

### Skill Checks

**What's Left Out?** 1–6 pp. 102–104

Each page of Skill Checks may be copied and cut in half so that each check may be used at a different time. Remember to have all students respond to STOP before solving the ten problems. The problems written horizontally lend themselves to mental computation.

### Games

**99 and Out** p. 105

**Target 20** pp. 106–107

**Target 200** pp. 106, 108

These are repeatable, engaging Games that families will enjoy playing several times. *99 and Out* requires strategic thinking and much subtraction. *Target 20* actively involves students in mental subtraction. *Target 200* extends this activity to three-place subtraction.

### Independent Activities

**Sorting Differences** pp. 109–110

**Finding Pairs** pp. 111–112

**Subtraction Arrays** pp. 113–114

These activities provide immediate feedback to students. Skill with *Finding Differences* (p. 98) should ensure success with *Finding Pairs*. Some problems can be solved in more than one way. Students gain additional practice by creating *Finding Pairs* puzzles for others. By solving the problems in *Sorting Differences* and *Subtraction Arrays*, students discover interesting trivia.

# Finding Differences

**Topic:** Mental Subtraction

**Object:** Identify two numbers whose difference equals a given amount

**Groups:** Whole class or small group

*Tip For additional experience with this activity, have students do the Finding Pairs activity, p. 111.*

### Materials

- chalkboard or overhead projector

### Directions

1. Leader displays group of numbers listed in descending order.
2. Leader announces a possible difference, like 3.
3. Students try to identify two listed numbers whose difference is 3. Then ask, "Can it be done any other way?"

   *Example:* 30 – 27 = 3 and 23 – 20 = 3

| | |
|---|---|
| 35 | 23 |
| 30 | 20 |
| 27 | 18 |

4. Leader continues stating differences and students respond with one or more possibilities. (Other possible differences for the box above: 2, 4, 5, 7, 8, 9, 10, 12, 15, and 17.)
5. Challenge students with an expanded listing:

   *Possible differences for the second box:* 1, 3, 4, 5, 6, 7, 8, 9, 11, 12, 14, 15, 17, 18, 20, 21, 23, and 26 (Many can be done more than one way.)

| | | |
|---|---|---|
| 48 | 39 | 28 |
| 43 | 35 | 25 |
| 40 | 31 | 22 |

### Making Connections

Promote reflection and make mathematical connections by asking:

- What helped you quickly locate differences?

# Diffy

**Topic:** Mental Subtraction

**Object:** Find differences until all differences equal the same amount

**Groups:** Whole class or small group

### Materials

- transparency of *Diffy* form, p. 100
- *Diffy* recording sheet for each student, p. 101

### Directions

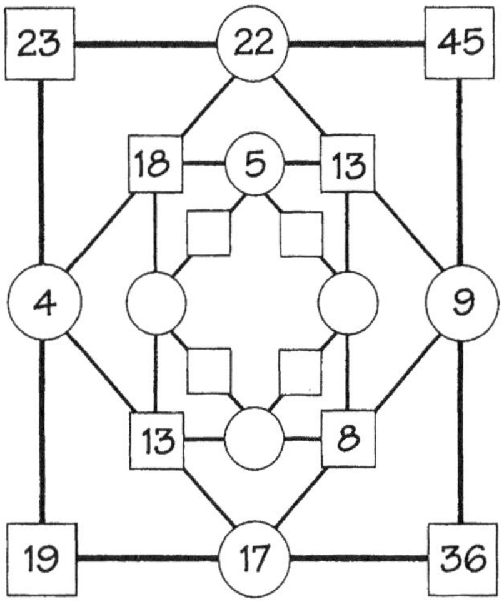

1. Students suggest four different 2-digit numbers. Leader records these numbers in the four corner squares. Students record these numbers on one of their recording sheet forms.
2. Students subtract the corner numbers from each other and record the differences in the circles between them.
3. Students subtract the four new differences from each other and record those differences in the squares between them.
4. Students continue this process until all four new differences match. Ask, "How many subtractions were required?"
5. Students start the process over again with four new numbers until four different *Diffy* puzzles are completed. Ask, "Did each *Diffy* puzzle require the same number of steps to complete?"
6. Students compare and contrast their results, seeking possible patterns.

### Making Connections

Promote reflection and make mathematical connections by asking:

- Which numbers require three or fewer subtraction steps?
- Did you create any *Diffy* puzzles that required more than four subtraction steps?

***Tips*** *To easily reuse transparency for a new puzzle, use a blank transparency on top of the* Diffy *transparency.*

*Use the* Diffy *recording sheet with numbers recorded in the four outside corner squares to provide an additional independent practice activity.*

*Acknowledgment: This activity is adapted from* Drill and Practice at the Problem Solving Level, *written by Robert W. Wirtz, Curriculum Development Associates.*

# Diffy

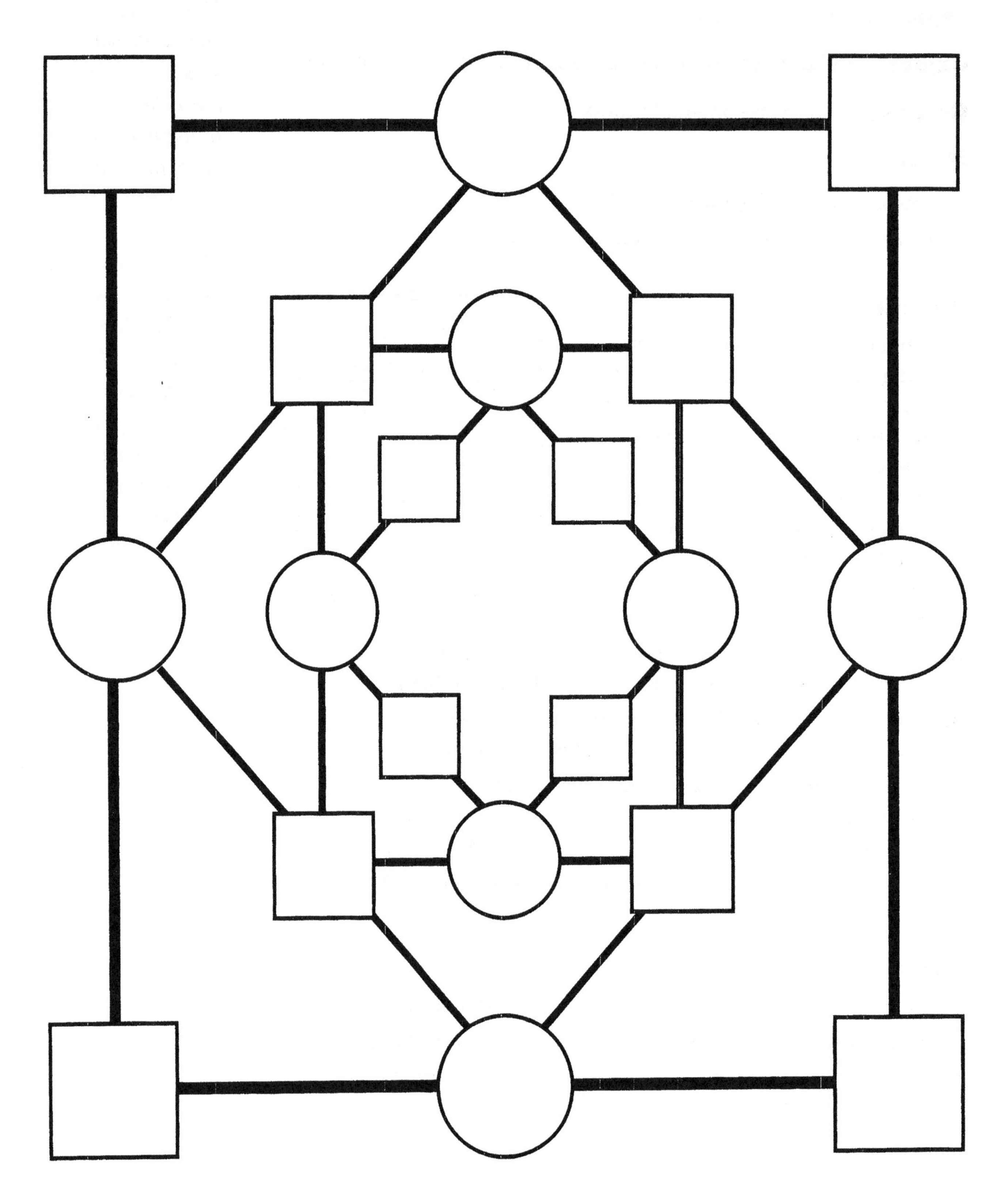

# Diffy

## Recording Sheet

Date ____________ Name ____________________

# What's Left Out? 1

Don't start yet!
Star three problems that may have even answers.

**1.** $\square + 12 = 20$ **2.** $35 + \square = 50$ **3.** $\square + 17 = 33$

**4.** $30 - 6 = \square$ **5.** $42 - 9 = \square$

**6.** $71 - 34$ **7.** $172 - 58$ **8.** $100 - 46$ **9.** $214 - 175$ **10.** $372 - 167$

Which number is closer to 1000? 974 or 1028?
Please explain your answer.

Date ____________ Name ____________________

# What's Left Out? 2

STOP

Don't start yet!
Star two problems in the last row that may have answers between 150 and 250.

**1.** $\square + 14 = 20$ **2.** $37 + \square = 50$ **3.** $\square + 15 = 32$

**4.** $40 - 7 = \square$ **5.** $53 - 8 = \square$

**6.** $61 - 25$ **7.** $217 - 44$ **8.** $200 - 63$ **9.** $328 - 165$ **10.** $710 - 467$

What numbers come next? 220, 213, 206, ______ , ______
Please explain your answer.

Date ____________ Name ____________

# What's Left Out? 3

Don't start yet!
Star three problems that are easy to compute mentally.

**1.** $\square + 7 = 20$  **2.** $26 + \square = 40$  **3.** $\square + 14 = 31$

**4.** $70 - 8 = \square$  **5.** $83 - 8 = \square$

**6.** $\begin{array}{r} 63 \\ -\ 45 \\ \hline \end{array}$  **7.** $\begin{array}{r} 237 \\ -\ 54 \\ \hline \end{array}$  **8.** $\begin{array}{r} 100 \\ -\ 36 \\ \hline \end{array}$  **9.** $\begin{array}{r} 321 \\ -\ 276 \\ \hline \end{array}$  **10.** $\begin{array}{r} 420 \\ -\ 276 \\ \hline \end{array}$

**Go On** Write three subtraction equations that equal 29.

Date ____________ Name ____________

# What's Left Out? 4

Don't start yet!
Star the problems in the last row that may have odd answers.

**1.** $\square + 11 = 20$  **2.** $38 + \square = 50$  **3.** $\square + 15 = 34$

**4.** $80 - 4 = \square$  **5.** $71 - 7 = \square$

**6.** $\begin{array}{r} 62 \\ -\ 35 \\ \hline \end{array}$  **7.** $\begin{array}{r} 382 \\ -\ 67 \\ \hline \end{array}$  **8.** $\begin{array}{r} 200 \\ -\ 74 \\ \hline \end{array}$  **9.** $\begin{array}{r} 438 \\ -\ 195 \\ \hline \end{array}$  **10.** $\begin{array}{r} 710 \\ -\ 476 \\ \hline \end{array}$

**Go On** What number is missing? 460, 435, 410, ______, 360, 335

Date ____________ Name ____________________

# What's Left Out? 5

**STOP** Don't start yet!
Star the problem that may have the largest answer.

**1.** ☐ + 4 = 20 **2.** 32 + ☐ = 50 **3.** ☐ + 17 = 35

**4.** 60 – 6 = ☐ **5.** 72 – 7 = ☐

| **6.** | **7.** | **8.** | **9.** | **10.** |
|---|---|---|---|---|
| 72 | 328 | 200 | 638 | 814 |
| – 26 | – 45 | – 37 | – 263 | – 576 |

**Go On** Write another subtraction equation that fits.
Please explain your answer.

| | |
|---|---|
| 40 – 18 | 57 – 35 |
| 31– 9 | |

✂ ............................................................

Date ____________ Name ____________________

# What's Left Out? 6

**STOP** Don't start yet!
Star two problems that are difficult to compute mentally.

**1.** ☐ + 13 = 20 **2.** 26 + ☐ = 40 **3.** ☐ + 17 = 32

**4.** 50 – 7 = ☐ **5.** 81 – 9 = ☐

| **6.** | **7.** | **8.** | **9.** | **10.** |
|---|---|---|---|---|
| 61 | 273 | 100 | 427 | 610 |
| – 37 | – 69 | – 62 | – 294 | – 357 |

**Go On** Which number is closer to 180? 163 or 196?
Please prove it.

# 99 and Out

**Topic:** 2-Place Subtraction

**Object:** Subtract close to zero

**Groups:** 2–3 players

### Materials for each group

- 2 Number Cubes (1–6) or spinners
- scratch paper and pencil (for each player)

*Tip When students become confident, play "100 and Out" for a more challenging game.*

### Directions

1. The first player rolls the two number cubes to form a two-digit number and subtracts this number from 99. The player records the difference. (See one player's sample.)
2. Each other player, in turn, rolls the number cubes, forms a new two-digit number, and subtracts it from 99.
3. For the second turn, each player rolls the number cubes, forms a new two-digit number, and subtracts it from the existing difference.
4. For succeeding turns, players decide if they want to subtract a 2-digit or one-digit number and then roll the appropriate quantity of number cubes. (The player in the sample game would probably choose to roll only one number cube on the next turn.)
5. Players continue rolling and subtracting until a player reaches zero or close to it. Players who roll a number higher than the remaining difference automatically lose that round.
6. The player with the lowest difference wins. (The number of turns or rolls is not a factor.)

$$\begin{array}{r} 99 \\ -24 \\ \hline 75 \\ -63 \\ \hline 12 \end{array}$$

### Making Connections

Promote reflection and make mathematical connections by asking:

- When and why did you use only one number cube?
- At what point did you decide to stop rolling? Why?

# Target 20

**Topic:** 2-place Subtraction

**Object:** Create two 2-digit numbers whose difference is close to 20

**Groups:** Small group or pair players

### Materials for each pair

- 1 set of Digit Squares, p. 147
- *Target 20* recording sheet, p. 107

*Tip* *For students ready to practice 3-place subtraction, play Target 200, p. 108. Students draw six digit squares and seek a difference close to 200.*

### Directions

1. Each pair draws four digit squares.
2. Each pair works together to arrange the four squares to form two 2-digit numbers whose difference is close to 20. The pair then records the problem and the difference.
3. Next, the pairs determine their scores by finding and recording the differences between their answers and 20.
4. Pairs repeat this process three more times.
5. Pairs play several rounds and total their scores. The pair with the lowest score wins.

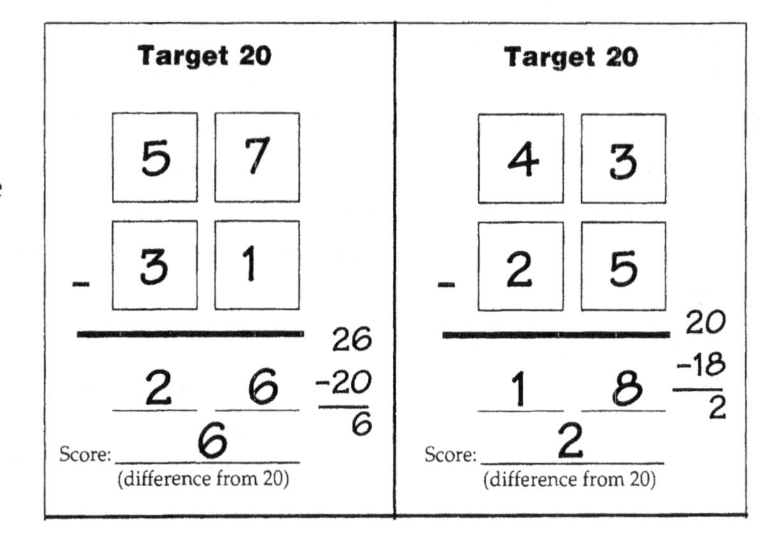


### Making Connections

Promote reflection and make mathematical connections by asking:

- What strategies did you use to produce low scores?

## Target 20

−

Score: ____________
(difference from 20)

## Target 20

−

Score: ____________
(difference from 20)

## Target 20

−

Score: ____________
(difference from 20)

## Target 20

−

Score: ____________
(difference from 20)

## Target 200

Score: ____________________
(difference from 200)

## Target 200

Score: ____________________
(difference from 200)

## Target 200

Score: ____________________
(difference from 200)

## Target 200

Score: ____________________
(difference from 200)

Date ____________________ Name ________________________________

# Sorting Differences I

Solve and cut out the twelve problems at the bottom of the page. Arrange these problems in the boxes so that only four fit with each rule.

*

| Difference less than 20 | | Difference between 20 and 30 | | Difference greater than 30 | |
|---|---|---|---|---|---|
| | | | | | |
| | | | | | |

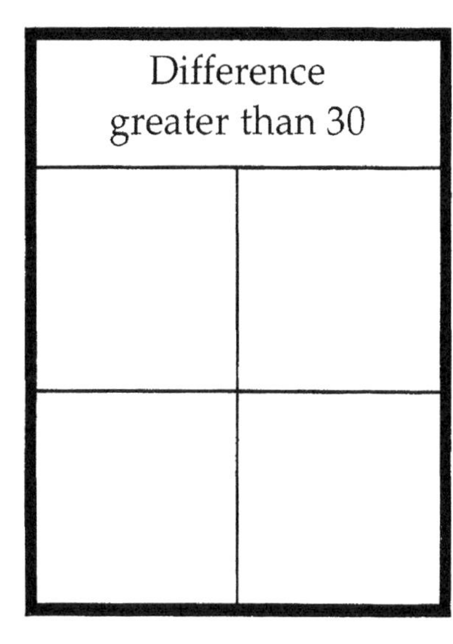

* **Trivia Bonus:** The sum of these four answers equals the running speed in miles per hour for the world's fastest land animal (cheetah).

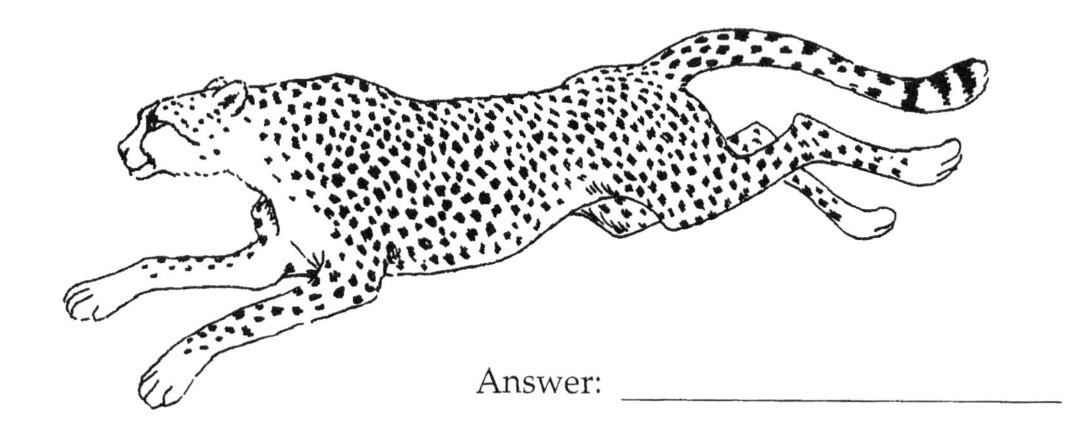

Answer: ____________________

| | | | | | |
|---|---|---|---|---|---|
| 51 − 28 | 42 − 24 | 63 − 37 | 59 − 24 | 35 − 19 | 83 − 36 |
| 78 − 42 | 64 − 35 | 84 − 67 | 97 − 53 | 66 − 38 | 75 − 56 |

Date ____________________ Name ________________________________

# Sorting Differences II

Solve and cut out the twelve problems at the bottom of the page. Arrange these problems in the boxes so that only four fit with each rule. (Careful: Some fit more than one rule.)

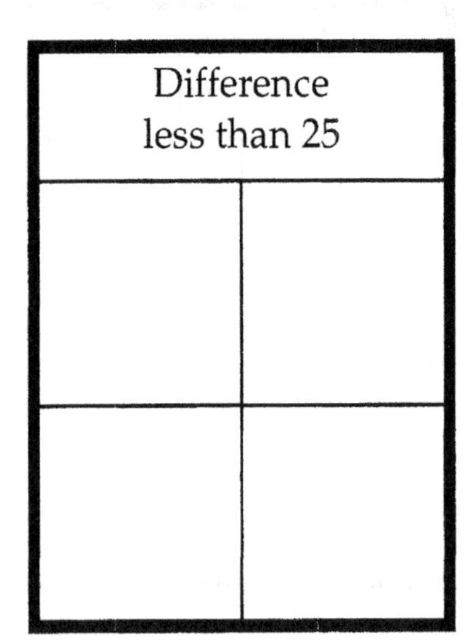


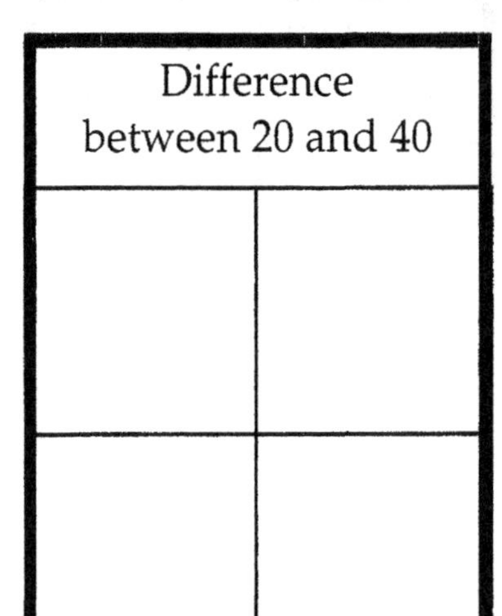


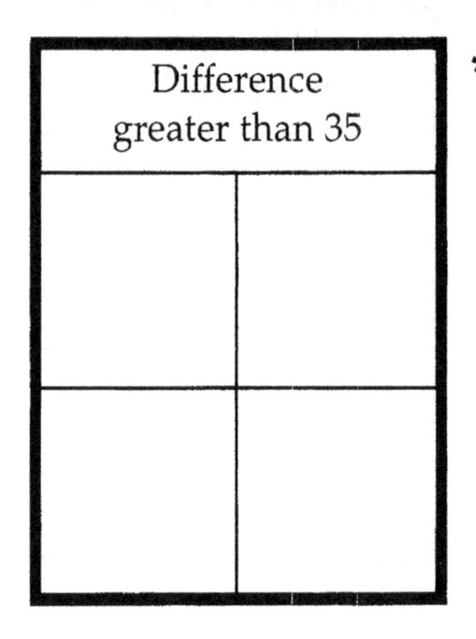


*

* **Trivia Bonus:** The sum of these four answers equals the number of long feathers on a male peacock.

Answer: ____________________

| | | | | | |
|---|---|---|---|---|---|
| 137<br>– 118 | 110<br>– 83 | 118<br>– 97 | 102<br>– 78 | 130<br>– 91 | 92<br>– 76 |
| 213<br>– 156 | 214<br>– 189 | 311<br>– 268 | 178<br>– 145 | 485<br>– 439 | 132<br>– 78 |

Date ________ Name ________

# Finding Pairs I

Use the numbers in the box to create correct subtraction problems.

| | |
|---|---|
| 30 | 18 |
| 26 | 14 |
| 21 | 13 |

____ – ____ = 4 ____ – ____ = 16

____ – ____ = 7 ____ – ____ = 9

____ – ____ = 3 ____ – ____ = 13

____ – ____ = 5 ____ – ____ = 17

Can you do it two different ways?

____ – ____ = 12 ____ – ____ = 8

____ – ____ = 12 ____ – ____ = 8

Use the numbers in the box to create correct subtraction problems.

| | |
|---|---|
| 50 | 33 |
| 46 | 28 |
| 40 | 25 |
| 37 | 21 |

____ – ____ = 4 ____ – ____ = 8

____ – ____ = 16 ____ – ____ = 19

____ – ____ = 5 ____ – ____ = 21

____ – ____ = 17 ____ – ____ = 15

____ – ____ = 29 ____ – ____ = 22

Can you do it two different ways?

____ – ____ = 9 ____ – ____ = 18

____ – ____ = 9 ____ – ____ = 13

Date ____________________ Name ________________________________

# Finding Pairs II

Use the numbers in the box to create correct subtraction problems.

| | |
|---|---|
| 100 | 76 |
| 92 | 69 |
| 87 | 63 |
| 81 | 58 |

_____ – _____ = 13 _____ – _____ = 12

_____ – _____ = 16 _____ – _____ = 24

_____ – _____ = 42 _____ – _____ = 23

_____ – _____ = 34 _____ – _____ = 29

Can you do it two different ways?

_____ – _____ = 18 _____ – _____ = 31

_____ – _____ = 18 _____ – _____ = 37

Use the numbers in the box to create correct subtraction problems.

| | |
|---|---|
| 120 | 93 |
| 112 | 86 |
| 105 | 77 |
| 101 | 64 |

_____ – _____ = 8 _____ – _____ = 24

_____ – _____ = 41 _____ – _____ = 13

_____ – _____ = 27 _____ – _____ = 16

_____ – _____ = 12 _____ – _____ = 19

_____ – _____ = 29 _____ – _____ = 22

Can you do it two different ways?

_____ – _____ = 15 _____ – _____ = 28

_____ – _____ = 15 _____ – _____ = 48

Date ____________ Name ____________

# Subtraction Arrays I

Fill in the missing numbers so each row and column makes a complete and correct subtraction sentence.

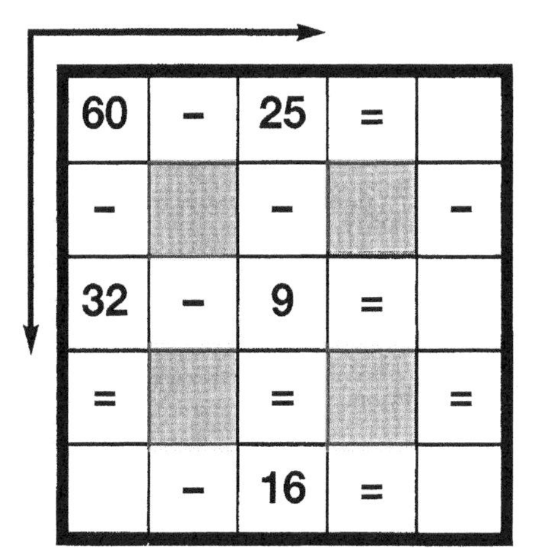

| 60 | - | 25 | = | |
|---|---|---|---|---|
| - | | - | | - |
| 32 | - | 9 | = | |
| = | | = | | = |
| | - | 16 | = | |

| 45 | - | 17 | = | |
|---|---|---|---|---|
| - | | - | | - |
| 29 | - | 13 | = | 16 |
| = | | = | | = |
| | - | | = | |

| 74 | - | 39 | = | |
|---|---|---|---|---|
| - | | - | | - |
| 42 | - | 16 | = | |
| = | | = | | = |
| | - | | = | |

| 91 | - | | = | 56 |
|---|---|---|---|---|
| - | | - | | - |
| 48 | - | 15 | = | |
| = | | = | | = |
| | - | 20 | = | |

| 100 | - | 43 | = | |
|---|---|---|---|---|
| - | | - | | - |
| 51 | - | 35 | = | |
| = | | = | | = |
| | - | | = | |

| 83 | - | 34 | = | |
|---|---|---|---|---|
| - | | - | | - |
| 17 | - | | = | |
| = | | = | | = |
| | - | 28 | = | |

**Trivia Bonus** Locate the heavy-framed squares in the last row. Use the digits in these two answers with the code below to find the most popular dog name in the United States.

| | | | |
|---|---|---|---|
| A = 1 | B = 2 | D = 3 | L = 4 |
| M = 5 | R = 6 | S = 7 | Y = 8 |

____ ____ ____ ____

Date ______________ Name ______________________

# Subtraction Arrays II

Fill in the missing numbers so each row and column makes a complete and correct subtraction sentence.

| | | | | |
|---|---|---|---|---|
| 240 | – | 86 | = | |
| – | | – | | – |
| 77 | – | 19 | = | |
| = | | = | | = |
| | – | | = | |

| | | | | |
|---|---|---|---|---|
| 623 | – | | = | 274 |
| – | | – | | – |
| 486 | – | 269 | = | |
| = | | = | | = |
| | – | | = | |

| | | | | |
|---|---|---|---|---|
| 892 | – | 468 | = | |
| – | | – | | – |
| | – | 198 | = | |
| = | | = | | = |
| 647 | – | | = | |

| | | | | |
|---|---|---|---|---|
| 406 | – | | = | 227 |
| – | | – | | – |
| 235 | – | | = | |
| = | | = | | = |
| | – | | = | 88 |

| | | | | |
|---|---|---|---|---|
| 794 | – | | = | 430 |
| – | | – | | – |
| 283 | – | | = | |
| = | | = | | = |
| | – | 169 | = | |

| | | | | |
|---|---|---|---|---|
| 931 | – | | = | 443 |
| – | | – | | – |
| | – | 215 | = | |
| = | | = | | = |
| 538 | – | | = | |

**Trivia Bonus** Locate the heavy-framed squares in the last row. Use the digits in these two answers with the code below to find an animal whose arms are twice as long as its body.

A = 1 B = 2 G = 3 I = 4
N = 5 O = 6 T = 7 Y = 8 ____ ____ ____ ____ ____ ____

# Multiplication Facts

**Assumptions** The multiplication/division facts have previously been taught and reviewed, emphasizing understanding. Concrete objects and visual models, such as counters and grid paper, have been used extensively.

## Section Overview and Suggestions

This section focuses on practice of multiplication facts and provides attention to the related division facts. Some practice activities are designed to accomodate two levels of difficulty, facts through 6s and facts through 9s. When students have successfully completed the activities in this section, they are ready for the Mixed Facts section (pp. 129–142).

### Sponges

**Name My Numbers** p. 116

**Rhythm Multiplication** p. 117

These open-ended warm-ups reinforce the multiplication facts. Neither *Name My Numbers* nor *Rhythm Multiplication* requires preparation and both can be used repeatedly. The level of difficulty for both Sponges is controlled by the leader.

### Skill Checks

**Proper Products 1–6** pp. 118–120

These Skill Checks provide a way for parents, students, and you to see students' improvement with the multiplication facts. Each page of *Proper Products* may be copied and cut in half so that each check may be used at a different time. Remember to have all students respond to STOP before solving the ten problems.

### Games

**Factors Pathway** pp. 121–123

**Four-in-a-Row** pp. 124–125

These open-ended and repeatable games actively involve students in practicing many multiplication and division facts. Both *Factors Pathway* and *Four-in-a-Row* offer engaging alternatives to practicing multiplication flashcards. *Factors Pathway A* includes facts through 5s while *Factors Pathway B* reinforces facts through 9s. *Four-in-a-Row* promotes practice of facts through 6s.

### Independent Activities

**Cross-Number Puzzle** pp. 126–127

**Facts Find** p. 128

These activity sheets promote independent practice of the multiplication and division facts. *Cross-Number Puzzle I* reinforces facts through 6s while *Cross-Number Puzzles II* includes facts through 9s.

# Name My Numbers

**Topic:** Multiplication and Addition Facts

**Object:** Identify factors when given the product and sum

**Groups:** Whole class or small group

*Tips* *As students gain confidence, have them volunteer the sum and product information, while their classmates respond.*
*To emphasize multiplication facts, give the product before the sum.*

### Materials

- chalkboard or overhead projector

### Directions

**1.** To facilitate this activity, provide a visual clue.

$\triangle + \bigcirc = \square$

$\triangle \times \bigcirc = \square$

**2.** Leader announces, "The sum of my numbers equals ... (11). The product of my numbers equals ... (30). What are my numbers?"

**3.** Leader records the given sum and product.

$\triangle + \bigcirc = 11$

$\triangle \times \bigcirc = 30$

*Other starters:*

| | | |
|---|---|---|
| sum = 6<br>product = 8 | sum = 6<br>product = 9 | sum = 9<br>product = 14 |
| sum = 11<br>product = 24 | sum = 12<br>product = 27 | sum = 12<br>product = 32 |

### Making Connections

Promote reflection and make mathematical connections by asking:

- What approach did you use to identify the numbers?

$\triangle = ?$ $\square = ?$

# Rhythm Multiplication

**Topic:** Multiplication Facts

**Object:** Name product while maintaining the rhythm

**Groups:** Whole class or small group

*Tip* *Set a slow pace to allow for greater success.*

## Directions

1. Leader identifies a pathway around the classroom that includes all students.
2. The entire class practices a "two slaps, two claps, two snaps" continuing rhythm.
3. When everyone seems to have the rhythmic pattern, leader begins by stating a multiplication fact during the "snapping stage." (It's best to state the facts as "three fives" rather than "3 times 5.") Without interrupting the rhythmic activity, the first student responds with the product timed with the snaps. (All responses and naming of facts occur during the "snapping stage.")
4. Leader continues this warm-up with each student answering a stated fact. The goal is to go all around the classroom or group without breaking the rhythmic pattern and by responding in the expected timely manner.

## Making Connections

Promote reflection and make mathematical connections by asking:

- What suggestions could be made to ensure success for the entire class?

Date ____________ Name ____________________

# Proper Products 1

STOP Don't start yet! Star two problems that may have odd answers.

**1.** $6 \times 3 =$ ____ **2.** $6 \times 5 =$ ____ **3.** $\begin{array}{r} 3 \\ \times 4 \\ \hline \end{array}$ **4.** $\begin{array}{r} 7 \\ \times 6 \\ \hline \end{array}$

**5.** $3 \times 7 =$ ____ **6.** $8 \times 6 =$ ____

**7.** ____ $\times 4 = 32$ **8.** $36 \div 4 =$ ____ **9.** $24 \div 6 =$ ____

**10.** $(7 \times 5) + (5 \times 4) =$ ____

**Go On**

△ + ○ = 15 △ = ____

△ × ○ = 56 ○ = ____

Date ____________ Name ____________________

# Proper Products 2

STOP Don't start yet! Star two problems that may have even answers.

**1.** $2 \times 8 =$ ____ **2.** $5 \times 4 =$ ____ **3.** $\begin{array}{r} 4 \\ \times 9 \\ \hline \end{array}$ **4.** $\begin{array}{r} 7 \\ \times 7 \\ \hline \end{array}$

**5.** $6 \times 6 =$ ____ **6.** $6 \times 9 =$ ____

**7.** ____ $\times 3 = 24$ **8.** $35 \div 5 =$ ____ **9.** $28 \div 7 =$ ____

**10.** $(8 \times 4) + (5 \times 6) =$ ____

△ + ○ = 15 △ = ____

△ × ○ = 54 ○ = ____

Date ______________ Name ______________________

# Proper Products 3

**STOP** Don't start yet! Star two problems that may have answers between 20 and 30.

**1.** $4 \times 4 =$ ____

**2.** $5 \times 3 =$ ____

**3.** $\begin{array}{r} 7 \\ \times 3 \\ \hline \end{array}$

**4.** $\begin{array}{r} 6 \\ \times 8 \\ \hline \end{array}$

**5.** $3 \times 9 =$ ____

**6.** $6 \times 7 =$ ____

**7.** ____ $\times 3 = 12$

**8.** $24 \div 8 =$ ____

**9.** $36 \div 6 =$ ____

**10.** $(5 \times 3) + (6 \times 4) =$ ____

**Go On**

$\triangle + \square = 14$ $\triangle =$ ____

$\triangle \times \square = 49$ $\square =$ ____

Date ______________ Name ______________________

# Proper Products 4

**STOP** Don't start yet! Star two problems that may have odd answers less than 15.

**1.** $6 \times 4 =$ ____

**2.** $5 \times 7 =$ ____

**3.** $\begin{array}{r} 4 \\ \times 8 \\ \hline \end{array}$

**4.** $\begin{array}{r} 8 \\ \times 7 \\ \hline \end{array}$

**5.** $3 \times 8 =$ ____

**6.** $4 \times 7 =$ ____

**7.** ____ $\times 3 = 27$

**8.** $28 \div 4 =$ ____

**9.** $36 \div 9 =$ ____

**10.** $(3 \times 4) + (8 \times 5) =$ ____

$\triangle + \square = 13$ $\triangle =$ ____

$\triangle \times \square = 42$ $\square =$ ____

Date ____________ Name ____________

# Proper Products 5

STOP Don't start yet! Star two problems that may have answers less than 30.

**1.** $9 \times 3 =$ ____

**2.** $5 \times 8 =$ ____

**3.** $4 \times 6$ = ____

**4.** $9 \times 7$ = ____

**5.** $4 \times 7 =$ ____

**6.** $8 \times 4 =$ ____

**7.** ____ $\times 7 = 42$

**8.** $21 \div 7 =$ ____

**9.** $32 \div 8 =$ ____

**10.** $(6 \times 3) + (2 \times 8) =$ ____

$\triangle + \square = 16$ $\triangle =$ ____

$\triangle \times \square = 63$ $\square =$ ____

Date ____________ Name ____________

# Proper Products 6

STOP Don't start yet! Star two problems that may have answers more than 40.

**1.** $5 \times 7 =$ ____

**2.** $5 \times 5 =$ ____

**3.** $8 \times 3$ = ____

**4.** $9 \times 5$ = ____

**5.** $4 \times 9 =$ ____

**6.** $8 \times 7 =$ ____

**7.** ____ $\times 4 = 16$

**8.** $35 \div 5 =$ ____

**9.** $27 \div 9 =$ ____

**10.** $(6 \times 6) + (3 \times 7) =$ ____

$\triangle + \square = 17$ $\triangle =$ ____

$\triangle \times \square = 72$ $\square =$ ____

# Factors Pathway

**Topic:** Multiplication Facts (3s, 4s, and 5s)

**Object:** Create a pathway of missing factors

**Groups:** 2 pair players or 2 players

### Materials for each group

- markers (different kind for each player)
- special Number Cube (3– 5), p. 149
- *Factors Pathway* gameboard, pp. 122–123

### Directions

1. After tossing the 3–5 Number Cube, the first pair seeks cells where the tossed digit correctly completes a multiplication fact. The pair selects and covers one of the identified cells with one of the markers.
2. The other pair follows the same procedure. (Only one colored marker can occupy a single cell.)
3. Pairs continue alternating turns until one pair forms a continuous pathway across the gameboard.

*Tips* *Use* Factors Pathway B, *p. 123, for students ready to practice the difficult multiplication facts. Note: A different special Number Cube is required, p. 149 (6, 6, 7, 7, 8, 8).*

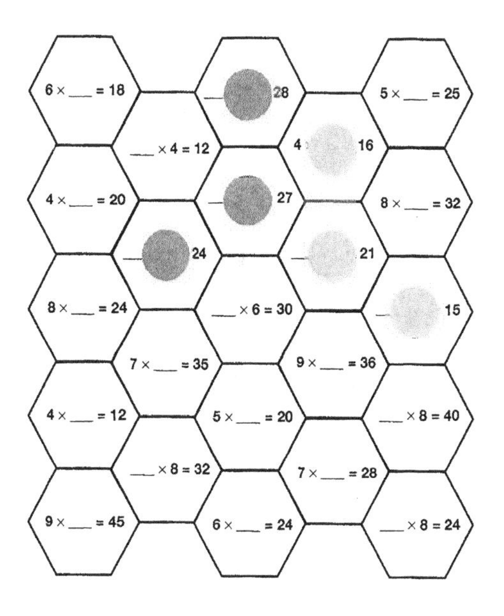


### Making Connections

Promote reflection and make mathematical connections by asking:

- What strategy helped you place your markers in a complete pathway?

# Factors Pathway A

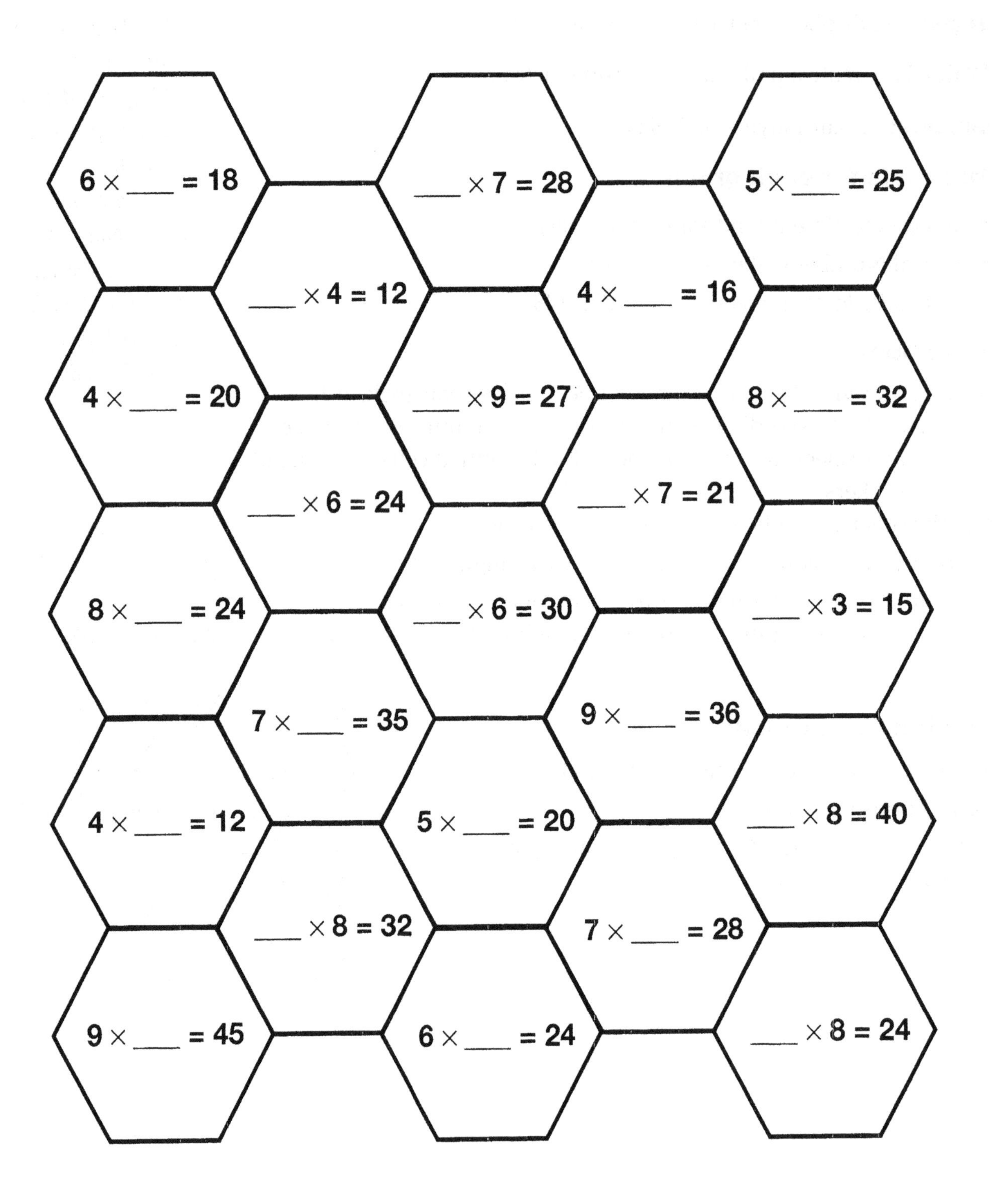

# Factors Pathway B

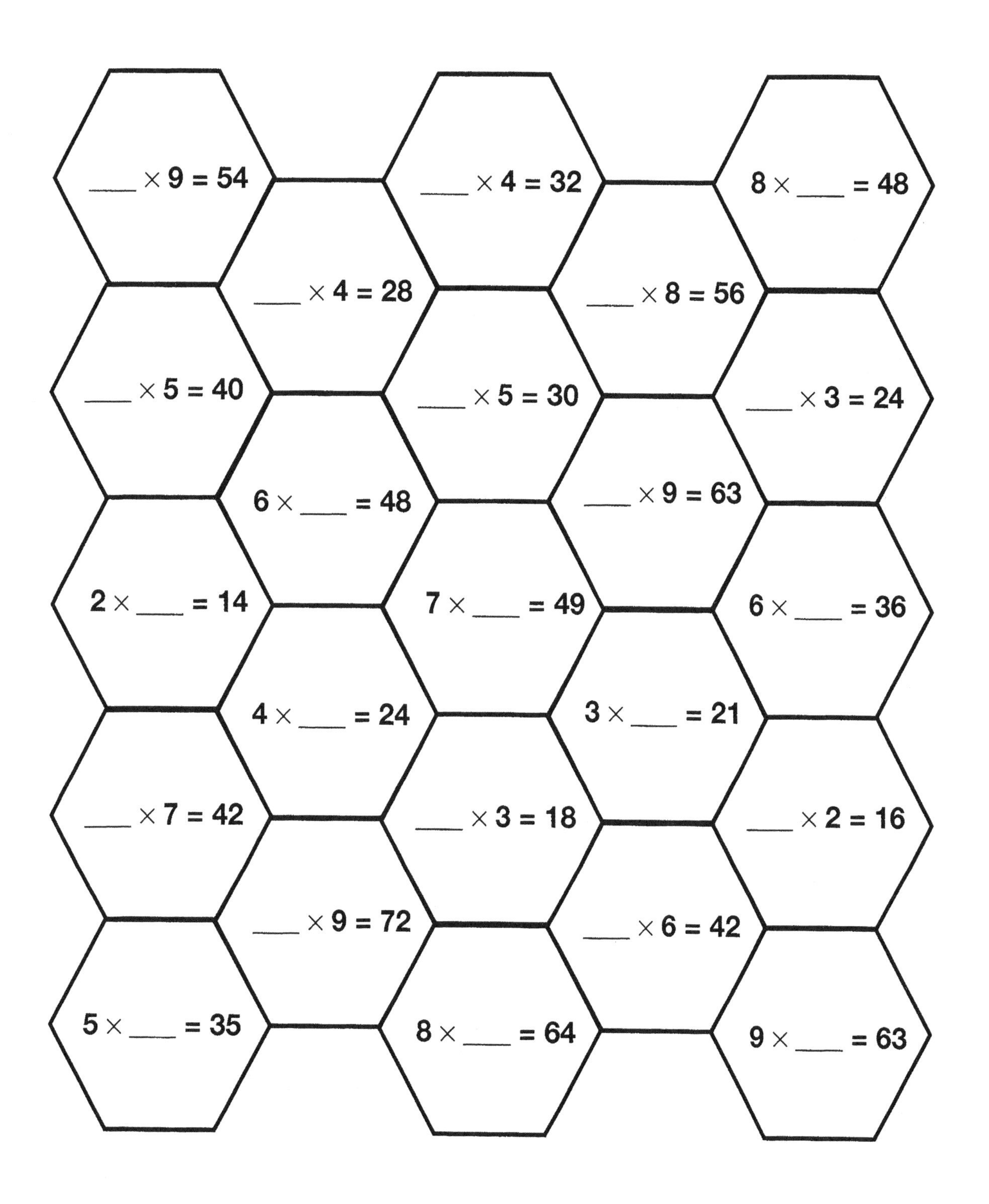

# Four-in-a-Row

**Topic:** Multiplication Facts

**Object:** Cover four-in-a-row with "your" markers

**Groups:** 2 pair players

*Tip* *If players feel insecure with the facts, you may allow three in a row to win.*

### Materials for each group

- *Four-in-a-Row* gameboard, p. 125
- 2 paper clips
- markers (different kind for each pair)

### Directions

1. The first pair places two paper clips at the bottom of the gameboard, indicating two factors. The same pair multiplies the selected factors and places a marker on the resulting product.
2. The other pair moves one of the paper clips to a new factor. Next, this pair multiplies the two factors and places a marker on that product. (It is permissible to have two paper clips on the same factor.)
3. Pairs continue alternating turns, moving one paper clip each time, multiplying the factors, and placing markers on the product on the gameboard.
4. The winner is the first pair to have four markers in a row horizontally, vertically, or diagonally.

| 1 | 2 | 3 | 4 | 5 |
|---|---|---|---|---|
| 6 | 7 | 8 | 9 | 10 |
| 12 | 14 | 15 | 16 | 18 |
| 20 | (21) | 24 | 25 | 27 |
| 28 | 30 | 32 | 35 | 36 |

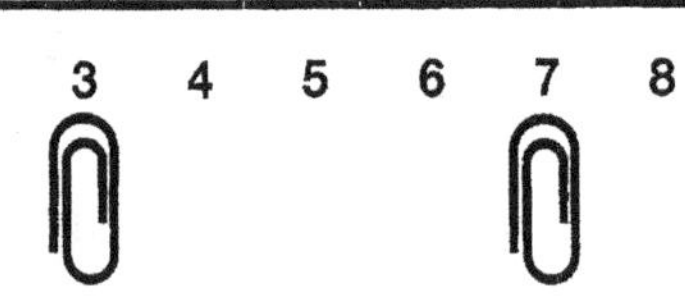


### Making Connections

Promote reflection and make mathematical connections by asking:

- What strategies helped you line up your markers in a row?
- What do you notice about the numbers used on the gameboard? Why do you think this is so?

# Four-in-a-Row

| | | | | |
|---|---|---|---|---|
| 1 | 2 | 3 | 4 | 5 |
| 6 | 7 | 8 | 9 | 10 |
| 12 | 14 | 15 | 16 | 18 |
| 20 | 21 | 24 | 25 | 27 |
| 28 | 30 | 32 | 35 | 36 |

1 2 3 4 5 6 7 8 9

Date ____________ Name ____________________

# Cross-Number Puzzle I

| | | | | | | | | |
|---|---|---|---|---|---|---|---|---|
| 1. | 2. | | 3. | | | | 4. | |
| 5. | | | 6. | | | | 7. | 8. |
| | | 9. | | | 10. | 11. | | |
| 12. | 13. | | 14. | 15. | | | | |
| | | 16. | | 17. | | | 18. | 19. |
| | 20. | | | | | 21. | | |

**Across →**

**1.** $6 \times 2$

**3.** $6 \times 5$

**4.** $9 \times \square = 27$

**5.** $5 \times 8$

**6.** $3 \times \square = 18$

**7.** $6 \times 4$

**9.** $5 \times \square = 25$

**10.** $4 \times 3$

**12.** $5 \times 3$

**14.** $4 \times 8$

**17.** $6 \times 3$

**18.** $7 \times 3$

**20.** $9 \times 4$

**21.** $3 \times \square = 24$

**Down ↓**

**1.** $2 \times 7$

**2.** $5 \times 4$

**3.** $6 \times 6$

**4.** $8 \times 4$

**8.** $9 \times 5$

**11.** $7 \times 4$

**12.** $9 \times 2$

**13.** $7 \times \square = 35$

**15.** $3 \times 7$

**16.** $4 \times 4$

**19.** $5 \times 2$

**21.** $2 \times \square = 16$

Date ____________ Name ____________________

# Cross-Number Puzzle II

| | | | | | | | | |
|---|---|---|---|---|---|---|---|---|
| 1. | 2. | ■ | 3. | | ■ | ■ | 4. | ■ |
| 5. | | ■ | 6. | ■ | ■ | ■ | 7. | 8. |
| ■ | ■ | 9. | ■ | ■ | 10. | 11. | ■ | |
| 12. | 13. | ■ | 14. | 15. | ■ | | ■ | ■ |
| | ■ | 16. | ■ | 17. | | ■ | 18. | 19. |
| ■ | 20. | | ■ | ■ | ■ | 21. | ■ | |

**Across** →

**1.** $3 \times 8$

**3.** $4 \times 4$

**4.** $9 \times \square = 27$

**5.** $6 \times 3$

**6.** $32 \div 8$

**7.** $8 \times 7$

**9.** $25 \div 5$

**10.** $4 \times 7$

**12.** $9 \times 5$

**14.** $7 \times 9$

**17.** $9 \times 3$

**18.** $6 \times 6$

**20.** $6 \times 9$

**21.** $24 \div 3$

**Down** ↓

**1.** $3 \times 7$

**2.** $6 \times 8$

**3.** $2 \times 7$

**4.** $7 \times 5$

**8.** $8 \times 8$

**11.** $9 \times 9$

**12.** $6 \times 7$

**13.** $40 \div 8$

**15.** $4 \times 8$

**16.** $6 \times 4$

**19.** $6 \times 10$

**21.** $16 \div 2$

Date ____________ Name ________________________

# Facts Find

Find three neighboring numbers that make a multiplication or division equation.
Look across and down. One has been circled and done for you.
Can you find the other 14 equations?
Be sure to write the operation sign and the equal sign.

| | | | | | | |
|---|---|---|---|---|---|---|
| 26 | 8 ÷ | 4 = | 2 | 42 | 3 | 5 |
| 7 | 2 | 14 | 9 | 18 | 2 | 9 |
| 3 | 35 | 7 | 4 | 28 | 5 | 18 |
| 21 | 6 | 6 | 36 | 24 | 4 | 6 |
| 15 | 8 | 4 | 32 | 8 | 9 | 3 |
| 5 | 16 | 4 | 4 | 3 | 5 | 9 |
| 3 | 12 | 30 | 6 | 5 | 45 | 27 |

Independent Activity

# Mixed Facts

**Assumptions** The addition, subtraction, and multiplication/division facts have previously been taught and reviewed, emphasizing understanding. Concrete objects and visual models, such as counters and grids, have been used extensively.

### Section Overview and Suggestions

Long-term use of this section will ensure future success with mental computation.

## Sponges

**Signal Math** pp. 130–131

**Can You Make ...?** pp. 132–133

These open-ended, repeatable, whole-class or small-group warm-ups reinforce many addition, subtraction, and multiplication/division facts and require minimum preparation.

## Skill Checks

**Quick Checks 1–6** pp. 134–136

The Skill Checks provide a way for parents, students, and you to see students' improvement with the basic facts. Each page of *Quick Checks* may be copied and cut in half so that each check may be used at a different time. Remember to have all students respond to STOP before solving the ten problems.

## Games

**Cover Up** pp. 137–138

This open-ended and repeatable Game actively involves students in practicing many basic facts and promotes mental computation. Use of the two Sponges will prepare students for more success with *Cover Up,* a Game that uses all operations.

## Independent Activities

**Can You Make It?** pp. 139–140

**Possible Equations** pp. 141–142

These activities require students to independently practice basic facts to solve inviting equations. Students practice many additional facts as they seek equations that work on these Independent Activities. With repeated use of the above Sponges and Games, students should be able to confidently use varied basic facts to complete these activities. *Possible Equations,* intended for repeatable use, provides long-term practice and requires all four operations.

# Signal Math

**Topic:** All Facts

**Object:** Identify required operation(s)

**Groups:** Whole class or small group

*Tip* *Some students might find it helpful to manipulate the corresponding Digit Squares when they begin the three-digit version.*

### Materials

- transparency of *Signal Math,* p. 131
- 3 colored transparent markers

### Directions

**1.** Leader displays *Signal Math* transparency and covers two numbers. Leader states one number that results when operating on these two numbers.

*Example:* Leader covers 2 and 8. A student might say, "I can make 16."

**2.** Other students determine the operation used and respond with the appropriate hand or arm signal. In this instance, multiplication is used so students signal multiplication by crossing their wrists.

**3.** Leader asks if any student can make another answer using the same numbers.

*Example:* A student might say, "I can make 10." Remaining students signal addition.

**4.** After exhausting all possibilities for the two covered numbers, leader covers two new numbers and begins the process again.

**5.** When students seem ready, leader covers three numbers for students to use in any order. This allows for multiple solutions and many more possible answers.

*Example:* Leader covers 2, 3, and 6. A student might say, "I can make 9." Multiple solutions include $3 \times 6 \div 2$ or $2 \times 6 - 3$.

Since solutions will usually involve two different operations, students indicate operations with alternating signals.

### Making Connections

Promote reflection and make mathematical connections by asking:

- What helped you eliminate possible operations?

# Signal Math

| 0 | 1 | 2 | 3 | 4 |
|---|---|---|---|---|
| 5 | 6 | 7 | 8 | 9 |

+ ×

− ÷

# Can You Make . . . ?

**Topic:** All Operations

**Object:** Identify a qualifying equation composed of neighboring digits

**Groups:** Whole class or small group

### Materials

- transparency of *Can You Make . . . ?*, p. 133
- two 5 × 8 cards (to mask unwanted digits)

### Directions

**1.** Leader displays only one row or column of digits and announces a target number.

*Example:* Leader says, "Can you make 10?" With 5, 3, 2, 4, 6, and 1, a student might respond with 6 + 4, 5 + 3 + 2, or 3 × 2 + 4.

**2.** Students score one point for each different operation used. Students individually tally points for their equations.

*Example:* One point is scored for 6 + 4 or 5 + 3 + 2, while two points are earned for 3 × 2 + 4.

Other target numbers for row #1: 11, 9, 8, 5, and 2



**3.** When displaying students' equations, the leader could add clarity by inserting parentheses to indicate the order of operations, even when parentheses are not necessary.

*Example:* 3 + (2 × 4) = 11 and (3 + 2) × 4 = 20

*Reminder:* Order of operations requires completing operations in parentheses first and then multiplying and dividing before adding and subtracting.

**4.** When students become skilled with the single rows/columns format, leader may display two rows or a three-by-three array. The leader follows the same procedure by announcing target numbers and having the students identify qualifying number sentences. If a three-by-three array is displayed, students can also check out diagonals.

### Making Connections

Promote reflection and make mathematical connections by asking:

- Which target numbers are often made more than one way?

# Can You Make . . . ?

| | | | | | |
|---|---|---|---|---|---|
| 5 | 3 | 2 | 4 | 6 | 1 |
| 8 | 6 | 5 | 3 | 2 | 4 |
| 4 | 2 | 7 | 5 | 9 | 2 |
| 6 | 3 | 4 | 2 | 5 | 3 |
| 2 | 9 | 6 | 4 | 3 | 5 |
| 3 | 5 | 4 | 6 | 7 | 2 |

Date ________________ Name ____________________

# Quick Check 1

**STOP** Don't start yet! Star a problem that will have an answer between 15 and 20.

**1.** Circle the larger amount: $30 \div 6$ or $13 - 9$

**2.** $(4 \times 5) - 2 =$ ____ **3.** $20 - (7 \times 2) =$ ____ **4.** $(8 \times 6) + 4 =$ ____

**5.** $(8 \times 3) +$ ____ $= 29$ **6.** $(4 \times 4) - (21 \div 3) =$____ **7.** $(5 \times 2) + ($ __ $\times$ __ $) = 31$

**8.** Use 2, 3, and 4: $\square \times \square \div \square = 6$

**9–10.** Use +, –, or ×: $3 \ \square \ 5 \ \square \ 4 = 11$

$6 \ \square \ 3 \ \square \ 2 = 20$

What numbers come next? 30, 25, 27, 22, 24, ____ , ____ , ____

---

Date ________________ Name ____________________

# Quick Check 2

**STOP** Don't start yet! Star a problem that will have an answer between 20 and 30.

**1.** Circle the larger amount: $35 \div 7$ or $12 - 3$

**2.** $(9 \times 4) - 3 =$ ____ **3.** $30 - (4 \times 6) =$ ____ **4.** $(9 \times 9) - 2 =$ ____

**5.** $(6 \times 3) +$ ____ $= 22$ **6.** $(2 \times 9) - (27 \div 3) =$____ **7.** $(5 \times 4) + ($ __ $\times$ __ $) = 34$

**8.** Use 2, 4, and 5: $\square \times \square \div \square = 10$

**9–10.** Use +, –, or ×: $4 \ \square \ 2 \ \square \ 3 = 11$

$3 \ \square \ 7 \ \square \ 4 = 6$

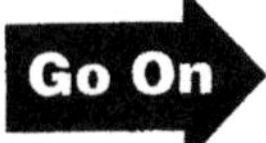

Complete these equations:

$\square \times \square + \square = 18$

$\square \times \square - \square = 18$

$\square \div \square + \square = 18$

Date ____________ Name ____________

# Quick Check 3

**STOP** Don't start yet. Star a problem that will have an answer less than 10.

**1.** Circle the larger amount: $24 \div 3$ or $14 - 8$

**2.** $(3 \times 9) - 2 =$ ____ **3.** $20 - (4 \times 4) =$ ____ **4.** $(7 \times 7) + 4 =$ ____

**5.** $(4 \times 6) +$ ____ $= 27$ **6.** $(7 \times 3) - (18 \div 3) =$ ____ **7.** $(4 \times 5) + ($ __ $\times$ __ $) = 35$

**8.** Use 2, 3, and 6: ☐ × ☐ ÷ ☐ = 9

**9–10.** Use +, –, or ×: 6 ☐ 2 ☐ 3 = 15

4 ☐ (3 ☐ 5) = 19

**Go On** Which one doesn't belong? Describe your rule.

| 24 | | 36 |
|---|---|---|
| | 32 | |
| 22 | | 28 |

Date ____________ Name ____________

# Quick Check 4

**STOP** Don't start yet. Star a problem that is easy to solve mentally.

**1.** Circle the larger amount: $28 \div 4$ or $15 - 6$

**2.** $(4 \times 9) - 3 =$ ____ **3.** $30 - (5 \times 5) =$ ____ **4.** $(8 \times 7) + 4 =$ ____

**5.** $(8 \times 4) +$ ____ $= 35$ **6.** $(2 \times 7) - (20 \div 4) =$ ____ **7.** $(3 \times 8) + ($ __ $\times$ __ $) = 34$

**8.** Use 2, 4, and 8: ☐ × ☐ ÷ ☐ = 4

**9–10.** Use +, –, or ×: 4 ☐ 5 ☐ 3 = 17

3 ☐ (2 ☐ 8) = 19

**Go On** Complete these equations: ☐ ÷ ☐ + ☐ = 20 ☐ × ☐ + ☐ = 20

☐ × ☐ – ☐ = 20

Date ____________ Name ____________

# Quick Check 5

STOP Don't start yet! Star a problem that will have an even answer.

**1.** Circle the larger amount: $54 \div 9$ or $14 - 6$

**2.** $(4 \times 8) - 3 =$ ____ **3.** $20 - (2 \times 8) =$ ____ **4.** $(6 \times 7) - 4 =$ ____

**5.** $(4 \times 6) +$ ____ $= 30$ **6.** $(3 \times 4) - (15 \div 3) =$ ____ **7.** $(6 \times 5) + (\_ \times \_) = 44$

**8.** Use 3, 4, and 6: $\square \times \square \div \square = 8$

**9–10.** Use +, –, or ×: $3 \ \square \ 6 \ \square \ 4 = 14$

$7 \ \square \ 5 \ \square \ 3 = 15$

Go On Which other number fits in this group? Please explain your answer.

| 27 | 18 |
|---|---|
| 24 | 15 |

Date ____________ Name ____________

# Quick Check 6

Don't start yet! Star two problems that will have an odd answer.

**1.** Circle the larger amount: $36 \div 6$ or $11 - 4$

**2.** $(3 \times 8) - 5 =$ ____ **3.** $30 - (7 \times 3) =$ ____ **4.** $(8 \times 8) - 5 =$ ____

**5.** $(5 \times 5) +$ ____ $= 28$ **6.** $(3 \times 5) - (21 \div 3) =$ ____ **7.** $(5 \times 2) + (\_ \times \_) = 40$

**8.** Use 2, 5, and 6: $\square \times \square - \square = 7$

**9–10.** Use +, –, or ×: $7 \ \square \ 2 \ \square \ 3 = 17$

$5 \ \square \ (4 \ \square \ 3) = 17$

What numbers are missing? 2, 4, 3, 6, 5, ____, 9, 18, ____, 34

# Cover Up

**Topic:** All Facts

**Object:** Cover as many numbers as possible

**Groups:** Pair players or 2 players

### Materials for each group

- *Cover Up* gameboard, p. 138
- markers (13 each)
- 2 Number Cubes (1–6)

*Tip* *An interesting variation is to have scores equal the numerical total of each pair's uncovered numbers. Thus, pairs would try to have the lowest total.*

### Directions

1. The first pair rolls the number cubes. The pair may add, subtract, multiply, or divide the rolled numbers to decide which number to cover on the gameboard. (There are two separate playing areas on each gameboard, one playing area for each pair.)

   *Example:* If 2 and 6 are rolled, the pair might cover 8 (sum), 4 (difference), 3 (quotient), or 12 (product).

2. Pairs alternate turns, rolling number cubes, making equations, and covering the selected result.
3. When a pair can no longer produce an uncovered number, the pair is out of the game. The game is over when neither pair can produce an uncovered number.
4. The winner is the pair who covers the most numbers.
5. Encourage students to play additional rounds.

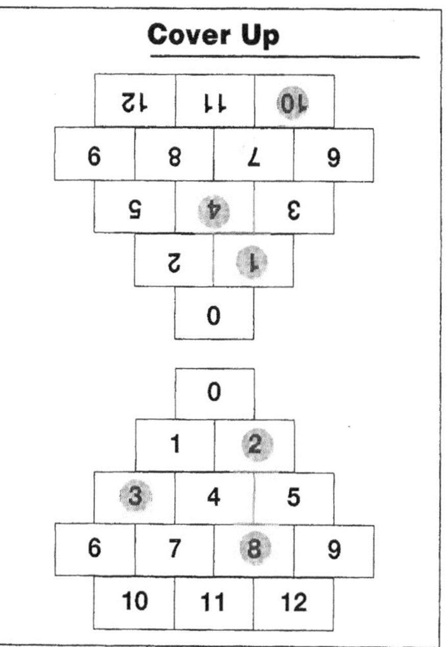


### Making Connections

Promote reflection and make mathematical connections by asking:

- Which operation did you use the most? Please explain.
- What strategies helped you cover more numbers?

# Cover Up

Date ______________ Name ______________________

# Can You Make It? I

Use neighboring numbers to add, subtract, multiply, or divide.
Parentheses help show what to do first when more than one operation is required.

| 2 | 4 |
|---|---|
| 5 | 3 |

Make 9. __________

Make 15. __________

Use three numbers to make 10.

______________________

Make 7 two ways.

__________ __________

Make 6 two ways.

__________ __________

| 6 | 9 |
|---|---|
| 3 | 2 |

Make 15. __________

Make 18. __________

Use three numbers to make 21.

______________________

Make 3 two ways.

__________ __________

Make 12 two ways.

__________ __________

| 3 | 5 | 4 |
|---|---|---|
| 6 | 2 | 8 |

Make 13. __________

Make 32. __________

Use three numbers to make 20.

______________________

Make 4 two ways.

__________ __________

Make 10 two ways.

__________ __________

| 7 | 2 | 4 |
|---|---|---|
| 5 | 6 | 3 |

Make 18. __________

Make 30. __________

Use three numbers to make 8.

______________________

Make 14 two ways.

__________ __________

Make 24 two ways.

__________ __________

Date ______________ Name ______________

# Can You Make It? II

Use three or more neighboring numbers and add, subtract, multiply, or divide. Parentheses help show what to do first.

| 2 | 4 | 6 |
|---|---|---|
| 5 | 3 | 2 |
| 1 | 4 | 6 |

Make 8 two ways. ________ ________

Make 10 two ways. ________ ________

Make 20. ________

Make 12. ________

| 5 | 3 | 4 |
|---|---|---|
| 7 | 2 | 8 |
| 9 | 6 | 5 |

Make 4 two ways. ________ ________

Make 20 two ways. ________ ________

Make 12. ________

Make 6. ________

| 6 | 5 | 9 |
|---|---|---|
| 4 | 2 | 5 |
| 8 | 4 | 3 |

Make 7 two ways. ________ ________

Make 16 two ways. ________ ________

Make 20. ________

Make 10. ________

| 6 | 7 | 4 |
|---|---|---|
| 9 | 2 | 5 |
| 7 | 5 | 8 |

Make 13 two ways. ________ ________

Make 15 two ways. ________ ________

Make 10. ________

Make 20. ________

# Possible Equations

**Topic:** All Facts (+, −, ×, ÷)

*Tip* *To be sure of success, use Digit Squares or place Today's Numbers individually on small movable squares of paper that can be easily rearranged.*

### Materials

- *Possible Equations* recording sheet, p. 142 (one for each student)

### Directions

**1.** The leader announces four single-digit numbers that are recorded as "Today's Numbers."

*Suggestion:* Include the digits 1 and/or 2 to provide more possibilities. A good starting group of numbers would be 1, 2, 3, and 6.

**2.** Students use three of Today's Numbers and two operations to complete the equations.

*Warning:* Be sure to insert parentheses as needed to indicate order of operations. Some solutions might not be possible.

### Making Connections

Promote reflection and make mathematical connections by asking:

- Which solutions are not possible? How can you prove it?
- Which equations have more than one solution?

### Challenge

Try to use all four digits to make some of the numbers 1 to 12.

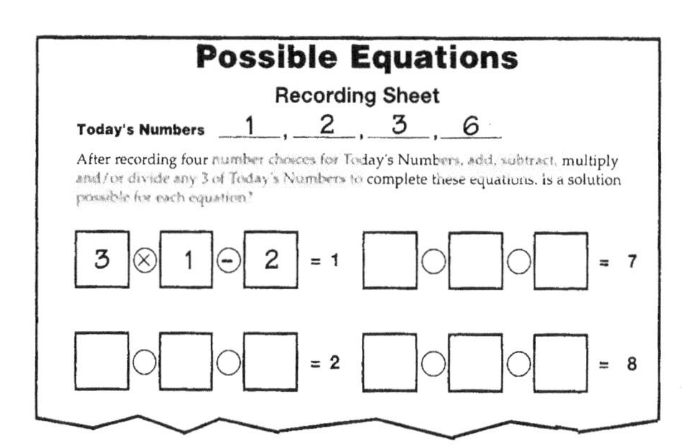

**Possible Equations**

Recording Sheet

**Today's Numbers** 1, 2, 3, 6

After recording four number choices for Today's Numbers, add, subtract, multiply and/or divide any 3 of Today's Numbers to complete these equations. Is a solution possible for each equation?

3 ⊗ 1 ⊖ 2 = 1    □ ○ □ ○ □ = 7

□ ○ □ ○ □ = 2    □ ○ □ ○ □ = 8

Date ____________________ Name ______________________________

# Possible Equations

## Recording Sheet

**Today's Numbers** ______, ______, ______, ______

After recording four number choices for Today's Numbers, add, subtract, multiply, and/or divide any three of Today's Numbers to complete these equations. Is a solution possible for each equation?

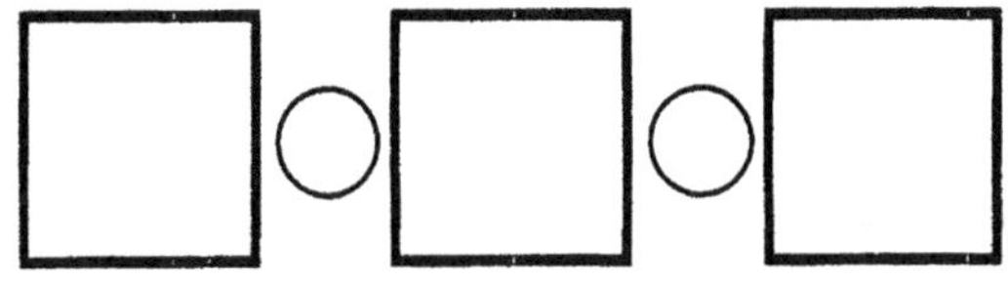

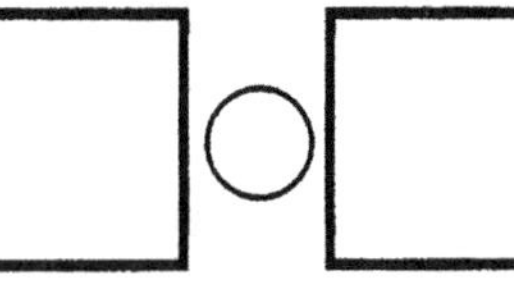
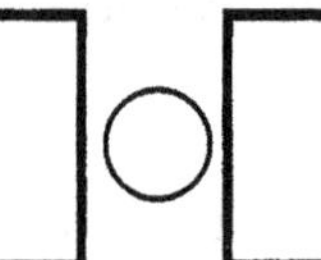

= 1 = 7

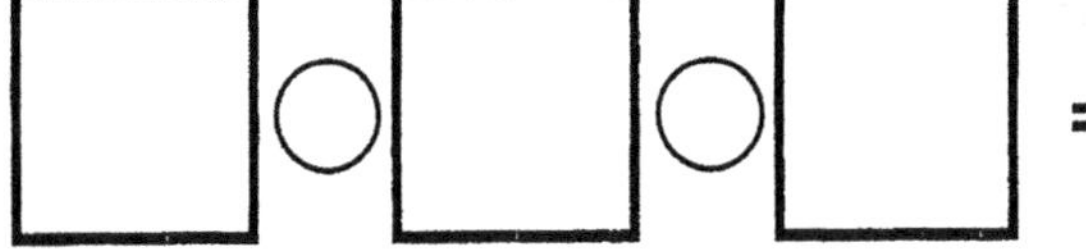

= 2 = 8

= 3 = 9

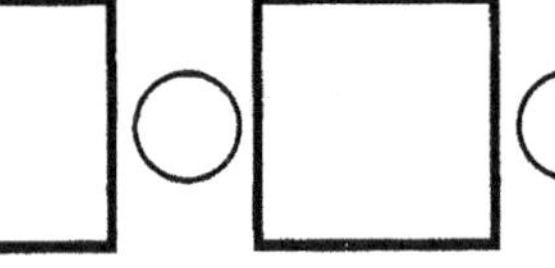

= 4 = 10

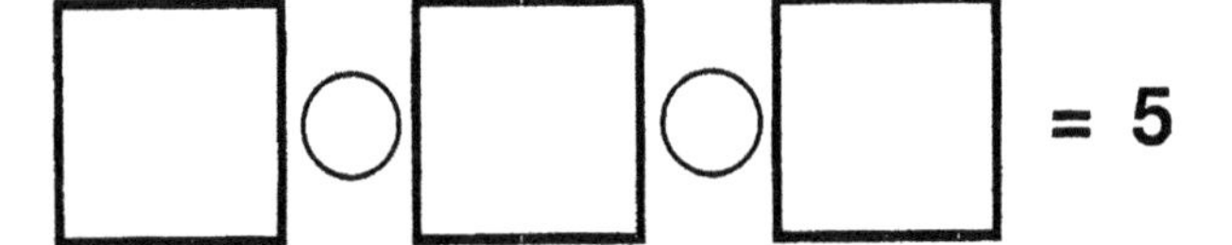
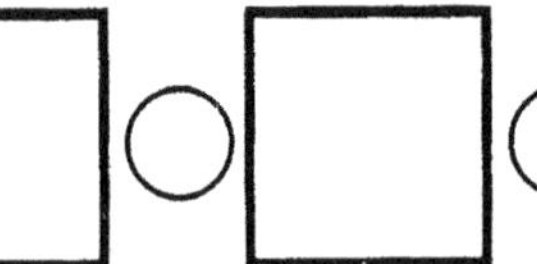

= 5 = 11

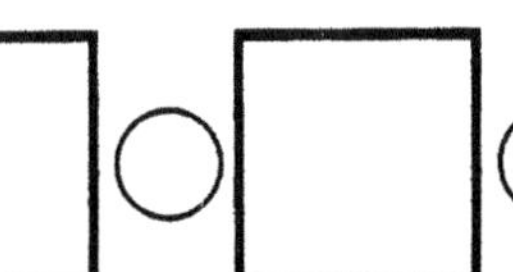
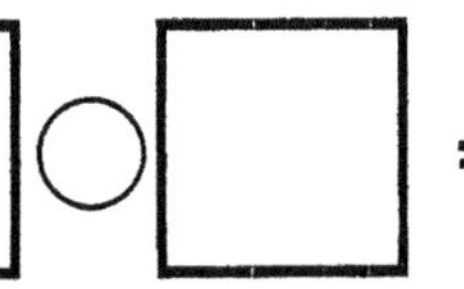

= 6 = 12

# Blackline Masters

200 Chart

Coins

Digit Cards

Digit Squares

Number Cubes (1–6), (4–9)

Number Cubes (3–5), blank

Spinners (1–6), blank

Subtraction Squares

Addition Chart

Multiplication Chart

# 200 Chart

| 1 | 2 | 3 | 4 | 5 | 6 | 7 | 8 | 9 | 10 |
|---|---|---|---|---|---|---|---|---|---|
| 11 | 12 | 13 | 14 | 15 | 16 | 17 | 18 | 19 | 20 |
| 21 | 22 | 23 | 24 | 25 | 26 | 27 | 28 | 29 | 30 |
| 31 | 32 | 33 | 34 | 35 | 36 | 37 | 38 | 39 | 40 |
| 41 | 42 | 43 | 44 | 45 | 46 | 47 | 48 | 49 | 50 |
| 51 | 52 | 53 | 54 | 55 | 56 | 57 | 58 | 59 | 60 |
| 61 | 62 | 63 | 64 | 65 | 66 | 67 | 68 | 69 | 70 |
| 71 | 72 | 73 | 74 | 75 | 76 | 77 | 78 | 79 | 80 |
| 81 | 82 | 83 | 84 | 85 | 86 | 87 | 88 | 89 | 90 |
| 91 | 92 | 93 | 94 | 95 | 96 | 97 | 98 | 99 | 100 |
| 101 | 102 | 103 | 104 | 105 | 106 | 107 | 108 | 109 | 110 |
| 111 | 112 | 113 | 114 | 115 | 116 | 117 | 118 | 119 | 120 |
| 121 | 122 | 123 | 124 | 125 | 126 | 127 | 128 | 129 | 130 |
| 131 | 132 | 133 | 134 | 135 | 136 | 137 | 138 | 139 | 140 |
| 141 | 142 | 143 | 144 | 145 | 146 | 147 | 148 | 149 | 150 |
| 151 | 152 | 153 | 154 | 155 | 156 | 157 | 158 | 159 | 160 |
| 161 | 162 | 163 | 164 | 165 | 166 | 167 | 168 | 169 | 170 |
| 171 | 172 | 173 | 174 | 175 | 176 | 177 | 178 | 179 | 180 |
| 181 | 182 | 183 | 184 | 185 | 186 | 187 | 188 | 189 | 190 |
| 191 | 192 | 193 | 194 | 195 | 196 | 197 | 198 | 199 | 200 |

# Coins

IN GOD WE TRUST
LIBERTY
1994
D
UNITED STATES OF AMERICA
E PLURIBUS UNUM
ONE CENT
MONTICELLO
FIVE CENTS
ONE DIME
QUARTER DOLLAR

# Digit Cards

| 0 | | |
|---|---|---|
| 1 | 2 | 3 |
| 4 | 5 | 6 |
| 7 | 8 | 9 |

# Digit Squares

| 0 | 1 | 2 | 3 | 4 |
|---|---|---|---|---|
| 5 | 6 | 7 | 8 | 9 |

| 0 | 1 | 2 | 3 | 4 |
|---|---|---|---|---|
| 5 | 6 | 7 | 8 | 9 |

| 0 | 1 | 2 | 3 | 4 |
|---|---|---|---|---|
| 5 | 6 | 7 | 8 | 9 |

# Number Cubes

Cut solid lines. Fold on dotted lines.

3

1 5

2 4

6

6

4 8

5 7

9

# Number Cubes

Cut solid lines. Fold on dotted lines.

| | | |
|---|---|---|
| | 3 | |
| 5 | | 4 |
| 4 | 3 | |
| | 5 | |
| | | |

# Spinners

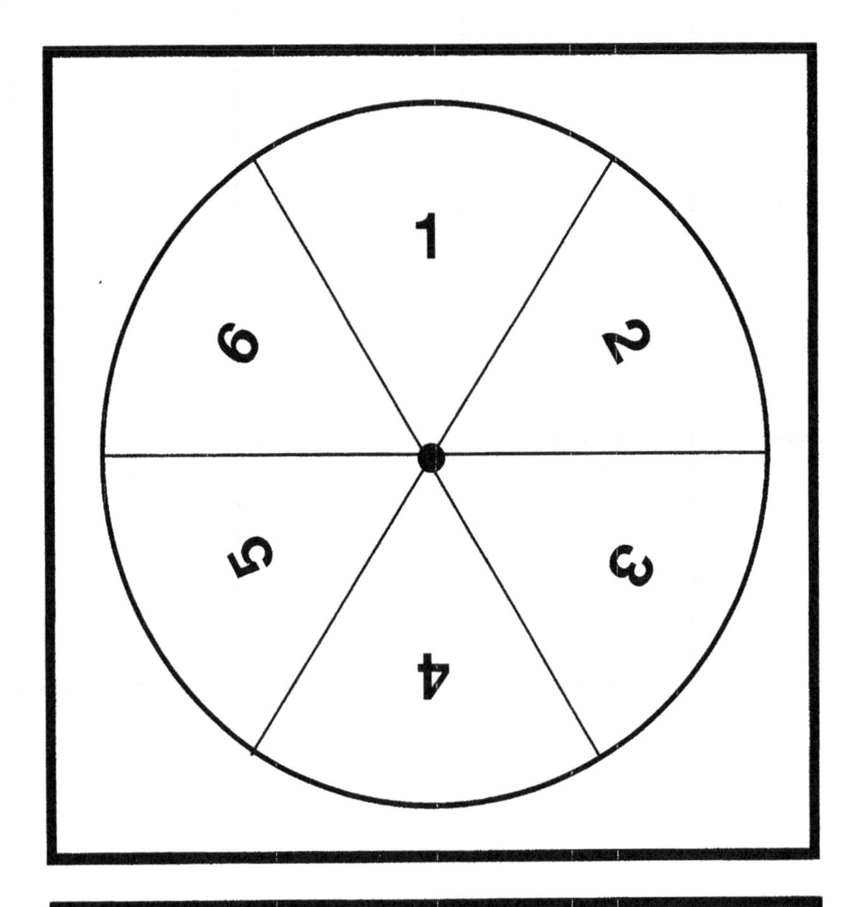


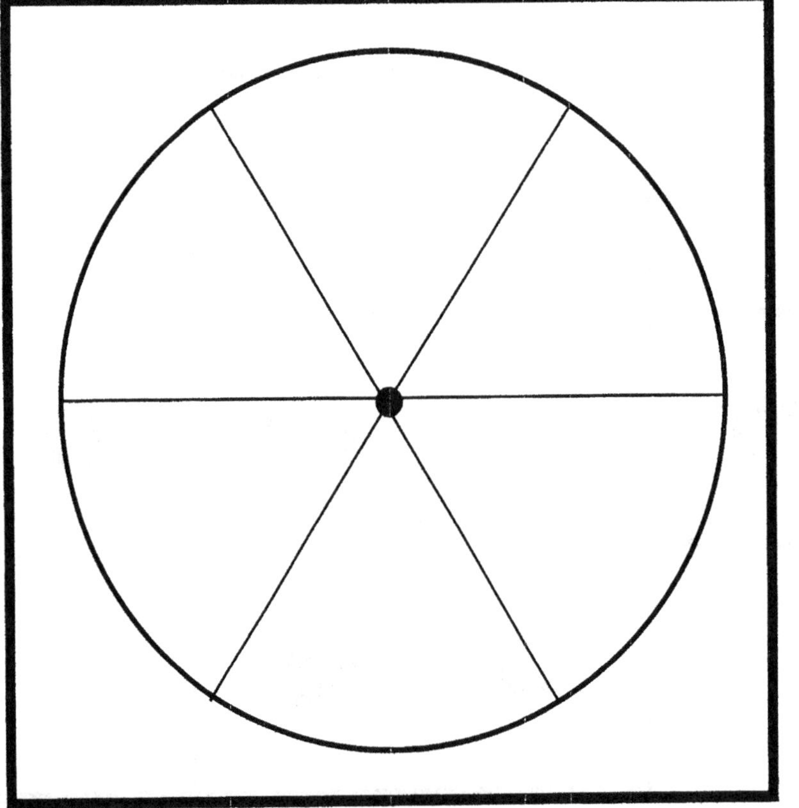

Date ________________ Name ____________________________

# Subtraction Squares

Subtract each row and column to fill in the missing numbers.

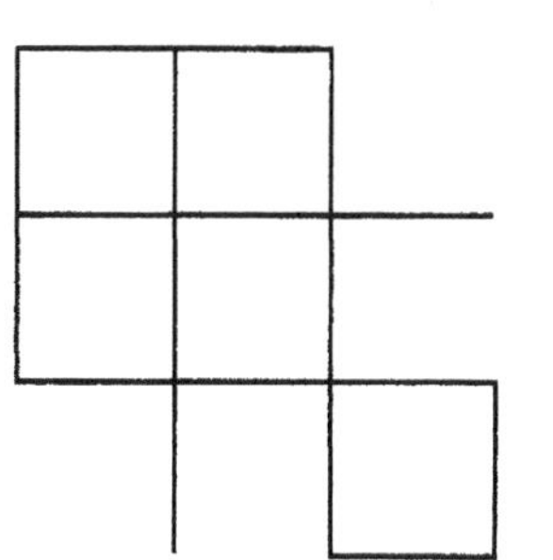
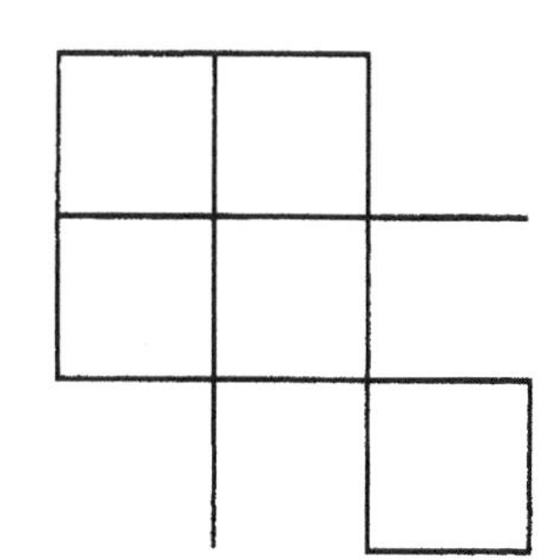
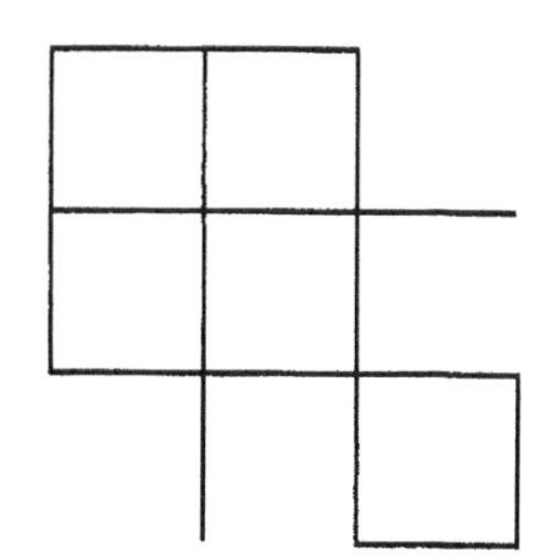
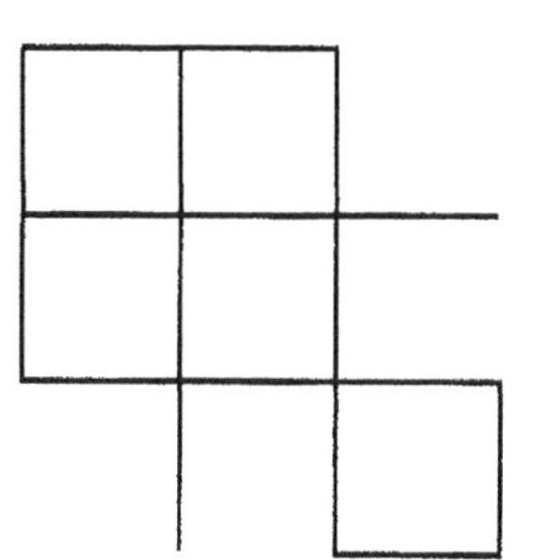
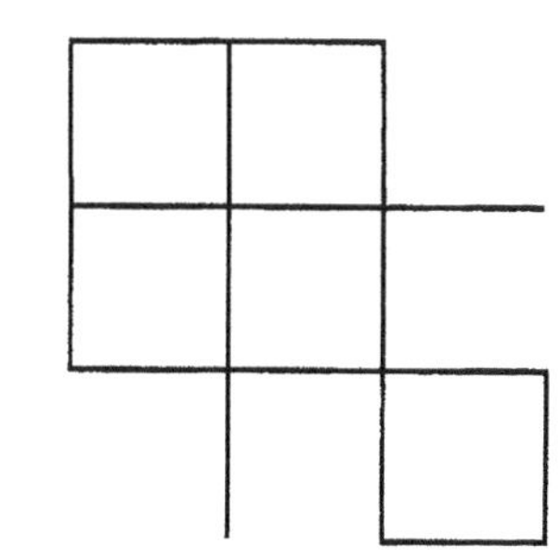
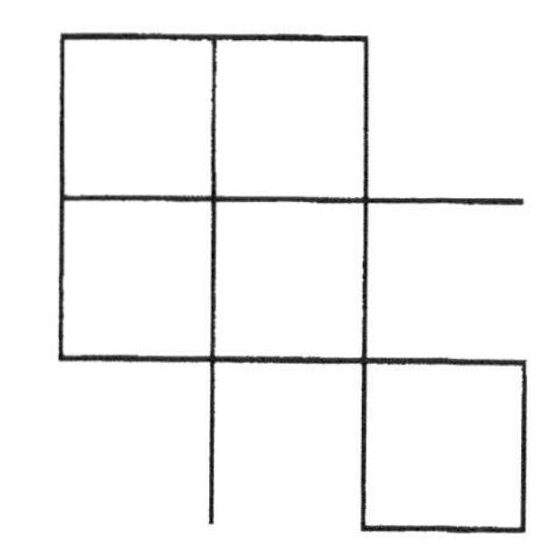
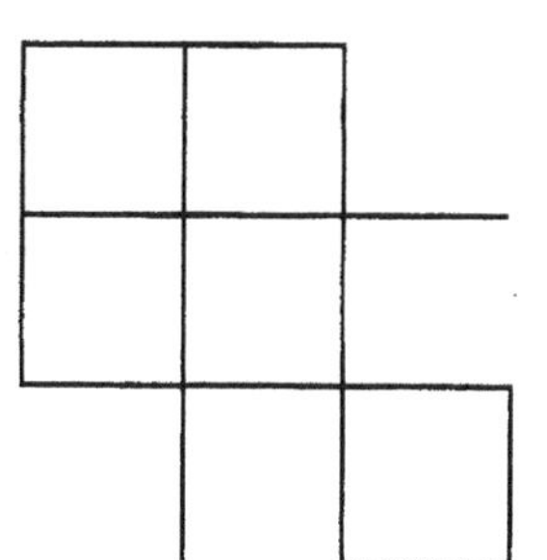
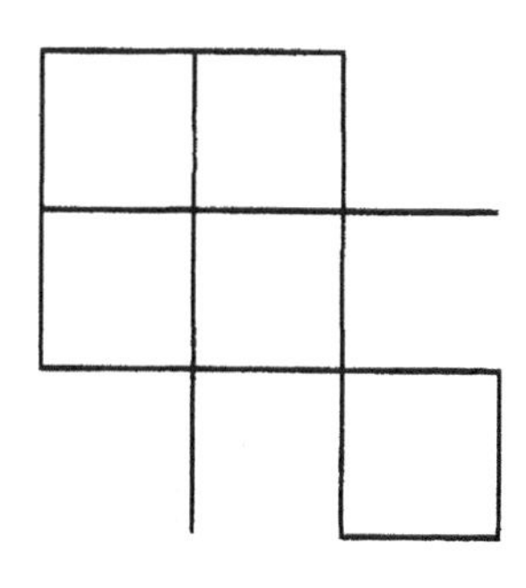
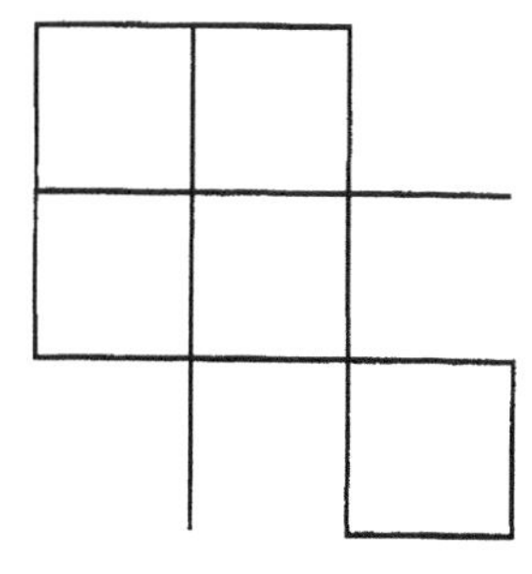
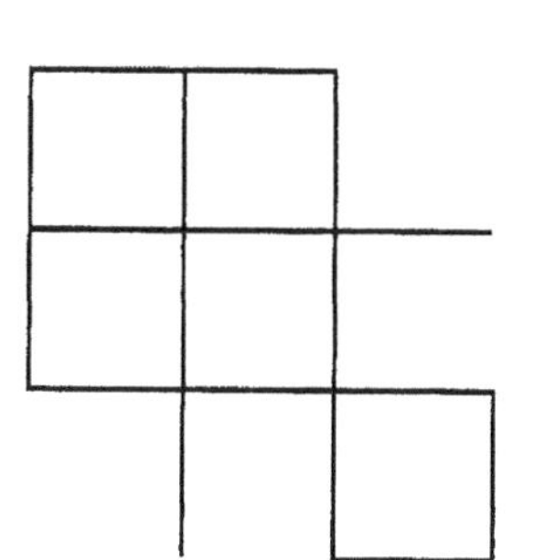
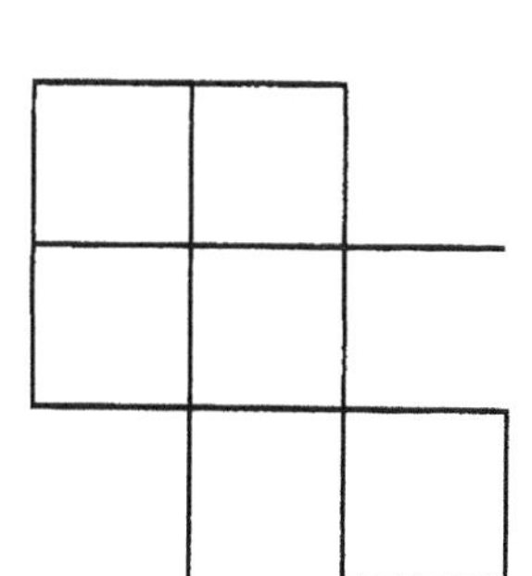

# Addition Chart

| + | 1 | 2 | 3 | 4 | 5 | 6 | 7 | 8 | 9 | 10 |
|---|---|---|---|---|---|---|---|---|---|---|
| 1 | 2 | 3 | 4 | 5 | 6 | 7 | 8 | 9 | 10 | 11 |
| 2 | 3 | 4 | 5 | 6 | 7 | 8 | 9 | 10 | 11 | 12 |
| 3 | 4 | 5 | 6 | 7 | 8 | 9 | 10 | 11 | 12 | 13 |
| 4 | 5 | 6 | 7 | 8 | 9 | 10 | 11 | 12 | 13 | 14 |
| 5 | 6 | 7 | 8 | 9 | 10 | 11 | 12 | 13 | 14 | 15 |
| 6 | 7 | 8 | 9 | 10 | 11 | 12 | 13 | 14 | 15 | 16 |
| 7 | 8 | 9 | 10 | 11 | 12 | 13 | 14 | 15 | 16 | 17 |
| 8 | 9 | 10 | 11 | 12 | 13 | 14 | 15 | 16 | 17 | 18 |
| 9 | 10 | 11 | 12 | 13 | 14 | 15 | 16 | 17 | 18 | 19 |
| 10 | 11 | 12 | 13 | 14 | 15 | 16 | 17 | 18 | 19 | 20 |

# Multiplication Chart

| × | 1 | 2 | 3 | 4 | 5 | 6 | 7 | 8 | 9 | 10 |
|---|---|---|---|---|---|---|---|---|---|---|
| 1 | 1 | 2 | 3 | 4 | 5 | 6 | 7 | 8 | 9 | 10 |
| 2 | 2 | 4 | 6 | 8 | 10 | 12 | 14 | 16 | 18 | 20 |
| 3 | 3 | 6 | 9 | 12 | 15 | 18 | 21 | 24 | 27 | 30 |
| 4 | 4 | 8 | 12 | 16 | 20 | 24 | 28 | 32 | 36 | 40 |
| 5 | 5 | 10 | 15 | 20 | 25 | 30 | 35 | 40 | 45 | 50 |
| 6 | 6 | 12 | 18 | 24 | 30 | 36 | 42 | 48 | 54 | 60 |
| 7 | 7 | 14 | 21 | 28 | 35 | 42 | 49 | 56 | 63 | 70 |
| 8 | 8 | 16 | 24 | 32 | 40 | 48 | 56 | 64 | 72 | 80 |
| 9 | 9 | 18 | 27 | 36 | 45 | 54 | 63 | 72 | 81 | 90 |
| 10 | 10 | 20 | 30 | 40 | 50 | 60 | 70 | 80 | 90 | 100 |

# *Nimble with Numbers* Answer Key

**p. 18** *Just the Facts 1*

1) 8  2) 12  3) 16  4) 16  5) 8  6) 11  7) 15  8) 13  9) 15  10) 17

Go On: Answers will vary.

*Just the Facts 2*

1) 7  2) 12  3) 14  4) 18  5) 9  6) 11  7) 14  8) 15  9) 16  10) 15

Go On: 10

**p. 19** *Just the Facts 3*

1) 9  2) 12  3) 15  4) 14  5) 10  6) 11  7) 17  8) 14  9) 9  10) 16

Go On: 9, 11, 13

*Just the Facts 4*

1) 9  2) 11  3) 13  4) 13  5) 10  6) 11  7) 15  8) 11  9) 13  10) 17

Go On: Answers will vary.

**p. 20** *Just the Facts 5*

1) 8  2) 11  3) 15  4) 13  5) 7  6) 12  7) 16  8) 14  9) 16  10) 17

Go On: Any even number.

*Just the Facts 6*

1) 9  2) 11  3) 17  4) 14  5) 10  6) 12  7) 13  8) 12  9) 15  10) 15

Go On: 11, 14, 17

**p. 27** *Seeking Sums Practice I*

Answers may vary for some problems.

1)
- 6  3 + 3
- 7  4 + 3 /6 + 1
- 8  4 + 4
- 9  6 + 3
- 10  6 + 4
- 11  6 + 4 + 1
- 12  Not possible
- 13  6 + 4 + 3
- 14  6 + 4 + 3 + 1

2)
- 6  5 + 1
- 7  7
- 8  7 + 1 / 5 + 3
- 9  5 + 3 + 1
- 10  3 + 7
- 11  7 + 3 + 1
- 12  7 + 5
- 13  7 + 5 + 1
- 14  Not possible
- 15  7 + 5 + 3

**p. 28** *Seeking Sums Practice II*

Answers will vary.

**p. 29** *Circling Sums*

Answers will vary.

**p. 30** *Matching Sums Practice*

Answers will vary.

**p. 35** *What's the Difference? 1*

1) 3  2) 6  3) 5  4) 8  5) 6  6) 7  7) 9  8) 9  9) 4  10) 5

Go On: 5, 0

*What's the Difference? 2*

1) 5  2) 5  3) 6  4) 7  5) 3  6) 3  7) 6  8) 9  9) 3  10) 5

Go On: 9

**p. 36** *What's the Difference? 3*

1) 4  2) 4  3) 7  4) 7  5) 3  6) 8  7) 5  8) 8  9) 6  10) 5

Go On: Answers will vary.

**p. 36** *What's the Difference? 4*

1) 4 2) 7 3) 6 4) 9 5) 5 6) 4 7) 7 8) 8 9) 5 10) 7

Go On: 8, 5

**p. 37** *What's the Difference? 5*

1) 2 2) 6 3) 8 4) 6 5) 4 6) 7 7) 7 8) 8 9) 4 10) 6

Go On: 5

*What's the Difference? 6*

1) 6 2) 4 3) 4 4) 8 5) 6 6) 4 7) 7 8) 7 9) 5 10) 7

Go On: 8

**p. 41** *Tic-Tac-Toe Subtract I*

1) Row 2 2) Row 3 3) Diagonal—Upper left to lower right 4) Column 3

**p. 42** *Tic-Tac-Toe Subtract II*

1) Diagonal—Upper left to lower right 2) Row 2

3) Diagonal—Lower left to upper right 4) Answers will vary.

**p. 43** *What's Left? I*

1) 2 2) 3 3) 7

**p. 44** *What's Left? II*

1) 9 2) 12 3) 10

**p. 45** *Subtraction Squares* **p. 46** *Subtraction Squares Challenge*

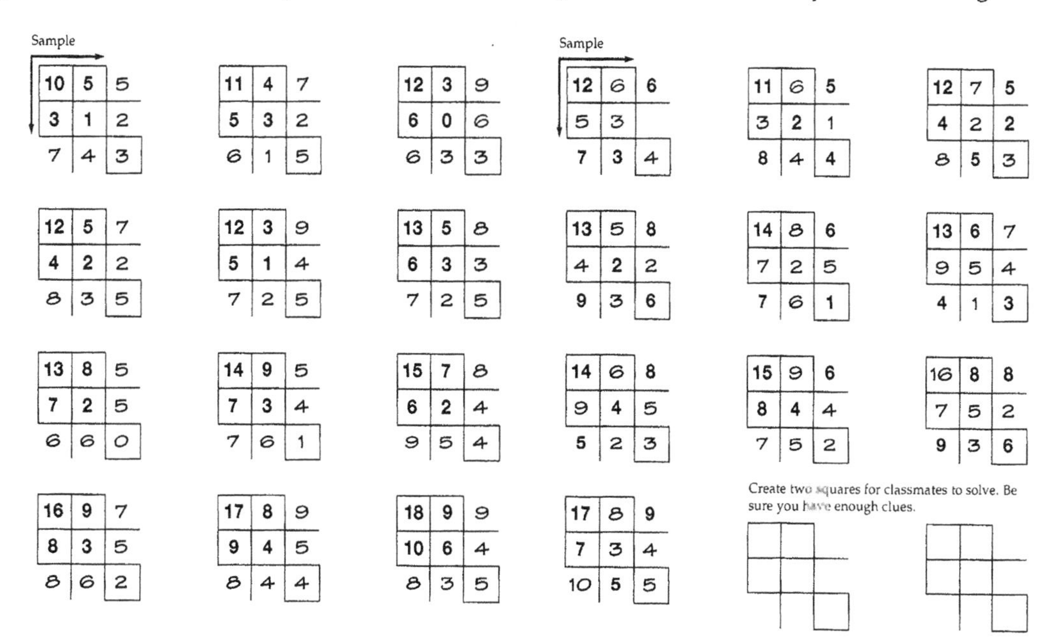


**p. 51** *Making Cents 1*

1) 55¢ 2) 32¢ 3) 25¢ 4) 1 quarter + 1 dime

5) 1 quarter + 2 nickels 6) 3 quarters + 1 nickel

7) 1 dime + 2 nickels 8) 1 quarter + 1 nickel + 1 dime

9) One possibility: 1 dime + 1 nickel 10) One possibility: 1 nickel + 2 pennies

Go On: Move 1 dime from the right to the left.

**p. 52** *Making Cents 2*

1) 41¢ 2) 65¢ 3) 25¢ 4) 1 quarter + 1 nickel
5) 2 quarters + 1 penny 6) 1 quarter + 3 dimes
7) 2 quarters + 1 dime 8) 1 quarter + 2 dimes
9) One possibility: 2 dimes + 1 penny 10) One possibility: 1 nickel + 3 pennies
Go On: Move 1 nickel from the left to the right.

**p. 53** *Making Cents 3*

1) 45¢ 2) 61¢ 3) 30¢ 4) 2 quarters
5) 2 quarters + 1 dime 6) 2 quarters + 1 dime + 1 nickel
7) 1 quarter + 1 nickel 8) 1 quarter + 2 dimes + 1 penny
9) One possibility: 1 dime + 1 nickel + 1 penny 10) One possibility: 2 dimes + 3 pennies
Go On: Move 1 nickel from the left to the right.

**p. 58** *Coin Combinations*

Answers will vary.

**p. 59** *Find the Combination* Some problems may have more than one answer.

45¢ Q D D
60¢ Q Q D
65¢ Q Q D N
80¢ Q Q Q N
86¢ Q Q Q D P
42¢ Q D N P P
56¢ Q D D D P
50¢ D D D D N N
$1.35 5Q + 1D
$1.06 4Q + 1N + 1P

31¢ Q N P
55¢ Q Q N
32¢ Q N P P
50¢ Q D D N
75¢ Q Q D D N
50¢ D D D D D
60¢ Q D D D N
75¢ Q D D D D D
95¢ Q Q Q D N N
66¢ Q D D D D P

**p. 60** *Vending Machine Math*

Answers may vary for some problems.
1) 5¢ 2) 15¢ 3) 10¢ 4) 5¢ 5) Q + D; N
6) 2Q; N 7) 2Q + D; N 8) 3Q; D 9) 4Q; 2D 10) 2Q + D; P
11) 3Q; N + 4P 12) 2Q; N + P

**p. 66** *Place It Right 1*

1) 32, 43 2) 114, 134 3) 96, 124, 142, 157 4) 72
5) 612 6) 95 7) 54 8) 53 9) 34 10) 435 or 453
Go On: 402, 412

*Place It Right 2*

1) 55, 63 2) 76, 87 3) 91, 109, 115, 188 4) 45
5) 379 6) 177 7) 42 8) 47 9) 24 10) 472
Go On: 240

**p. 67** *Place It Right 3*

1) 128, 147 2) 64, 86 3) 84, 99, 104, 120 4) 63
5) 518 6) 112 7) 75 8) 76
9) 57 10) 576
Go On: Any 3-digit number with a 1 in the hundreds place and/or a 4 in the tens place

**p, 67** *Place It Right 4*

1) 133, 144 2) 17, 37 3) 119, 127, 136, 143 4) 54
5) 209 6) 510 7) 24 8) 21
9) 42 10) 214
Go On: 103, 93

**p. 68** *Place It Right 5*

1) 144, 152 2) 72, 83 3) 118, 125, 149, 152 4) 36
5) 750 6) 225 7) 89 8) 98
9) 48 10) 894
Go On: 325

*Place It Right 6*

1) 71, 90 2) 164, 173 3) 113, 122, 127, 143 4) 89
5) 410 6) 350 7) 67 8) 76
9) 26 10) 276
Go On: Any 3-digit number with a 1 in the hundreds place and/or a 7 in the ones place

**p. 74** *What Numbers Are Missing? I*

**p. 75** *What Numbers Are Missing? II*

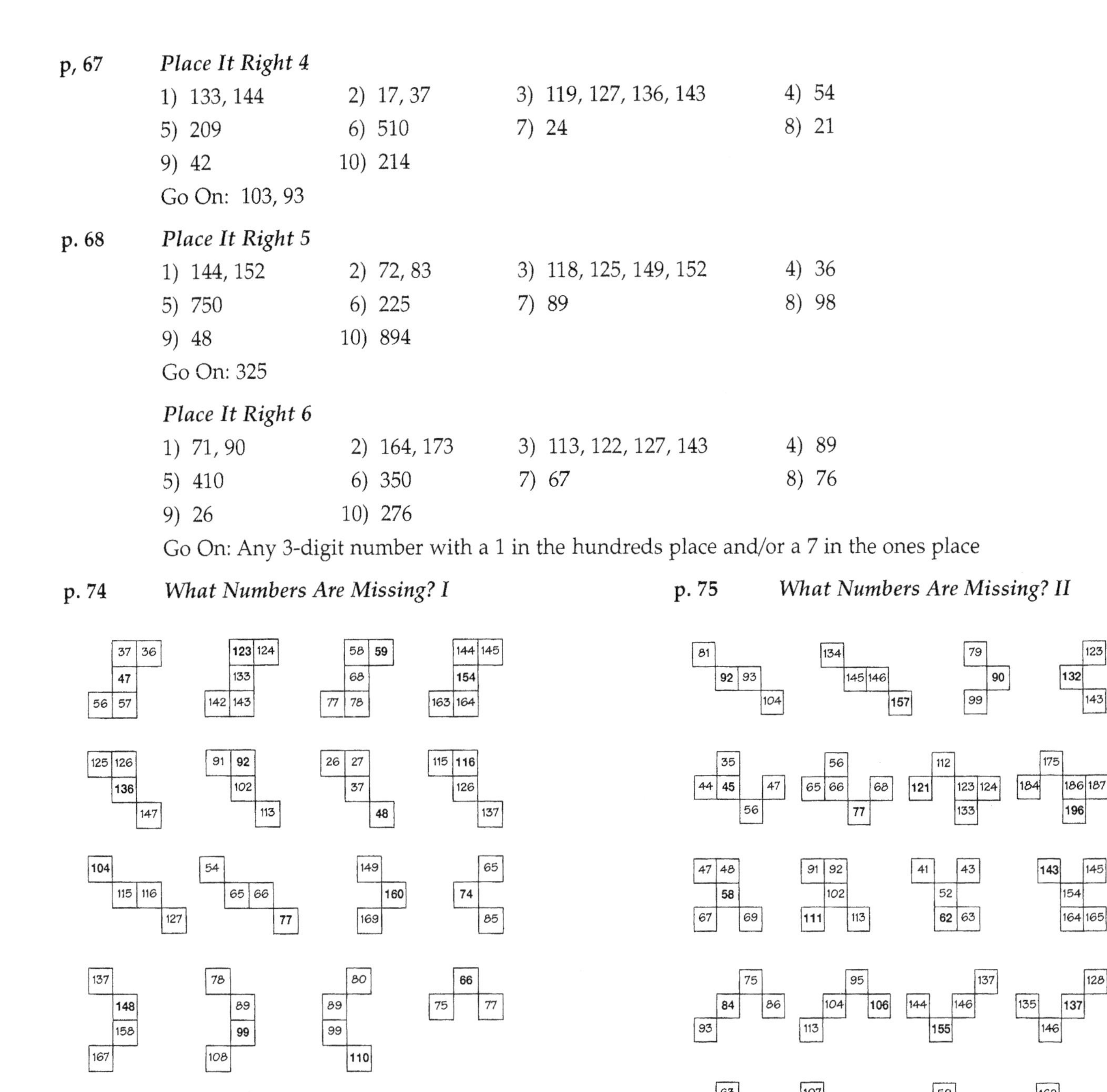


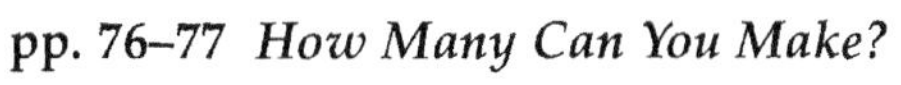

**pp. 76–77** *How Many Can You Make?*

Answers will vary.

**p. 78** *What's My Number?*

1) 452 2) 254 3) 538 4) 853 5) 740 6) 407 7) 491 8) 914

**p. 84** *Sum It Up 1*

1) 33 2) 50 3) 111 4) 94 5) 150 6) 153 7) 64 8) 495 9) 849 10) 1183
Go On: 413, 428

*Sum It Up 2*

1) 42 2) 61 3) 54 4) 115 5) 160 6) 134 7) 91 8) 835 9) 1191 10) 1033
Go On: Answers will vary for addition equations equal to 150.

**p. 85** *Sum It Up 3*

1) 43 2) 41 3) 65 4) 103 5) 180 6) 164 7) 91 8) 532 9) 803 10) 1411

Go On: Answers will vary.

*Sum It Up 4*

1) 52 2) 50 3) 73 4) 67 5) 150 6) 192 7) 82 8) 639 9) 902 10) 1493

Go On: 201

**p. 86** *Sum It Up 5*

1) 62 2) 48 3) 95 4) 96 5) 170 6) 173 7) 71 8) 601 9) 1193 10) 1430

Go On: 305, 320

*Sum It Up 6*

1) 72 2) 37 3) 43 4) 135 5) 180 6) 185 7) 95 8) 422 9) 1049 10) 1424

Go On: Answers will vary.

**p. 91** *Loop Addition I*

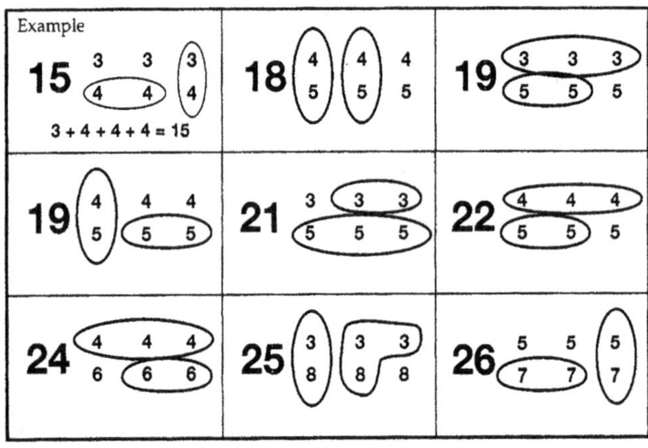


Draw a loop around one group of numbers to match the sum.

Example: Sum = 16

3
5
7
4
2

| Sum = 15 | Sum = 15 | Sum = 19 | Sum = 21 | Sum = 23 | Sum = 25 | Sum = 28 |
|---|---|---|---|---|---|---|
| 4 | 2 | 6 | 3 | 5 | 9 | 8 |
| 3 | 6 | 4 | 4 | 7 | 3 | 5 |
| 6 | 5 | 6 | 7 | 3 | 7 | 9 |
| 2 | 4 | 5 | 2 | 8 | 4 | 6 |
| 7 | 8 | 4 | 3 | 6 | 6 | 4 |
| | | | 9 | 4 | 8 | 7 |

**p. 92** *Loop Addition II*

| | | |
|---|---|---|
| Example<br>19 4 4 4 4<br>5 5 5 5<br>4 + 5 + 5 + 5 = 19 | 30 4 4 4 4<br>9 9 9 9 | 27 3 3 3 3<br>7 7 7 7 |
| 32 6 6 6 6<br>7 7 7 7 | 36 5 5 5 5<br>7 7 7 7 | 36 3 3 3 3<br>8 8 8 8 |
| 38 6 6 6 6<br>8 8 8 8 | 39 6 6 6 6<br>9 9 9 9 | 46 7 7 7 7<br>9 9 9 9 |

Draw a loop around one group of numbers to match the sum.

Example: Sum = 16

3
5
7
4
2

| Sum = 32 | Sum = 29 | Sum = 33 | Sum = 33 | Sum = 33 | Sum = 34 | Sum = 37 |
|---|---|---|---|---|---|---|
| 6 | 7 | 4 | 9 | 5 | 9 | 8 |
| 4 | 7 | 6 | 6 | 9 | 6 | 4 |
| 9 | 9 | 8 | 8 | 8 | 8 | 8 |
| 5 | 5 | 7 | 4 | 7 | 7 | 9 |
| 8 | 8 | 8 | 7 | 9 | 4 | 7 |
| 7 | 6 | 5 | 8 | 6 | 8 | 9 |

p. 93 *Making Sums I*

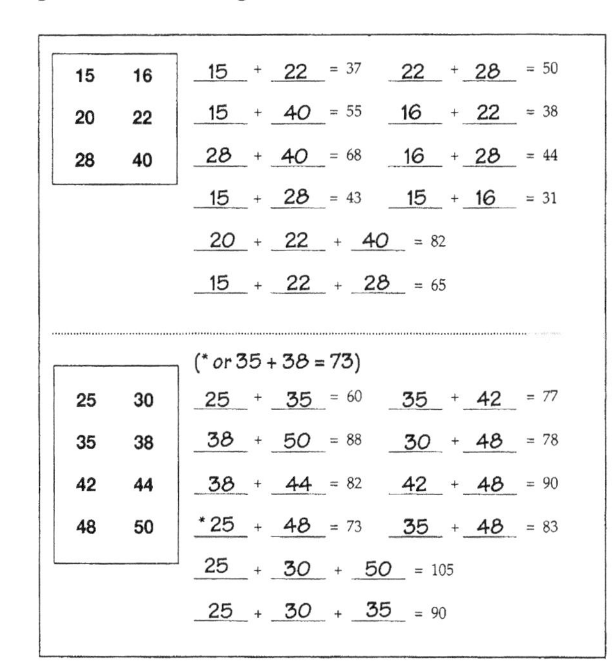

| 15 | 16 |
|---|---|
| 20 | 22 |
| 28 | 40 |

15 + 22 = 37   22 + 28 = 50
15 + 40 = 55   16 + 22 = 38
28 + 40 = 68   16 + 28 = 44
15 + 28 = 43   15 + 16 = 31
20 + 22 + 40 = 82
15 + 22 + 28 = 65

| 25 | 30 |
|---|---|
| 35 | 38 |
| 42 | 44 |
| 48 | 50 |

(* or 35 + 38 = 73)
25 + 35 = 60   35 + 42 = 77
38 + 50 = 88   30 + 48 = 78
38 + 44 = 82   42 + 48 = 90
*25 + 48 = 73   35 + 48 = 83
25 + 30 + 50 = 105
25 + 30 + 35 = 90

p. 94 *Making Sums II*

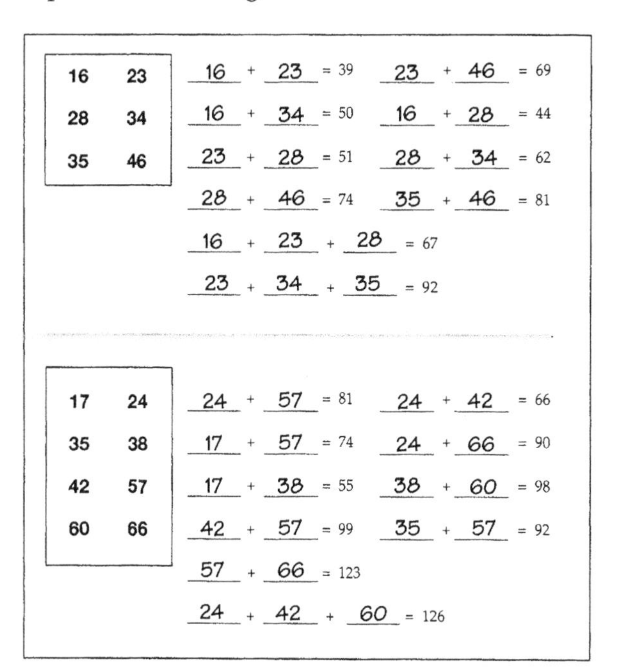

| 16 | 23 |
|---|---|
| 28 | 34 |
| 35 | 46 |

16 + 23 = 39   23 + 46 = 69
16 + 34 = 50   16 + 28 = 44
23 + 28 = 51   28 + 34 = 62
28 + 46 = 74   35 + 46 = 81
16 + 23 + 28 = 67
23 + 34 + 35 = 92

| 17 | 24 |
|---|---|
| 35 | 38 |
| 42 | 57 |
| 60 | 66 |

24 + 57 = 81   24 + 42 = 66
17 + 57 = 74   24 + 66 = 90
17 + 38 = 55   38 + 60 = 98
42 + 57 = 99   35 + 57 = 92
57 + 66 = 123
24 + 42 + 60 = 126

p. 95 *Estimating Sums*

1) B   2) Y   3) I   4) T   5) S   6) B   7) A   8) R   9) K   By its bark.

p. 96 *Linked Equations*

| 19 | + | 17 | = | 36 | | | | 59 | + | 84 | = | 143 |
|---|---|---|---|---|---|---|---|---|---|---|---|---|
| + | | | | + | | | | + | | | | + |
| 26 | | | | 18 | + | 28 | = | 46 | | | | 78 |
| = | | | | = | | | | = | | | | = |
| 45 | + | 9 | = | 54 | | | | 105 | + | 116 | = | 221 |
| | | + | | | | | | | | + | | |
| | | 18 | | | | | | | | 288 | | |
| | | = | | | | | | | | = | | |
| 155 | + | 27 | = | 182 | | | | 327 | + | 404 | = | 731 |
| + | | | | + | | | | + | | | | + |
| 73 | | | | 221 | + | 138 | = | 359 | | | | 249 |
| = | | | | = | | | | = | | | | = |
| 228 | + | 175 | + | 403 | | | | 686 | + | 294 | = | 980 |

p. 102 *What's Left Out? 1*

1) 8   2) 15   3) 16   4) 24   5) 33   6) 37   7) 114   8) 54   9) 39   10) 205

Go On: 974; 1000 – 974 = 26, and 1028 – 1000 = 28

*What's Left Out? 2*

1) 6   2) 13   3) 17   4) 33   5) 45   6) 36   7) 73   8) 137   9) 163   10) 243

Go On: 199, 192

**p. 103** *What's Left Out? 3*

1) 13 2) 14 3) 17 4) 62 5) 75 6) 18 7) 183 8) 64 9) 45 10) 144

Go On: Answers will vary.

*What's Left Out? 4*

1) 9 2) 12 3) 19 4) 76 5) 64 6) 27 7) 315 8) 126 9) 243 10) 234

Go On: 385

**p. 104** *What's Left Out? 5*

1) 16 2) 18 3) 18 4) 54 5) 65 6) 46 7) 283 8) 163 9) 375 10) 238

Go On: Answers will vary for subtraction equations equal to 22.

*What's Left Out? 6*

1) 7 2) 14 3) 15 4) 43 5) 72 6) 24 7) 204 8) 38 9) 133 10) 253

Go On: 196; 180 – 163 = 17, and 196 – 180 = 16

**p. 109** *Sorting Differences I*

| * Difference less than 20 | | Difference between 20 and 30 | | Difference greater than 30 | |
|---|---|---|---|---|---|
| 16 | 17 | 23 | 29 | 44 | 35 |
| 18 | 19 | 28 | 26 | 47 | 36 |

*** Trivia Bonus:** The sum of these four answers equals the running speed in miles per hour for the world's fastest land animal (cheetah). 70 mph

| 51 − 28 | 42 − 24 | 63 − 37 | 59 − 24 | 35 − 19 | 83 − 36 |
|---|---|---|---|---|---|
| 23 | 18 | 26 | 35 | 16 | 47 |
| **78 − 42** | **64 − 35** | **84 − 67** | **97 − 53** | **66 − 38** | **75 − 56** |
| 36 | 29 | 17 | 44 | 28 | 19 |

**p. 110** *Sorting Differences II*

| Difference less than 25 | | Difference between 20 and 40 | | Difference greater than 35 * | |
|---|---|---|---|---|---|
| 19 | 21 | 27 | 39 | 57 | 43 |
| 24 | 16 | 25 | 33 | 46 | 54 |

*** Trivia Bonus:** The sum of these four answers equals the number of long feathers on a male peacock. 200 feathers

| 137 − 118 | 110 − 83 | 118 − 97 | 102 − 78 | 130 − 91 | 92 − 76 |
|---|---|---|---|---|---|
| 19 | 27 | 21 | 24 | 39 | 16 |
| **213 − 156** | **214 − 189** | **311 − 268** | **178 − 145** | **485 − 439** | **132 − 78** |
| 57 | 25 | 43 | 33 | 46 | 54 |

**p. 111** *Finding Pairs I*

| | |
|---|---|
| 30 | 18 |
| 26 | 14 |
| 21 | 13 |

Can you do it two different ways?

18 – 14 = 4
21 – 14 = 7
21 – 18 = 3
26 – 21 = 5
26 – 14 = 12
30 – 18 = 12

30 – 14 = 16
30 – 21 = 9
26 – 13 = 13
30 – 13 = 17
26 – 18 = 8
21 – 13 = 8

| | |
|---|---|
| 50 | 33 |
| 46 | 28 |
| 40 | 25 |
| 37 | 21 |

Can you do it two different ways?

37 – 33 = 4
37 – 21 = 16
33 – 28 = 5
50 – 33 = 17
50 – 21 = 29
37 – 28 = 9
46 – 37 = 9

33 – 25 = 8
40 – 21 = 19
46 – 25 = 21
40 – 25 = 15
50 – 28 = 22
46 – 28 = 18
46 – 33 = 13

**p. 112** *Finding Pairs II*

| | |
|---|---|
| 100 | 76 |
| 92 | 69 |
| 87 | 63 |
| 81 | 58 |

Can you do it two different ways?

100 – 87 = 13
92 – 76 = 16
100 – 58 = 42
92 – 58 = 34
81 – 63 = 18
76 – 58 = 18

81 – 69 = 12
100 – 76 = 24
92 – 69 = 23
92 – 63 = 29
100 – 69 = 31
100 – 63 = 37

| | |
|---|---|
| 120 | 93 |
| 112 | 86 |
| 105 | 77 |
| 101 | 64 |

Can you do it two different ways?

120 – 112 = 8
105 – 64 = 41
120 – 93 = 27
105 – 93 = 12
93 – 64 = 29
101 – 86 = 15
120 – 105 = 15

101 – 77 = 24
77 – 64 = 13
93 – 77 = 16
112 – 93 = 19
86 – 64 = 22
105 – 77 = 28
112 – 64 = 48

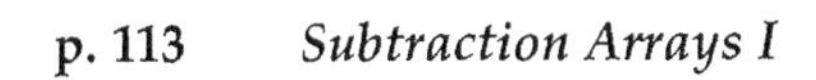

**p. 113** *Subtraction Arrays I*

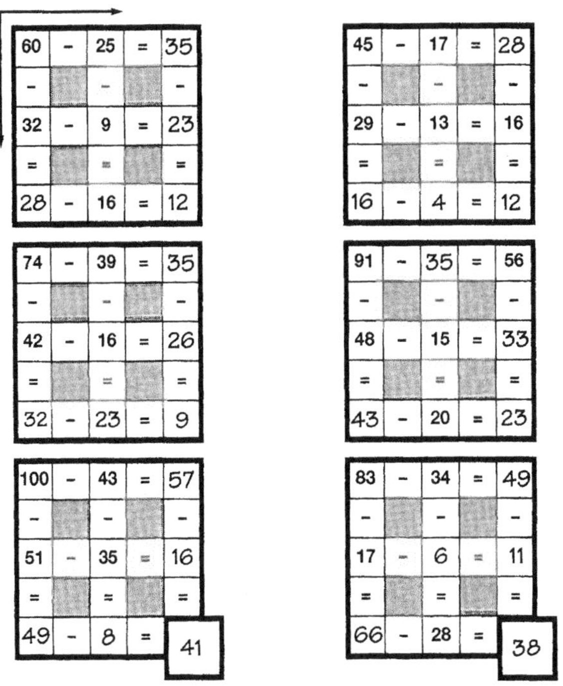

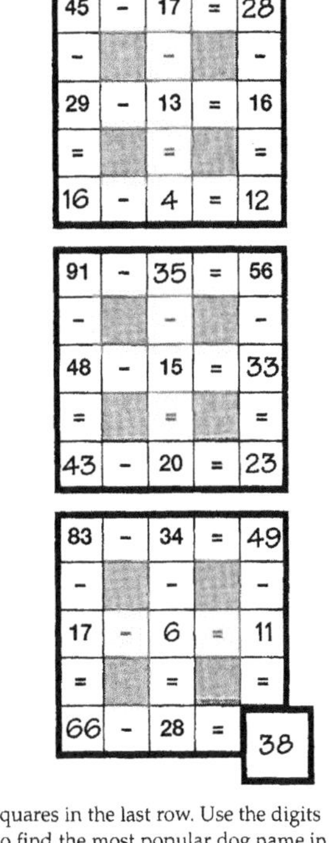

| 60 | - | 25 | = | 35 |
|---|---|---|---|---|
| - | | - | | - |
| 32 | - | 9 | = | 23 |
| = | | = | | = |
| 28 | - | 16 | = | 12 |

| 45 | - | 17 | = | 28 |
|---|---|---|---|---|
| - | | - | | - |
| 29 | - | 13 | = | 16 |
| = | | = | | = |
| 16 | - | 4 | = | 12 |

| 74 | - | 39 | = | 35 |
|---|---|---|---|---|
| - | | - | | - |
| 42 | - | 16 | = | 26 |
| = | | = | | = |
| 32 | - | 23 | = | 9 |

| 91 | - | 35 | = | 56 |
|---|---|---|---|---|
| - | | - | | - |
| 48 | - | 15 | = | 33 |
| = | | = | | = |
| 43 | - | 20 | = | 23 |

| 100 | - | 43 | = | 57 |
|---|---|---|---|---|
| - | | - | | - |
| 51 | - | 35 | = | 16 |
| = | | = | | = |
| 49 | - | 8 | = | 41 |

| 83 | - | 34 | = | 49 |
|---|---|---|---|---|
| - | | - | | - |
| 17 | - | 6 | = | 11 |
| = | | = | | = |
| 66 | - | 28 | = | 38 |

**Trivia Bonus** Locate the heavy-framed squares in the last row. Use the digits in these two answers with the code below to find the most popular dog name in the United States.

A = 1 B = 2 D = 3 L = 4
M = 5 R = 6 S = 7 Y = 8

l a d y

**p. 114** *Subtraction Arrays II*

| 240 | - | 86 | = | 154 |
|---|---|---|---|---|
| - | | - | | - |
| 77 | - | 19 | = | 58 |
| = | | = | | = |
| 163 | - | 67 | = | 96 |

| 623 | - | 349 | = | 274 |
|---|---|---|---|---|
| - | | - | | - |
| 486 | - | 269 | = | 217 |
| = | | = | | = |
| 137 | - | 80 | = | 57 |

| 892 | - | 468 | = | 424 |
|---|---|---|---|---|
| - | | - | | - |
| 245 | - | 198 | = | 47 |
| = | | = | | = |
| 647 | - | 270 | = | 377 |

| 406 | - | 179 | = | 227 |
|---|---|---|---|---|
| - | | - | | - |
| 235 | - | 96 | = | 139 |
| = | | = | | = |
| 171 | - | 83 | = | 88 |

| 794 | - | 364 | = | 430 |
|---|---|---|---|---|
| - | | - | | - |
| 283 | - | 195 | = | 88 |
| = | | = | | = |
| 511 | - | 169 | = | 342 |

| 931 | - | 488 | = | 443 |
|---|---|---|---|---|
| - | | - | | - |
| 393 | - | 215 | = | 178 |
| = | | = | | = |
| 538 | - | 273 | = | 265 |

**Trivia Bonus** Locate the heavy-framed squares in the last row. Use the digits in these two answers with the code below to find an animal whose arms are twice as long as its body.

A = 1 B = 2 G = 3 I = 4
N = 5 O = 6 T = 7 Y = 8

g i b b o n

**p. 118** *Proper Products 1*

1) 18 2) 30 3) 12 4) 42 5) 21 6) 48 7) 8 8) 9 9) 4 10) 55

Go On: The numbers are 7 and 8.

*Proper Products 2*

1) 16 2) 20 3) 36 4) 49 5) 36 6) 54 7) 8 8) 7 9) 4 10) 62

Go On: The numbers are 9 and 6.

**p. 119** *Proper Products 3*

1) 16 2) 15 3) 21 4) 48 5) 27 6) 42 7) 4 8) 3 9) 6 10) 39

Go On: Both numbers are 7.

*Proper Products 4*

1) 24 2) 35 3) 32 4) 56 5) 24 6) 28 7) 9 8) 7 9) 4 10) 52

Go On: The numbers are 6 and 7.

**p. 120** *Proper Products 5*

1) 27 2) 40 3) 24 4) 63 5) 28 6) 32 7) 6 8) 3 9) 4 10) 34

Go On: The numbers are 9 and 7.

*Proper Products 6*

1) 35 2) 25 3) 24 4) 45 5) 36 6) 56 7) 4 8) 7 9) 3 10) 57

Go On: The numbers are 8 and 9.

p. 126 *Cross-Number Puzzle I*

| | | | | | | | | |
|---|---|---|---|---|---|---|---|---|
| 1 | 2 | | 3 | 0 | | | 3 | |
| 4 | 0 | | 6 | | | | 2 | 4 |
| | | 5 | | | 1 | 2 | | 5 |
| 1 | 5 | | 3 | 2 | | 8 | | |
| 8 | | 1 | | 1 | 8 | | 2 | 1 |
| | 3 | 6 | | | | 8 | | 0 |

p. 127 *Cross-Number Puzzle II*

p. 128 *Facts Find*

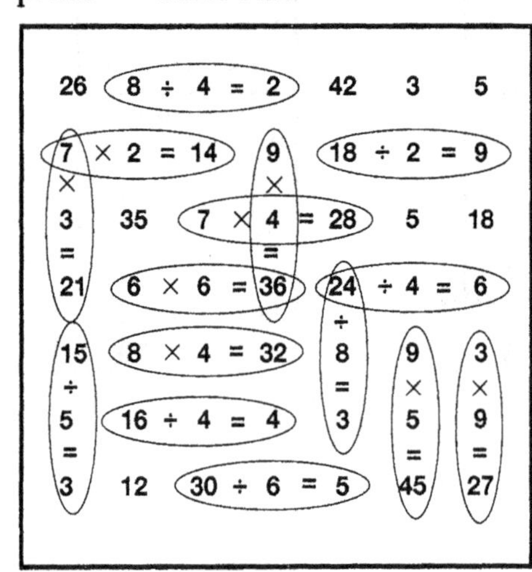


p. 134 *Quick Check 1*
1) 30 ÷ 6 2) 18 3) 6 4) 52 5) 5 6) 9 7) 7 × 3 8) 4 × 3 ÷ 2 = 6
9) 3 × 5 – 4 = 11 10) 6 × 3 + 2 = 20 Go On: 19, 21, 16

*Quick Check 2*
1) 12 – 3 2) 33 3) 6 4) 79 5) 4 6) 9 7) 2 × 7 8) 4 × 5 ÷ 2 = 10
9) 4 × 2 + 3 = 11 10) 3 + 7 – 4 = 6 Go On: Answers will vary.

p. 135 *Quick Check 3*
1) 24 ÷ 3 2) 25 3) 4 4) 53 5) 3 6) 15 7) 3 × 5 8) 6 × 3 ÷ 2 = 9
9) 6 × 2 + 3 = 15 10) 4 + (3 × 5) = 19 Go On: 22; It is the only one not a multiple of 4.

*Quick Check 4*
1) 15 – 6 2) 33 3) 5 4) 60 5) 3 6) 9 7) 2 × 5 8) 2 × 8 ÷ 4 = 4
9) 4 × 5 – 3 = 17 10) 3 + (2 × 8) = 19 Go On: Answers will vary.

p. 136 *Quick Check 5*
1) 14 – 6 2) 29 3) 4 4) 38 5) 6 6) 7 7) 2 × 7 8) 6 × 4 ÷ 3 = 8
9) 3 × 6 – 4 = 14 10) 7 + 5 + 3 = 15 Go On: 21, or any multiple of 3

*Quick Check 6*
1) 11 – 4 2) 19 3) 9 4) 59 5) 3 6) 8 7) 6 × 5/3 × 10 8) 2 × 6 – 5 = 7
9) 7 × 2 + 3 = 17 10) 5 + (4 × 3) = 17 Go On: 10, 17

p. 139 *Can You Make It? I*
Answers will vary.

p. 140 *Can You Make It? II*
Answers will vary.

p. 142 *Possible Equations*
Answers will vary.